ANT COLONY OPTIMIZATION - TECHNIQUES AND APPLICATIONS

Edited by **Helio J.C. Barbosa**

Ant Colony Optimization - Techniques and Applications

http://dx.doi.org/10.5772/3423
Edited by Helio J.C. Barbosa

Contributors

Ozgur Baskan, Cenk Ozan, Soner Haldenbilen, Satoshi Kurihara, Mieczyslaw Drabowski, Edward Wantuch, Jaqueline Silva Angelo, Douglas Adriano Augusto, Helio J.C. Barbosa, Romdhane Rekaya, Anikó Csébfalvi, Kazuyuki Murase, Pierre Delisle

Published by InTech

Janeza Trdine 9, 51000 Rijeka, Croatia

Copyright © 2013 InTech

Notice

Publishing Process Manager Dejan Grgur
Typesetting InTech DTP Team
Cover InTech Design Team

Additional hard copies can be obtained from orders@intechopen.com

Ant Colony Optimization - Techniques and Applications, Edited by Helio J.C. Barbosa
p. cm.
ISBN 978-953-51-1001-9

For EU product safety concerns:
IN TECH d.o.o., Prolaz Marije Krucifikse Kozulić 3, 51000 Rijeka, Croatia,
info@intechopen.com or visit our website at intechopen.com.

Meet the editor

Helio J.C. Barbosa (www.lncc.br/~hcbm) is a Senior Technologist at the Laboratório Nacional de Computação Científica, Brazil.
He received a Civil Engineering degree (1974) from the Federal University of Juiz de Fora, where he is an Associate Professor in the Computer Science Department, and M.Sc. (1978) and D.Sc. (1986) degrees in Civil Engineering from the Federal University of Rio de Janeiro, Brazil.
During 1988-1990 he was a visiting scholar at the Division of Applied Mechanics, Stanford University, USA. He is currently mainly interested in the design and application of nature-inspired metaheuristics in engineering and biology.

Contents

Preface

Scientists have long been interested in understanding the behavior of ants and other social insects that, in spite of the relative simplicity of each individual, are able to collectively accomplish complex tasks required by the survival of the colony. For instance, biologists have shown that behavior at the colony level, such as foraging, can be explained via the concept of stigmergy, a form of indirect communication mediated by modifications of the environment.

Ant Colony Optimization (ACO) is thus one of the best examples of how studies aimed at modeling such complex natural systems can provide inspiration for the development of computational algorithms for the solution of hard mathematical problems. The first ACO system, inspired by the observation of pheromone trails, was introduced by Marco Dorigo in his Ph.D. thesis (1992) and initially applied to the travelling salesman problem. Since then, the field has experienced a continuous growth, with the development of many ACO variants, the organization of specialized conferences and scientific journals, and the emergence of several successful applications. Today ACO stands as an important nature-inspired stochastic metaheuristic for many difficult optimization problems.

This book is divided into two parts: (I) Techniques, and (II) Applications, and presents state-of-the-art ACO methods and recent contributions to diverse fields, such as traffic congestion and control, structural optimization, manufacturing, and genomics.

I would like to thank all contributing authors for their effort in preparing their chapters, and to acknowledge the assistance provided by the InTech Publishing Process Managers Mr. Marijan Polic, Mr. Vedran Greblo, and Mr. Dejan Grgur during the entire editing process of this book.

Dr. Helio J.C. Barbosa,
Federal University of Juiz de Fora,
Computer Science Department,
LNCC - National Laboratory for Scientific Computation
Petrópolis, Brazil

Section 1

Techniques

Chapter 1

Ant Colony Optimization Toward Feature Selection

Monirul Kabir, Md Shahjahan and Kazuyuki Murase

Additional information is available at the end of the chapter

http://dx.doi.org/10.5772/51707

1. Introduction

Over the past decades, there is an explosion of data composed by huge information, because of rapid growing up of computer and database technologies. Ordinarily, this information is hidden in the cast collection of raw data. Because of that, we are now drowning in information, but starving for knowledge [1]. As a solution, data mining successfully extracts knowledge from the series of data-mountains by means of data preprocessing [1]. In case of data preprocessing, feature selection (FS) is ordinarily used as a useful technique in order to reduce the dimension of the dataset. It significantly reduces the spurious information, that is to say, irrelevant, redundant, and noisy features, from the original feature set and eventually retaining a subset of most salient features. As a result, a number of good outcomes can be expected from the applications, such as, speeding up data mining algorithms, improving mining performances (including predictive accuracy) and comprehensibility of result [2].

In the available literature, different types of data mining are addressed, such as, regression, classification, and clustering [1]. The task of interest in this study is classification. In fact, classification problem is the task of assigning a data-point to a predefined class or group according to its predictive characteristics. In practice, data mining for classification techniques are significant in a wide range of domains, such as, financial engineering, medical diagnosis, and marketing.

In details, FS is, however, a search process or technique in data mining that selects a subset of salient features for building robust learning models, such as, neural networks and decision trees. Some irrelevant and/or redundant features generally exist in the learning data that not only make learning harder, but also degrade generalization performance of learned models. More precisely, good FS techniques can detect and ignore noisy and misleading features. As a result, the dataset quality might even increase after selection. There are two feature qualities that need to be considered in FS methods: relevancy and redundancy. A feature is said to be relevant if it is predictive of the decision feature(s); otherwise, it is irrelevant. A feature is considered to be redundant if it is highly correlated with other features. An informative feature is the one that is highly correlated with the decision concept(s), but is highly uncorrelated with other features.

For a given classification task, the problem of FS can be described as follows: given the original set, N, of n features, find a subset F consisting of f relevant features, where $F \subset N$ and $f < n$. The aim of selecting F is to maximize the classification accuracy in building learning models. The selection of relevant features is important in the sense that the generalization performance of learning models is greatly dependent on the selected features [3-6]. Moreover, FS assists for visualizing and understanding the data, reducing storage requirements, reducing training times and so on [7].

It is found that, two features to be useless individually and yet highly predictive if taken together. In FS terminology, they may be both redundant and irrelevant on their own, but their combination provides important information. For instance, in the Exclusive-OR problem, the classes are not linearly separable. The two features on their own provide no information concerning this separability, because they are uncorrelated with each other. However, considering together, the two features are highly informative and can provide good predictive accuracy. Therefore, the search of FS is particularly for high-quality feature subsets and not only for ranking of features.

2. Applications of Feature Selection

Feature selection has a wide-range of applications in various fields since the 1970s. The reason is that, many systems deal with datasets of large dimensionality. However, the areas, in which the task of FS can mainly be applied, are categorized into the following ways (see Figure 1.).

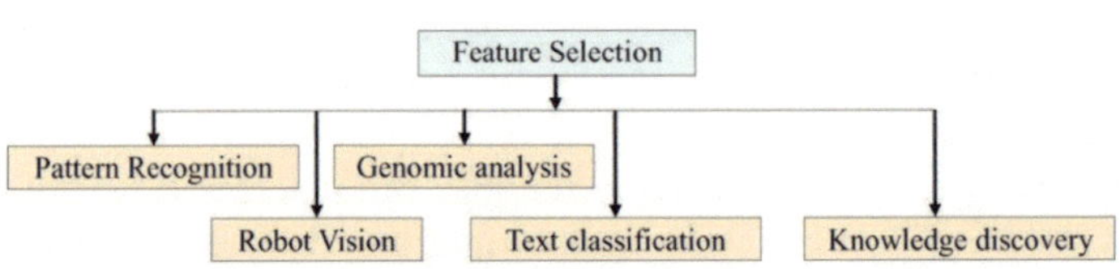

Figure 1. Applicable areas of feature selection.

Figure 2. Picture taken by a camera from a fish processing industry, adapted from [8].

In the pattern recognition paradigm, the FS tasks are mostly concerned with the classification problems. Basically, pattern recognition is the study of how machines can monitor the environment, learn to differentiate patterns of interest, and make decision correctly about the categories of patterns. A pattern, ordinarily, contains some features based on classifying a target or object. As an example, a classification problem, that is to say, sorting incoming fish on a conveyor belt in a fish industry according to species. Assume that, there are only two kinds of fish available, such as, salmon and sea bass, exhibited in Figure 2. A machine gives the decision in classifying the fishes automatically based on training of some features, for example, length, width, weight, number and shape of fins, tail shape, and so on. But, problem is that, if there are some irrelevant, redundant, and noisy features are available, classification performance then might be degraded. In such cases, FS has a significant performance to recognize the useless features from the patterns, delete the features, and finally bring the improved classification performance significantly in the context of pattern recognition.

FS technique has successfully been implemented in mobile robot vision to generate efficient navigation trajectories with an extremely simple neural control system [9]. In this case, evolved mobile robots select the salient visual features and actively maintain them on the same retinal position, while the useless image features are discarded. According to the analysis of evolved solutions, it can be found that, robots develop simple and very efficient edge detection to detect obstacles and to move away among them. Furthermore, FS has a significant role in image recognition systems [10]. In these systems, patterns are designed by image data specially describing the image pixel data. There could be hundreds of different features for an image. These features may include: *color* (in various channels), *texture* (dimensionality, line likeness, contrast, roughness, coarseness), *edge, shape, spatial relations, temporal information, statistical measures* (moments- mean, variance, standard deviation, skewness, kurtosis). The FS expert can identify a subset of relevant features from the whole feature set.

In analysis of human genome, gene expression microarray data have increased many folds in recent years. These data provide the opportunity to analyze the expression levels of thousand or tens of thousands of genes in a single experiment. A particular classification task distinguishes between healthy and cancer patients based on their gene expression profile. On the other hand, a typical gene expression data suffer from three problems:

a. limited number of available examples,

b. very high dimensional nature of data,

c. noisy characteristics of the data.

Therefore, suitable FS methods (e.g., [11, 12]) are used upon these datasets to find out a minimal set of gene that has sufficient classifying power to classify subgroups along with some initial filtering.

Text classification is, nowadays, a vital task because of the availability of the proliferated texts in the digital form. We need to access these texts in the flexible ways. A major problem in regard to the text classification is the high dimensionality of the feature space. It is found that, text feature space has several tens of thousands of features, among which most of them are irrelevant and spurious for the text classification tasks. This high number of features resulting the reduction of classification accuracy and of learning speed of the classifiers. Because of those features, a number of classifiers are being unable to utilize in their learning tasks. For this, FS is such a technique that is very much efficient for the text classification task in order to reduce the feature dimensionality and to improve the performance of the classifiers [13].

Knowledge discovery (KD) is an efficient process of identifying valid, novel, potentially useful, and ultimately understandable patterns from the large collections of data [14]. Indeed, the popularity of KD is caused due to our daily basis demands by federal agencies, banks, insurance companies, retail stores, and so on. One of the important KD steps is the data mining step. In the context of data mining, feature selection cleans up the dataset by reducing the set of least significant features. This step ultimately helps to extract some rules from the dataset, such as, *if---then* rule. This rule signifies the proper understanding about the data and increases the human capability to predict what is happening inside the data.

It is now clear that, FS task has an important role in various places, where one can easily produce better performances from the systems by distinguishing the salient features. Among the various applications, in this chapter, we are interested to discuss elaborately in a particular topic of "pattern recognition", in which how FS task can play an important role especially for the classification problem. The reason is that, in the recent years, solving classification problem using FS is a key source for the data mining and knowledge mining paradigm.

3. Feature Selection for Classification

In the recent years, the available real-world problems of the classification tasks draw a high demand for FS, since the datasets of those problems are mixed by a number of irrelevant and redundant features. In practice, FS tasks work on basis of the classification datasets that are publicly available. The most popular benchmark dataset collection is the University of California, Irvine (UCI) machine learning repository [15]. The collection of UCI is mostly row data that must be preprocessed to use in NNs. Preprocessed datasets in it include Proben1 [16]. The characteristics of the datasets particularly those were used in the experiments of this chapter, and their partitions are summarized in Table 1. The details of the table show a considerable diversity in the number of examples, features, and classes among the datasets. All datasets were partitioned into three sets: a training set, a validation set, and a testing set, according to the suggestion mentioned in [16]. For all datasets, the first P_1 examples were used for the training set, the following P_2 examples for the validation set, and the final P_3 examples for the testing set. The above mentioned datasets were used widely in many previous studies and they represent some of the most challenging datasets in the NN and machine learning [12, 17].

Datasets	**Features**	**Classes**	**Examples**	**Partition sets**		
				Training	Validation	Testing
Cancer	9	2	699	349	175	175
Glass	9	6	214	108	53	53
Vehicle	18	4	846	424	211	211
Thyroid	21	3	7200	3600	1800	1800
Ionosphere	34	2	351	175	88	88
Credit Card	51	2	690	346	172	172
Sonar	60	2	208	104	52	52
Gene	120	3	3175	1587	794	794
Colon cancer	2000	2	62	30	16	16

Table 1. Characteristics and partitions of different classification datasets.

The description of the datasets reported in Table 1 is available in [15], except colon cancer, which can be found in [18]. There are also some other gene expression datasets like colon cancer (e.g., lymphoma and leukemia), that are described in [19] and [20].

4. Existing Works for Feature Selection

A number of proposed approaches for solving FS problem that can broadly be categorized into the following three classifications [2]:

a. wrapper,

b. filter, and

c. hybrid.

d. Other than these classifications, there is also another one, called as, meta-heuristic.

In the wrapper approach, a predetermined learning model is assumed, wherein features are selected that justify the learning performance of the particular learning model [21], whereas in the filter approach, statistical analysis of the feature set is required, without utilizing any learning model [22]. The hybrid approach attempts to utilize the complementary strengths of the wrapper and filter approaches [23]. The meta-heuristics (or, global search approaches) attempt to search a salient feature subset in a full feature space in order to find a high-quality solution using mutual cooperation of individual agents, such as, genetic algorithm, ant colony optimization, and so on [64]. Now, the schematic diagrams of how the filter, wrapper, and hybrid approaches find relevant (salient) features are given in Figures 3(a,b,c). These figures are summarized according to the investigations of different FS related works.

Subsets can be generated and the search process carried out in a number of ways. One method, called sequential forward search (SFS[24,25]), is to start the search process with an empty set and successfully add features; another option called sequential backward search (SBS[4,26]), is to start with a full set and successfully remove features. In addition, a third alternative, called bidirectional selection [27], is to start on both ends and add and remove features simultaneously. A fourth method [28, 29], is to have a search process start with a randomly selected subset using a sequential or bidirectional strategy. Yet another search strategy, called complete search [2], may give a best solution to an FS task due to the thoroughness of its search, but is not feasible when dealing with a large number of features. Alternatively, the sequential strategy is simple to implement and fast, but is affected by the nesting effect [3], wherein once a feature is added (or, deleted) it cannot be deleted (or, added) later. In order to overcome such disadvantages of the sequential search strategy, another search strategy, called the floating search strategy [3], has been implemented.

Search strategy considerations for any FS algorithm are a vital part in finding salient features of a given dataset [2]. Numerous algorithms have been proposed to address the problem of searching. Most algorithms use either a sequential search (for example, [4,5,24,26,30]) or a global search (e.g., [11,23,31-35]). On the basis of guiding the search strategies and evaluating the subsets, in contrast, the existing FS algorithms can be grouped into the following three approaches: wrapper (e.g., [4,6,30,36-38]), filter (e.g., [40,41]), and hybrid (e.g., [23,42]). It is well-known that wrapper approaches always return features with a higher saliency than filter approaches, as the former utilize the association of features collectively during the learning process, but are computationally more expensive [2]).

In solutions for FS, filter approaches are faster to implement, since they estimate the performance of features without any actual model assumed between outputs and inputs of the data. A feature can be selected or deleted on the basis of some predefined criteria, such as, mutual information [39], principal component analysis [43], independent component analysis [44], class separability measure [45], or variable ranking [46]. Filter approaches have the advantage of computational efficiency, but the saliency of the selected features is insufficient, because they do not take into account the biases of classification models.

In order to implement the wrapper approaches, a number of algorithms ([4,24,26,30,47]) have been proposed that use sequential search strategies in finding a subset of salient features. In [24], features are added to a neural network (NN) according to SFS during training. The addition process is terminated when the performance of the trained classifier is degraded. Recently, Kabir et al. [47] proposed approach has drawn much attention in SFS-based feature selections. In this approach, correlated (distinct) features from two groups, namely, similar and dissimilar, are added to the NN training model sequentially. At the end of the training process, when the NN classifier has captured all the necessary information of a given dataset, a subset of salient features is generated with reduced redundancy of information. In a number of other studies (e.g., [4,26,30]), SBS is incorporated in FS using a NN, where the least salient features have been deleted in stepwise fashion during training. In this context, different algorithms employ different heuristic techniques for measuring saliency of features. In [24], saliency of features is measured using a NN training scheme, in which only one feature is used in the input layer at a time. Two different weight analysis-based heuristic techniques are employed in [4] and [26] for computing the saliency of features. Furthermore, in [30], a full feature set NN training scheme is used, where each feature is temporarily deleted with a cross-check of NN performance.

The value of a loss function, consisting of cross entropy with a penalty function, is considered directly for measuring the saliency of a feature in [5] and [6]. In [5], the penalty function encourages small weights to converge to zero, or prevents weights from converging to large values. After the penalty function has finished running, those features that have smaller weights are sequentially deleted during training as being irrelevant. On the other hand, in [6], the penalty function forces a network to keep the derivatives of the values of its neurons' transfer functions low. The aim of such a restriction is to reduce output sensitivity to input changes. In the FS process, feature removal operations are performed sequentially, especially for those features that do not degrade accuracy of the NN upon removal. A class-dependent FS algorithm in [38], selects a desirable feature subset for each class. It first divides a C class classification problem into C two-class classification problems. Then, the features are integrated to train a support vector machine (SVM) using a SFS strategy in order to find the feature subset of each binary classification problem. Pal and Chintalapudi [36] has proposed a SBS-based FS technique that multiplies an attenuation function by each feature before allowing the features to be entered into the NN training. This FS technique is the root for proposing another FS algorithm in [48]. Rakotomamonjy [37] has proposed new FS criteria that are derived from SVMs and that are based on the sensitivity of generalization error bounds with respect to features.

Unlike sequential search-based FS approaches, global search approaches (or, meta-heuristics) start a search in a full feature space instead of a partial feature space in order to find a high-quality solution. The strategy of these algorithms is based on the mutual cooperation of individual agents. A standard genetic algorithm (GA) has been used for FS [35], where fixed length strings in a population set represent a feature subset. The population set evolves over time to converge to an optimal solution via crossover and mutation operations. A number of other algorithms exist (e.g., [22,23]), in which GAs are used for solving FS. A hybrid approach [23] for FS has been proposed that incorporates the filter and wrapper approaches in a cooperative manner. A filter approach involving mutual information computation is used here as a local search to rank features. A wrapper approach involving GAs is used here as global search to find a subset of salient features from the ranked features. In [22], two basic operations, namely, deletion and addition are incorporated that seek the least significant and most significant features for making a stronger local search during FS.

ACO is predominantly a useful tool, considered as a modern algorithm that has been used in several studies (e.g., [11,31,42,49-52]) for selecting salient features. During the operation of this algorithm, a number of artificial ants traverse the feature space to construct feature subsets iteratively. During subset construction (SC), the existing approaches ([11,42,49-52]) define the size of the constructed subsets by a fixed number for each iteration, whereas the SFS strategy has been followed in [31,49], and [51]. In order to measure the heuristic values of features during FS, some of the algorithms ([11,31,50,52]) use filter tools. Evaluating the constructed subsets is, on the other hand, a vital part in the study of ACO-based FS, since most algorithms design the pheromone update rules on the basis of outcomes of subset evaluations. In this regard, a scheme of training classifiers (i.e., wrapper tools) has been used in almost all of the above ACO-based FS algorithms, except for the two cases, where rough set theory and the latent variable model (i.e., filter tools) are considered, which are in [11] and [31], respectively.

A recently proposed FS [34] approach is based on rough sets and a particle swarm optimization (PSO) algorithm. A PSO algorithm is used for finding a subset of salient features over a large and complex feature space. The main heuristic strategy of PSO in FS is that particles fly up to a certain velocity through the feature space. PSO finds an optimal solution through the interaction of individuals in the population. Thus, PSO finds the best solution in the FS as the particles fly within the subset space. This approach is more efficient than a GA in the sense that it does not require crossover and mutation operators; simple mathematical operators are required only.

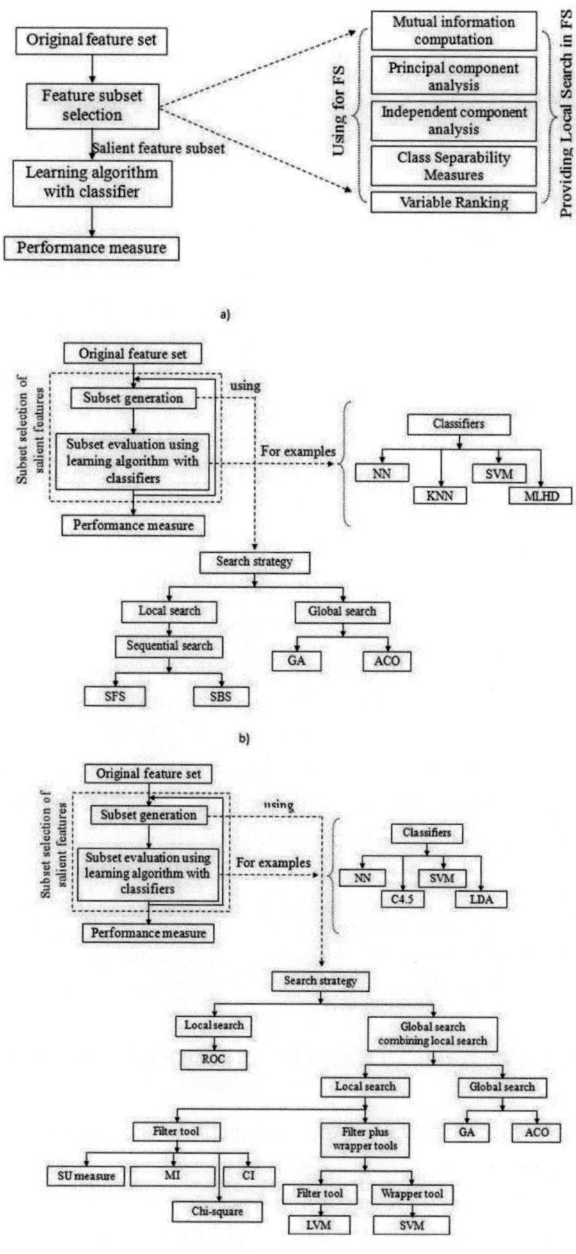

Figure 3. a)Schematic diagram of filter approach. Each approach incorporates the specific search strategies. (b)Schematic diagram of wrapper approach. Each approach incorporates the specific search strategies and classifiers. Here, NN, KNN, SVM, and MLHD refer to the neural network, K-nearest neighbour, support vector machine, and maximum likelihood classifier, respectively. (c)Schematic diagram of hybrid approach. Each approach incorporates the specific search strategies and classifiers. Here, LDA, ROC, SU, MI, CI, and LVM, refer to the linear discriminant analysis classifier,

receiver operating characteristic method, symmetrical uncertainty, mutual information, correlation information, and latent variable model, respectively.

5. Common Problems

Most of the afore-mentioned search strategies, however, attempt to find solutions in FS that range between sub-optimal and near optimal regions, since they use local search throughout the entire process, instead of global search. On the other hand, these search algorithms utilize a partial search over the feature space, and suffer from computational complexity. Consequently, near-optimal to optimal solutions are quite difficult to achieve using these algorithms. As a result, many research studies now focus on global search algorithms (or, metaheuristics) [31]). The significance of global search algorithms is that they can find a solution in the full search space on the basis of activities of multi-agent systems that use a global search ability utilizing local search appropriately, thus significantly increasing the ability of finding very high-quality solutions within a reasonable period of time[53]. To achieve global search, researchers have attempted simulated annealing [54], genetic algorithm [35], ant colony optimization ([49,50]), and particle swarm optimization [34] algorithms in solving FS tasks.

On the other hand, most of the global search approaches discussed above do not use a bounded scheme to decide the size of the constructed subsets. Accordingly, in these algorithms, the selected subsets might be larger in size and include a number of least significant features. Furthermore, most of the ACO-based FS algorithms do not consider the random and probabilistic behavior of ants during SCs. Thus, the solutions found in these algorithms might be incomplete in nature. On the other hand, the above sequential search-based FS approaches suffer from the nesting effect as they try to find subsets of salient features using a sequential search strategy. It is said that such an effect affects the generalization performance of the learning model [3].

6. A New Hybrid ACO-based Feature Selection Algorithm-ACOFS

It is found that, hybridization of several components gives rise to better overall performance in FS problem. The reason is that hybrid techniques are capable of finding a good solution, even when a single technique is often trapped with an incomplete solution [64]. Furthermore, incorporation of any global search strategy in a hybrid system (called as hybrid metaheuristic approach) can likely provide high-quality solution in FS problem.

In this chapter, a new hybrid meta-heuristic approach for feature selection (ACOFS) has been presented that utilizes ant colony optimization. The main focus of this algorithm is to generate subsets of salient features of reduced size. ACOFS utilizes a hybrid search technique that combines the wrapper and filter approaches. In this regard, ACOFS modifies the standard pheromone update and heuristic information measurement rules based on the above two approaches. The reason for the novelty and distinctness of ACOFS versus previous algorithms (e.g., [11,31,42,49-52]) lie in the following two aspects.

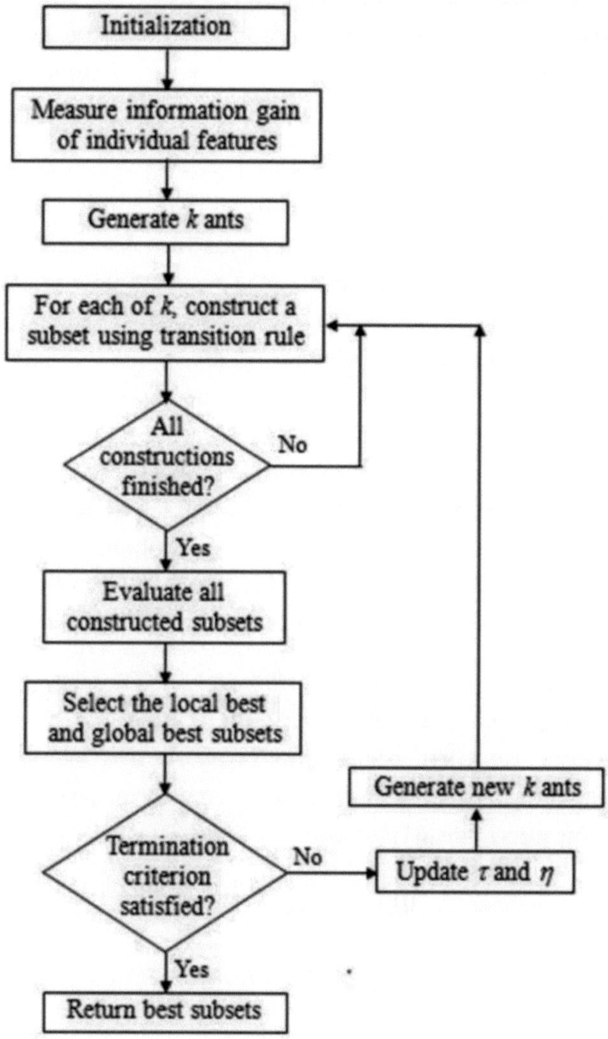

Figure 4. Major steps of ACOFS, adapted from [64].

First, ACOFS emphasizes not only the selection of a number of salient features, but also the attainment of a reduced number of them. ACOFS selects salient features of a reduced number using a subset size determination scheme. Such a scheme works upon a bounded region and provides sizes of constructed subsets that are smaller in number. Thus, following this scheme, an ant attempts to traverse the node (or, feature) space to construct a path (or, subset). This approach is quite different from those of the existing schemes ([31,49,51]), where the ants are guided by using the SFS strategy in selecting features during the feature subset construction. However, a problem is that, SFS requires an appropriate stopping criterion to stop the SC. Otherwise, a number of irrelevant features may be included in the constructed subsets, and the solutions may not be effective. To solve this problem, some algorithms ([11,42,50,52]) define the size of a constructed subset by a fixed number for each iteration for all ants, which is incremented at a fixed rate for following iterations. This technique could be inefficient if the fixed number becomes too large or too small. Therefore, deciding the subset size within a reduced area may be a good step for constructing the subset while the ants traverse through the feature space.

Second, ACOFS utilizes a hybrid search technique for selecting salient features that combines the advantages of the wrapper and filter approaches. An alternative name for such a search technique is "ACO search". This technique is designed with two sets of new rules for pheromone update and heuristic information measurement. The idea of these rules is based mainly on the random and probabilistic behaviors of ants while selecting features during SC. The aim is to provide the correct information to the features and to maintain an effective balance between exploitation and exploration of ants during SC. Thus, ACOFS achieves a strong search capability that helps to select a smaller number of the most salient features among a feature set. In contrast, the existing approaches ([11,31,42,49-52]) try to design rules without distinguishing between the random and probabilistic behaviors of ants during the construction of a subset. Consequently, ants may be deprived of the opportunity of utilizing enough previous experience or investigating more salient features during SC in their solutions.

The main structure of ACOFS is shown in Figure 4, in which the detailed description can be found in [64]. However, at the first stage, while each of the k ants attempt to construct subset, it decides the subset size r first according to the subset size determination scheme. This scheme guides the ants to construct subsets in a reduced form. Then, it follows the conventional probabilistic transition rule [31] for selecting features as follows,

$$P_i^k(t) = \begin{cases} \dfrac{[\tau_i(t)]^\alpha [\eta_i(t)]^\beta}{\sum_{u \in j^k} [\tau_u(t)]^\alpha [\eta_u(t)]^\beta} \\ 0 \end{cases} \tag{1}$$

$$if\ i \in j^k$$

where j^k is the set of feasible features that can be added to the partial solution, τ_i and η_i are the pheromone and heuristic values associated with feature i (i 1, 2,.....,n), and α and β are two parameters that determine the relative importance of the pheromone value and heuristic information. Note that, since the initial value of and for all individual features are equal, Eq. (1) shows random behaviour in SC initially. The approach used by the ants in constructing individual subsets during SC can be seen in Figure 5.

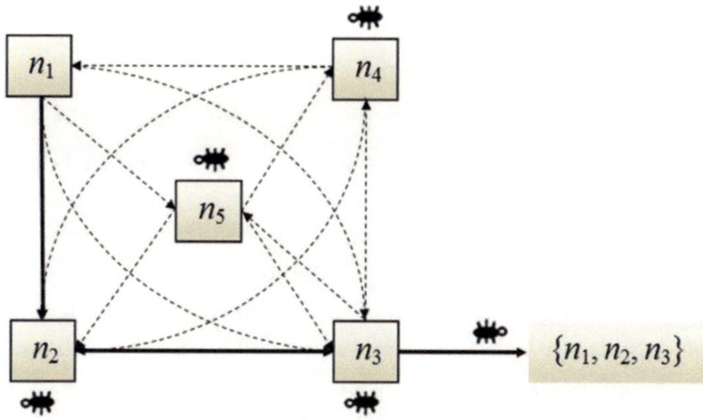

Figure 5. Representation of subset constructions by individual ants in ACO algorithm for FS. Here, n_1, n_2,..., n_5 represent the individual features. As an example, one ant placed in n_1 constructed one subset $\{n_1, n_2, n_3\}$.

ACOFS imposes a restriction upon the subset size determination in determining the subset size, which is not an inherent constraint. Because, other than such restriction, likewise the conventional approaches, the above determination scheme works on an extended boundary after a certain range that results in ineffective solutions for FS. In order to solve another problem, that is to say, incomplete solutions to ACO-based FS algorithms; our ACOFS incorporates a hybrid search strategy (i.e., a combination of the wrapper and filter approaches) by designing different rules to strengthen the global search ability of the ants. Incorporation of these two approaches results in an ACOFS that achieves high-quality solutions for FS from a given dataset. For better understanding, details about each aspect of ACOFS are now given in the following sections.

6.1. Determination of Subset Size

In an ACO algorithm, the activities of ants have significance for solving different combinatorial optimization problems. Therefore, in solving the FS problem, guiding ants in the correct directions is very advantageous in this sense. In contrast to other existing ACO- based FS algorithms, ACOFS uses a straightforward mechanism to determine the subset size r. It employs a simpler probabilistic formula with a constraint and a random function. The aim of using such a probabilistic formula is to provide information to the random function in such a way that the minimum subset size has a higher probability of being selected. This is important in the sense that ACOFS can be guided toward a particular direction by the choice of which reduced-size subset of salient features is likely to be generated. The subset size determination scheme used can be described in two ways as follows.

First, ACOFS uses a probabilistic formula modified from [32] to decide the size of a subset r $(\leq n)$ as follows:

$$P_r = \frac{n-r}{\sum_{i=1}^{l}(n-i)} \tag{2}$$

Here, P_r is maximized linearly as r is minimized, and the value of r is restricted by a constraint, namely, $2 \le r \le \delta$. Therefore, r 2, 3,......,δ, where $\delta = \mu\ xn$ and $l = n - r$. Here, μ is a user-specified parameter that controls δ. Its value depends on the n for a given dataset. If is closed to n, then the search space of finding the salient features becomes larger, which certainly causes a high computational cost, and raises the risk that ineffective feature subsets might be generated. Since the aim of ACOFS is to select a subset of salient features within a smaller range, the length of the selected subset is preferred to be between 3 and 12 depending on the given dataset. Thus, is set as [0.1, 0.6]. Then, normalize all the values of P_r in such a way that the summation of all possible values of P_r is equal to 1.

Second, ACOFS utilizes all the values of P_r for the random selection scheme mentioned in Figure 6 to determine the size of the subset, r eventually. This selection scheme is almost similar to the classical roulette wheel procedure [55].

```
Random_selection
{
    generate random value h [0,1];
    sum=0;P0=0;P1=0;
    for(r=2 to δ){
        sum=sum+Pr;
        if(h<=sum)
            break;
    }
    return r;
}
```

Figure 6. Pseudo-code of the random selection procedure.

6.2. Subset Evaluation

Subset evaluation has a significant role, along with other basic operations of ACO for selecting salient features in FS tasks. In common practices, filter or wrapper approaches are involved for evaluation tasks. However, it is found in [7] that the performance of a wrapper approach is always better than that of a filter approach. Therefore, the evaluation of the constructed subsets is inspired by a feed-forward NN training scheme for each iteration. Such a NN classifier is not an inherent constraint; instead of NN, any other type of classifier, such as SVM, can be used as well for this evaluation tasks. In this study, the evaluation of the subset is represented by the percentage value of NN classification accuracy (CA) for the testing set. A detailed discussion of the evaluation mechanism integrated into ACOFS as follows.

First, during training the features of a constructed subset, the NN is trained partially for τ_p epochs. Training is performed sequentially using the examples of a training set and a back-propagation (BP) learning algorithm [56]. The number of training epochs, τ_p, is specified by the user. In partial training, which was first used in conjunction with an evolutionary algorithm [17], the NN is trained for a fixed number of epochs, regardless of whether the algorithm has converged on a result.

Second, check the progress of training to determine whether further training is necessary. If training error is reduced by a predefined amount, ε, after the τ_p training epochs (as mentioned in Eq. (4)), we assume that the training process has been progressing well, and that further training is thus necessary, and then proceed to the first step. Otherwise, we go to the next step for adding a hidden neuron. The error, E, is calculated as follows:

$$E = \frac{1}{2}\sum_{p=1}^{P}\sum_{c=1}^{C}(o_c(p) - t_c(p))^2 \tag{3}$$

where $o_c(p)$ and $t_c(p)$ are the actual and target responses of the c-th output neuron for the training example p. The symbols P and C represent the total number of examples and of output neurons in the training set, respectively. The reduction of training error can be described as follows:

$$E(t) - E(t + \tau_p) > \varepsilon, \; t = \tau, \; 2\tau, \; 3\tau, ... \tag{4}$$

On the other hand, in the case of adding the hidden neuron, the addition operation is guided by computing the contributions of the current hidden neurons. If the contributions are high, then it is assumed that another one more hidden neuron is required. Otherwise, freeze the extension of the hidden layer size for further partial training of the NN. Computation of the contribution of previously added hidden neurons in the NN is based on the CA of the validation set. The CA can be calculated as follows:

$$CA = 100\left(\frac{P_{vc}}{P_v}\right) \tag{5}$$

where P_{vc} refers to the number of examples in the validation set correctly classified by the NN and P_v is the total number of patterns in the validation set.

At this stage, the ACOFS measures error and CA in the validation set using Eqs. (3) and (5) after every τ_p epochs of training. It then terminates training when either the validation CA decreases or the validation error increases or both are satisfied for T successive times, which are measured at the end of each of T successive τ_p epochs of training [16]. Finally, the testing accuracy of the current NN architecture is checked with selected hidden neurons, using the example of the testing set according to Eq. (5).

The idea behind this evaluation process is straightforward: minimize the training error, and maximize the validation accuracy. To achieve these goals, ACOFS uses a constructive approach to determine NN architectures automatically. Although other approaches, such as, pruning [57] and regularization [58] could be used in ACOFS, the selection of an initial NN architecture in these approaches is difficult [59]. This selection, however, is simple in the case of a constructive approach. For example, the initial network architecture in a constructive approach can consist of a hidden layer with one neuron. On the other hand, an input layer is set with r neurons, and an output layer with c neurons. More precisely, among r and c neurons, one neuron for each feature of the corresponding subset and one neuron for each class, respectively. If this minimal architecture cannot solve the given task, hidden neurons can be added one by one. Due to the simplicity of initialization, the constructive approach is used widely in multi-objective learning tasks [60].

6.3 Best Subset Selection

Generally, finding salient subsets with a reduced size is always preferable due to the low cost in hardware implementation and less time consumed in operation. Unlike other existing algorithms (e.g., [49,50]), in ACOFS, the best salient feature subset is recognized eventually as a combination of the local best and global best selections as follows:

Local best selection: Determine the local best subset, $S^l(t)$ for a particular t ($t \in 1, 2, 3, \ldots..$) iteration according to Max($S^k(t)$), where $S^k(t)$ is the number of subsets constructed by k ants, and k 1, 2,…,n.

Global best selection: Determine the global best subset (S^g), that is, the best subset of salient features from the all local best solutions in such a way that S^g is compared with the currently decided local best subset, $S^l(t)$ at every t iteration by their classification performances. If $S^l(t)$ is found better, then $S^l(t)$ is replaced by S^g. One thing is that, during this selection process, if the performances are found similar at any time, then select the one among the two, i.e., S^g and $S^l(t)$ as a best subset that has reduced size. Note that, at the first iteration $S^l(t)$ is considered as S^g.

6.4 Hybrid Search Process

The new hybrid search technique, incorporated in ACOFS, consists of wrapper and filter approaches. A significant advantage of this search technique is that ants achieve a significant ability of utilizing previous successful moves and of expressing desirability of moves towards a high-quality solution in FS. This search process is composed of two sets of newly designed rules, such as, the pheromone update rule and the heuristic information rule, which are further described as follows.

6.4.1. Pheromone Update Rule

Pheromone updating in the ACO algorithm is a vital aspect of FS tasks. Ants exploit features in SC that have been most suitable in prior iterations through the pheromone update rule, consisting of local update and global update. More precisely, global update applies only to those features that are a part of the best feature subset in the current iteration. It allows the features to receive a large amount of pheromone update in equal shares. The aim of global update is to encourage ants to construct subsets with a significant CA. In contrast to the global update, local update not only causes the irrelevant features to be less desirable, but also helps ants to select those features, which have never been explored before. This update either decreases the strength of the pheromone trail or maintains the same level, based on whether a particular feature has been selected.

In ACOFS, a set of new pheromone update rules has been designed on the basis of two basic behaviors (that is to say, random and probabilistic) of ants during SCs. These rules have been modified from the standard rule in [49] and [53], which aims to provide a proper balance between exploration and exploitation of ants for the next iteration. Exploration is reported to prohibit ants from converging on a common path. Actual ants also have a similar behavioral characteristic [61], which is an attractive property. If different paths can be explored by different ants, then there is a higher probability that one of the ants may find a better solution, as opposed to all ants converging on the same tour.

Random case: The rule presenting in Eq. (6) is modified only in the second term, which is divided by m_i. Such a modification provides for sufficient exploration of the ants for the following constructions. The reason is that during the random behavior of the transition rule, the features are being chosen to be selected randomly in practice, instead of according to their experiences. Thus, to provide an exploration facility for the ants, the modification has been adopted as follows:

$$
\begin{aligned}
&\tau_i(t+1)=(1-\rho)\tau_i(t)+\frac{1}{m_i}\sum_{k=1}^{n}\Delta\tau_i^k(t)+e\Delta\tau_i^g(t)\\
&\Delta\tau_i^k(t)=\begin{cases}\gamma(S^k(t)) & if\ i\in S^k(t)\\ 0 & otherwise\end{cases}\\
&\Delta\tau_i^g(t)=\begin{cases}\gamma(S^l(t)) & f\ i\in S^l(t)\\ 0 & otherwise\end{cases}
\end{aligned}
\tag{6}
$$

Here, i refers to the number of feature (i 1, 2,......n), and m_i is the count for the specific selected feature i in the current iteration. $\Delta\tau_i^k(t)$is the amount of pheromone received by the local update for feature i, which is included in $S^k(t)$ at iteration t. Similarly, the global update, $\Delta\tau_i^g(t)$, is the amount of pheromone for feature i that is included in $S^l(t)$. Finally, ρ and e refer to the pheromone decay value, and elitist parameter, respectively.

Probabilistic case: Eq. (7) shows the modified pheromone rule for the probabilistic case. The rule is similar to the original form, but actual modification has been made only for the inner portions of the second and third terms.

$$\tau_i(t+1)=(1-\rho)\tau_i(t)+\sum_{k=1}^{n}\Delta\tau_i^k(t)+e\Delta\tau_i^g(t)$$
$$\Delta\tau_i^k(t)=\begin{cases}\gamma(S^k(t))\times\lambda_i & f\ i\in S^k(t)\\ 0 & otherwise\end{cases} \tag{7}$$
$$\Delta\tau_i^g(t)=\begin{cases}\gamma(S^l(t))\times\lambda_i & f\ i\in S^l(t)\\ 0 & otherwise\end{cases}$$

Here, feature i is rewarded by the global update, and $\Delta\tau^g$ is in the third term, where i $S^l(t)i$. It is important to emphasize that, i is maintained strictly here. That is, i at iteration i $t_t i$ is compared with i at iteration $(t_t - \tau_p)$, where $t_t = t + \tau_p$, *and* τ_p 1, 2, 3,……In this regard, if $\gamma(S^l(t_t))$ max$((\gamma S^l(t_{tp}\varepsilon)),)$, where ε refers to the number of CAs for those local best subsets that maintain $|S^l(t_t)| = |S^l(t_{tp})|$, then a number of features, n_c are ignored to get $\Delta\tau^g$, since those features are available in $S^l(t_t)$, which causes to degrade its performance. Here, $n_c \in S^l(t_t)$ but $n_c \notin S^{lb}$, where S^{lb} provides max$((\gamma S^l(t_{tp})),)$, and $|S^l(t_t)|$ implies the size of the subset $S^l(t_t)$. Note that, the aim of this restriction is to provide $\Delta\tau^g$ only to those features that are actually significant, because, global update has a vital role in selecting the salient features in ACOFS. Distinguish such salient features and allow them to receive $\Delta\tau^g$ by imposing the above restriction.

6.4.2. Heuristic Information Measurement

A heuristic value, η , for each feature generally represents the attractiveness of the features, and depends on the dependency degree. It is therefore necessary to use ; otherwise, the algorithm may become too greedy, and ultimately a better solution may not be found [31]. Here, a set of new rules is introduced for measuring heuristic information using the advantages of wrapper and filter tools. More precisely, the outcome of subset evaluations using the NN is used here as a wrapper tool, whereas the value of information gain for each feature is used as a filter tool. These rules are, therefore, formulated according to the random and probabilistic behaviors of the ants, which are described as follows.

Random case: In the initial iteration, while ants are involved in constructing the feature subsets randomly, the heuristic value of all features i can be estimated as follows:

$$\eta_i = \frac{1}{m_i}\sum_{k=1}^{n}\gamma(S^k(t))(1+\varphi e^{-\frac{|S^k(t)|}{n}}) \qquad if\ i \in S^k(t) \tag{8}$$

Probabilistic case: In the following iterations, when ants complete the feature SCs on the basis of the probabilistic behavior, the following formula is used to estimate for all features i:

$$\eta_i = m_i\phi_i\sum_{k=1}^{n}\gamma_a(S^k(t))\lambda_i(1+\varphi e^{-\frac{|S^k(t)|}{n}}) \qquad if\ i \in S^k(t) \tag{9}$$

In these two rules, φ_i refers to the number of a particular selected feature i that is a part of the subsets that are constructed within the currently completed iterations, except for the initial iteration. The aim of multiplying m_i and φ_i is to provide a proper exploitation capability for the ants during SCs. λ_i refers to the information gain for feature i. A detailed discussion on measurement of information gain can be seen in [64]. However, the aim of including is based on the following two factors:

a. reducing the greediness of some particular feature i in n during SCs, and

b. increasing the diversity between the features in n.

Thus, different features may get an opportunity to be selected in the SC for different iterations, thus definitely enhancing the exploration behavior of ants. Furthermore, one additional exponential term has been multiplied by these rules in aiming for a reduced size subset. Here, is the user specified parameter that controls the exponential term.

6.5. Computational Complexity

In order to understand the actual computational cost of a method, an exact analysis of computational complexity is required. In this sense, the big-O notation [62] is a prominent approach in terms of analyzing computational complexity. Thus, ACOFS here uses the above process for this regard. There are seven basic steps in ACOFS, namely, information gain measurement, subset construction, subset evaluation, termination criterion, subset determination, pheromone update, and heuristic information measurement. The following paragraphs present the computational complexity of ACOFS in order to show that inclusion of different techniques does not increase computational complexity in selecting a feature subset.

i. Information Gain Measurement: In this step, information gain (IG) for each feature is measured according to [64]. If the number of total features for a given dataset is n, then the cost of measuring IG is $O(n \times P)$, where P denotes the number of examples in the given dataset. It is further mentioning that this cost is required only once, specifically, before starting the FS process.

ii. Subset Construction: Subset construction shows two different types of phenomena according to Eq. (1). For the random case, if the total number of features for a given dataset is n, then the cost of an ant constructing a single subset is $O(r \times n)$. Here,r refers to the size of subsets. Since the total number of ants is k, the computational cost is $O(r \times k \times n)$ operations. However, in practice, $r<n$; hence, the cost becomes $O(k \times n) \approx O(n^2)$. In terms of the probabilistic case, ACOFS uses the Eq. (1) for selecting the features in SC, which shows a constant computational cost of O(1) for each ant. If the number of ants is k, then the computational cost becomes $O(k)$.

iii. In ACOFS, five types of operations are necessarily required for evaluating a single subset using a constructive NN training scheme: (a) partial training, (b) stopping criterion, (c) further training, (d) contribution computation, and (e) addition of a hidden neuron. The subsequent paragraphs describe these types in details.

a. Partial training: In case of training, standard BP [56] is used. During training each epoch BP takes O(W) operations for one example. Here, W is the number of weights in the current NN. Thus, training all examples in the training set for τ_p epochs requires $O(\tau_p \times P_t \times W)$ operations, where P_t denotes the number of examples in the training set.

b. Stopping criterion: During training, the stopping criterion uses either validation accuracy or validation errors for subset evaluation. Since training error is computed as a part of the training process, evaluating the termination criterion takes $O(P_v \times W)$ operations, where P_v denotes the number of examples in the validation set. Since $P_v< P_t$, $O(P \times {}_v \times W) < O({}_p \times kP_t \times W)$.

c. Further training: ACOFS uses Eq. (4) to check whether further training is necessary. The evaluation of Eq. (4) takes a constant number of computational operations O(1), since the error values used in Eq. (3) have already been evaluated during training.

d. Contribution computation: ACOFS computes the contribution of the added hidden neuron using Eq. (5). This computation takes $O(P_v)$ operations, which is less than $O(\tau_p \times P_t \times W)$.

e. Addition of a hidden neuron: The computational cost for adding a hidden neuron is $O(r \times c)$ for initializing the connection weights, where r is the number of features in the current subset, and c is the number of neurons in the output layer. Also note that $O(r + c) < O({}_p \times P_t \times W)$.

The aforementioned computation is done for a partial training session consisting of τ_p epochs. In general, ACOFS requires a number, say M, of such partial training sessions for evaluating a single subset. Thus, the cost becomes $O(\tau_p \times M \times P_t \times W)$. Furthermore, by considering all subsets, the computational cost required is $O(k \times \tau_p \times M \times P_t \times W)$ operations.

iv. Termination criterion: A termination criterion is employed in ACOFS for terminating the FS process eventually. Since only one criterion is required to be executed (i.e., the algorithm achieves a predefined accuracy, or executes a iteration threshold, I), the execution of such a criterion requires a constant computational cost of O(1).

v. Subset determination: ACOFS requires two steps to determine the best subset, namely, finding the local best subset and the global best subset. In order to find the local best subset in each iteration t, ACOFS requires O(k) operations. The total computational cost for finding the local best subsets thus becomes O(k × t). In order to find the global best subset, ACOFS requires O(1) operations. Thus, the total computational cost for subset determination becomes $O(k \times t)$, which is less than $O(k \times \tau_p \times M \times P_t \times W)$.

vi. Pheromone update rule: ACOFS executes Eqs. (6) and (7) to update the pheromone trails for each feature in terms of the random and probabilistic cases. Since the number of features is n for a given learning dataset, the computation takes O(n) constant operations, which is less than $O(k \times \tau_p \times M \times P_t \times W)$.

vii. Heuristic information measurement: Similar to the pheromone update operation, ACOFS uses Eqs. (8) and (9) to update the heuristic value of n features. Thereafter, the computational cost becomes O(n). Note that, O(n) $O(k \times \tau_p \times M \times P_t \times W)$.

In accordance with the above analysis, summarize the different parts of the entire computational cost as $O(n \times P) + O(n^2) + O(k) + O(k \times \tau_p \times M \times P_t \times W)$. It is important to note here that the first and second terms, namely, $n \times P$ and $\times n^2$, are the cost of operations performed only once, and are much less than $k \times \tau_p \times M \times P_t \times P$. On the other hand, $O(k) << O(k \times \tau_p \times M \times P_t \times W)$. Hence, the total computational cost of ACOFS is $O((\tau_p \times M \times P_t \times W)$, which is similar to the cost of training a fixed network architecture using BP [56], and that the total cost is similar to that of other existing ACO-based FS approaches [42]. Thus, it can be said that incorporation of several techniques in ACOFS does not increase the computational cost.

7. Experimental Studies

The performance of ACOFS has been presented in this context on eight well-known benchmark classification datasets, including the breast cancer, glass, vehicle, thyroid, ionosphere, credit card, sonar, and gene datasets; and one gene expressional classification dataset, namely, the colon cancer dataset. These datasets have been the subject of many studies in NNs and machine learning, covering examples of small, medium, high, and very high-dimensional datasets. The characteristics of these datasets, summarized in Table 1, show a considerable diversity in the number of features, classes, and examples. Now, the experimental details, results, roles of subset size determination scheme in FS, the user specified parameter μ in FS, and hybrid search in FS are described in this context. Finally, one additional experiment on ACOFS concerning performance for FS over real-world datasets mixed with some noisy features, and comparisons of ACOFS with other existing works, are also discussed in this context.

7.1. Experimental Setup

In order to ascertain the effectiveness of ACOFS for FS, extensive experiments have been carried out on ACOFS that are adapted from [64]. To accomplish the FS task suitably in ACOFS, two basic steps need to be considered, namely, dimensionality reduction of the datasets and assigning values for user-specified parameters. In case of dimensionality reduction, in contrast to other datasets used in this study, colon cancer is being very high-dimensional datasets containing a very large number of genes (features). The number of genes of colon cancer (i.e., 2000 genes) is too high to manipulate in the learning classifier and not all genes are useful for classification [63]. To remove such difficulties, we first reduced the dimension of the colon cancer dataset to within 100 features, using an information gain (IG) measurement technique. Ordinarily, IG measurement determines statistically those features that are informative for classifying a target. On the basis of such a concept, we have used such a technique for reducing the dimension of the colon cancer dataset. Details about IG measurement can be found in [64].

In case of user-specified parameters, we used a number of parameters, which are common for the all datasets, reported in the Table 2. It should be noted that, these parameters are not specific to our algorithm, rather usual for any ACO-based FS algorithm using NN. We have chosen these parameters after some preliminary runs. They were not meant to be optimal. It is worth mentioning that, among the parameters mentioned in Table 2, proper selection of the values of parameters and , is helpful for achieving a level of balance between exploitation and exploration of ants in selecting salient features. For example, if 0, then no pheromone information is used, that is to say, previous search experience is neglected. The search then changes to a greedy search. If 0, then attractiveness, the potential benefit of moves, is neglected. In this work, the values of and were chosen according to the suggestion of [53].

Parameter	Value
Initial pheromone level for all features, τ	0.5
Initial heuristic value for all features, η	0.1
(,used in subset size determination	0.08 to 0.6
Strength of pheromone level, α	1
Strength of heuristic value, β	3
Pheromone decay parameter, ρ	0.4
Exponential term control parameter, φ	0.1
Iteration threshold,	10 to 18
Accuracy threshold	Depends on dataset
Learning rate for BP algorithm	0.1 to 0.2
Momentum term for BP algorithm	0.5 to 0.9
Initial weights of NNs	-1.0 to 1.0
The number of epochs for partial training, τ	20 to 40
Training error threshold, λ	Depends on dataset
Training threshold for terminating NN training, T	3

Table 2. Common parameters for all datasets.

7.2 Experimental Results

Tables 3 shows the results of ACOFS over 20 independent runs on nine real-world benchmark classification datasets. The classification accuracy (CA) in Table 3 refers to the percentage of exact classifications produced by trained NNs on the testing set of a classification dataset. In addition, the weights of features for the above nine datasets over 20 independent runs are exhibited in Tables 4-11. On the other hand, Figure 7 shows how the best solution was selected in ACOFS for the glass dataset. In order to observe whether the internal process of FS in ACOFS is appropriately being performed, Figures. 8-11 have been considered. Now, the following observations can be made from Tables 3-11 and Figures 7-11.

Dataset	Avg. result with all features				Avg. result with selected features			
	n	SD	CA (%)	SD	n_s	SD	CA(%)	SD
Cancer	9.00	0.00	97.97	0.42	3.50	1.36	98.91	0.40
Glass	9.00	0.00	76.60	2.55	3.30	1.14	82.54	1.44
Vehicle	18.00	0.00	60.71	11.76	2.90	1.37	75.90	0.64
Thyroid	21.0	0.00	98.04	0.58	3.00	1.34	99.08	0.11
Ionosphere	34.0	0.00	97.67	1.04	4.15	2.53	99.88	0.34
Credit card	51.0	0.00	85.23	0.67	5.85	1.76	87.99	0.38
Sonar	60.0	0.00	76.82	6.97	6.25	3.03	86.05	2.26
Gene	120.0	0.00	78.97	5.51	7.25	2.53	89.20	2.46
Colon cancer	100.0	0.00	59.06	5.75	5.25	2.48	84.06	3.68

Table 3. Performance of ACOFS for different classification datasets. Results were averaged over 20 independent runs. Here, n and n_s refer to the total number of original features and selected features, respectively. On the other hand, CA and SD signify the classification accuracy and standard deviation, respectively.

i. As can be seen from Table 3, ACOFS was able to select a smaller number of features for solving different datasets. For example, ACOFS selected, on average, 3.00 features from a set of 21 features in solving the thyroid dataset. It also selected, on average, 7.25 genes (features) from a set of 120 genes in solving the gene dataset. On the other hand, a very large-dimensional dataset, that of colon cancer, was preprocessed from the original one to be utilized in ACOFS. In this manner, the original 2000 features of colon cancer were reduced to within 100 features. ACOFS then obtained a small number of salient genes, 5.25 on average, from the set of 100 genes for solving the colon cancer dataset. In fact, ACOFS selected a small number of features for all other datasets having more features. Feature reduction in such datasets was several orders of magnitude (see Table 3).

ii. The positive effect of a small number of selected features (n_s) is clearly visible when we observe the CA. For example, for the vehicle dataset, the average CA of all features was 60.71%, whereas it had been 75.90% with 2.90 features. Similarly, ACOFS produced an average CA of 86.05% with the average number of features of 6.25

substantially reduced for the sonar dataset, while the average CA had been 76.82% with all 60 features. Other similar types of scenarios can also be seen for all remaining datasets in ACOFS. Thus, it can be said that ACOFS has a powerful searching capability for providing high-quality solutions. CA improvement for such datasets was several orders of magnitude (see Table 3). Furthermore, the use of n_s caused a relatively small standard deviation (SD), as presented in Table 3 for each entry. The low SDs imply robustness of ACOFS. Robustness is represented by consistency of an algorithm under different initial conditions.

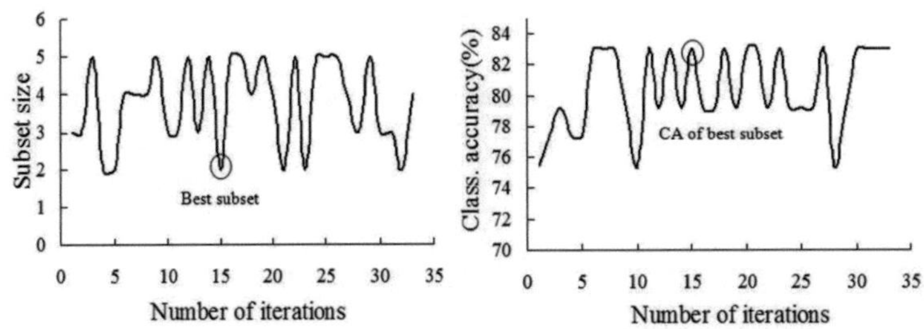

Figure 7. Finding best subset of the glass dataset for a single run. Here, the classification accuracy is the accuracy of the local best subset.

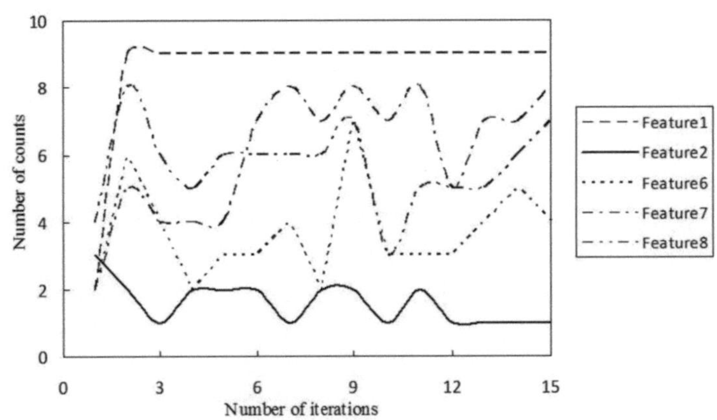

Figure 8. Number of selections of each feature by different ants for different iterations in the glass dataset for a single run.

iii. The method of determination for the final solution of a subset in ACOFS can be seen in Figure 7. We can observe that for the performances of the local best subsets, the CAs varied together with the size of those subsets. There were also several points, where the CAs were maximized, but the best solution was selected (indicated by circle) by considering the reduced size subset. It can also be seen in Figure 7 that CAs varied due to size variations of local best subsets in different iterations.

http://dx.doi.org/10.5772/51707

Furthermore, different features that were included in different local best subsets caused variations in CAs.

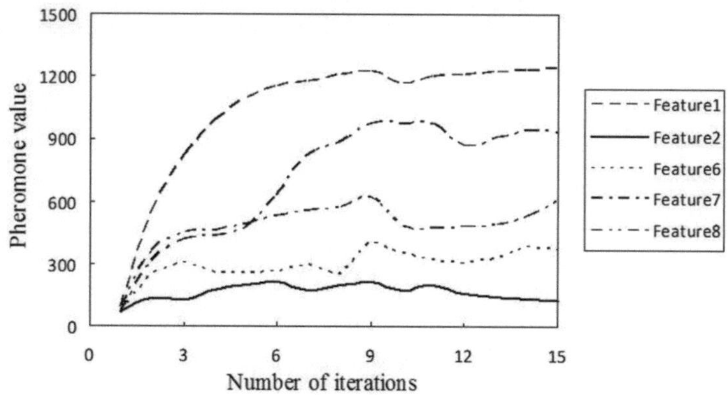

Figure 9. Distribution of pheromone level of some selected features of the glass dataset in different iterations for a single run.

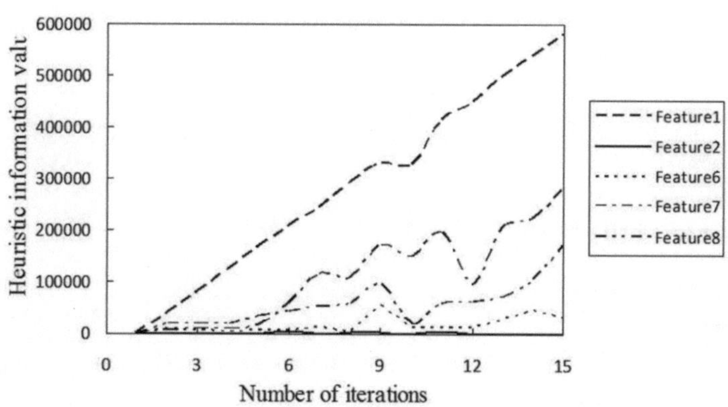

Figure 10. Distribution of heuristic level of some selected features of the glass dataset in different iterations for a single run.

iv. In order to observe the manner, in which how the selection of salient features in different iterations progresses in ACOFS, Figure 8 shows the scenario of such information for the glass dataset for a single run. We can see that features 1, 7, 8, 6, and 2 received most of the selections by ants during SCs compared to the other features. The selection of features was basically performed based on the values of pheromone update (τ) and heuristic information (η) for individual features. Accordingly, those features that had higher values of τ and η ordinarily obtained a higher priority of selection, as could be seen in Figures 9 and 10. For clarity, these figures represented five features, of which four (features 1, 7, 8, 6) had a higher rate of selection by ants during SCs and one (feature 2) had a lower rate.

Dataset	Feature								
	1	2	3	4	5	6	7	8	9
Cancer	0.186	0.042	0.129	0.142	0.129	0.2	0.115	0.042	0.015
Glass	0.258	0.045	0.258	0.107	0.06	0.015	0.182	0.06	0.015

Table 4. Weights of the features selected by ACOFS for the cancer and glass datasets.

Feature	1	2	4	7	9	10	11	12
Weight	0.189	0.103	0.069	0.051	0.086	0.086	0.103	0.086

Table 5. Weights of the features selected by ACOFS for the vehicle dataset.

Feature	1	7	17	19	20	21
Weight	0.052	0.052	0.332	0.1	0.069	0.15

Table 6. Weights of the features selected by ACOFS for the thyroid dataset.

Feature	1	3	4	5	7	8	12	27	29
Weight	0.108	0.036	0.036	0.036	0.06	0.12	0.06	0.12	0.036

Table 7. Weights of the features selected by ACOFS for the ionosphere dataset.

Feature	5	8	29	41	42	43	44	49	51
Weight	0.042	0.06	0.034	0.051	0.17	0.111	0.128	0.034	0.12

Table 8. Weights of the features selected by ACOFS for the credit card dataset.

Feature	2	9	10	11	12	15	17	18	44
Weight	0.037	0.046	0.056	0.084	0.112	0.037	0.037	0.037	0.06

Table 9. Weights of the features selected by ACOFS for the sonar dataset.

Feature	22	59	60	61	62	63	64	69	70	119
Weight	0.027	0.064	0.045	0.1	0.073	0.073	0.119	0.110	0.128	0.036

Table 10. Weights of the features selected by ACOFS for the gene dataset.

Feature	47	72	249	267	493	765	1247	1325	1380	1843
Weight	0.051	0.038	0.051	0.038	0.051	0.038	0.038	0.038	0.051	0.051

Table 11. Weights of the features selected by ACOFS for the colon cancer dataset.

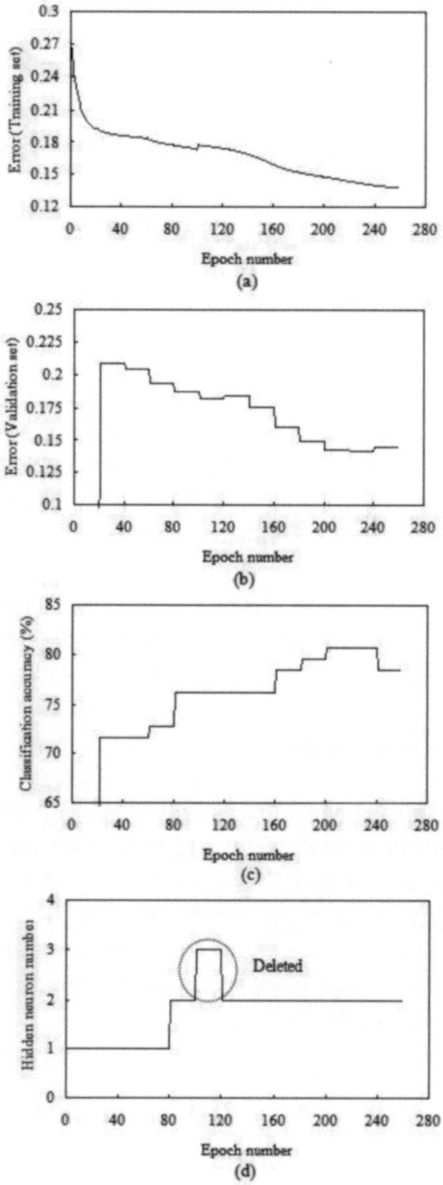

Figure 11. Training process for evaluating the subsets constructed by ants in the ionosphere dataset: (a) training error on training set, (b) training error on validation set, (c) classification accuracy on validation set, and (d) the hidden neuron addition process.

v. Upon completion of the entire FS process, the features that were most salient could be identified by means of weight computation for individual features. That is to say, features having higher weight values were more significant. On the other hand, for a particular feature to have a maximum weight value implied that the feature had the maximum number of selections by ants in any algorithm for most of the runs. Tables 4-11 show the weight of features for the cancer, glass, vehicle, thyroid, ionosphere, credit card, sonar, gene, and colon cancer datasets, respectively, over 20 independent runs. We can see in Table 4 that ACOFS selected features 6, 1, 4, 3, 5, and 7 from the cancer dataset very frequently, that these features had relatively higher weight values, and preformed well as discriminators. Similarly, our ACOFS selected features 42, 44, 51, 43, 8, and 5 as most important from the credit card dataset (Table 8), as well as features 70, 64, 69, 61, 63, 59, and 60 from the gene dataset (Table 10). Note that, weights for certain features are reported in Tables 5-11, whereas weights that were of negligible value for the rest of each dataset are not included.

vi. Finally, we wish to note that a successful evaluation function leads to finding high-quality solutions for ACOFS in FS. Our ACOFS uses a constructive NN model that evaluates the subsets constructed by ants in each and every step during training. As training process progresses, the training error for the training set converges to a certain limit (Figure 11(a)). However, there is an instance in which the training error increases. This is due to the addition of one unnecessary hidden neuron. Such an addition also hampers the training error on the validation set (Figure 11(b)). Therefore, ACOFS deletes such an unnecessary hidden neuron (Figure 11(d)) from the NN architecture, since it cannot improve the classification accuracy on the validation set (Figure 11(c)).

7.3. Effects of Subset Size Determination

The results presented in Table 3 show the ability of ACOFS in selecting salient features. However, the effects resulting from determining the subset size to control ants in such a manner as to construct the subset in a reduced boundary were not clear. To observe such effects, we carried out a new set of experiments. The setups of these experiments were almost exactly the same as those described before. The only difference was that ACOFS had not determined the subset size earlier using a bounded scheme; instead the size of the subset for each ant had been decided randomly.

Dataset	ACOFS without bounded scheme				ACOFS			
	n_s	SD	CA(%)	SD	n_s	SD	CA(%)	SD
Vehicle	6.05	4.76	75.73	0.48	2.90	1.37	75.90	0.64
Credit card	15.30	8.25	88.34	0.22	5.85	1.76	87.99	0.38

Table 12. Effect of determining subset size on the average performances of ACOFS.

Table 12 shows the average results of the new experiments for vehicle and credit card datasets over only 20 independent runs. The positive effects of determining the subset size during the FS process are clearly visible. For example, for the credit card dataset, the average values of n_s of ACOFS without and with subset size determination were 15.30 and 5.85, respectively. A similar scenario can also be seen for the other dataset. In terms of CAs, the average CAs for ACOFS with subset size determination were either better than or comparable to ACOFS without subset size determination for these two datasets.

7.4. Effect of μ

The essence of the proposed techniques in ACOFS can be seen in Table 3 for recognizing the subsets of salient features from the given datasets; however, the effects of the inner component μ of subset size determination (see Section 6.1) on the overall results were not clear. The reason is that the size of the subsets constructed by the ants depended roughly on the value of μ. To observe such effects, we conducted a new set of experiments. The setups of these experiments were almost exactly the same as those described before. The only difference was that the value of μ varied within a range of 0.2 to 0.94 by a small threshold value over 20 individual runs.

Values of μ		**Average performance**			
Initial	Final	n_s	SD	CA (%)	SD
0.40	0.64	2.60	0.91	80.09	2.69
0.50	0.74	3.05	1.16	82.16	1.51
0.60	0.84	3.30	1.14	82.54	1.44
0.70	0.94	3.45	1.39	81.98	1.39

Table 13. Effect of varying the value of μ on the average performances of ACOFS for the glass dataset. The value is incremented by a threshold value of 0.01 over 20 individual runs.

Values of μ		**Average performance**			
Initial	Final	n_s	SD	CA (%)	SD
0.20	0.30	4.70	2.59	99.54	0.83
0.23	0.33	3.65	2.32	99.65	0.63
0.26	0.36	4.15	2.53	99.88	0.34
0.29	0.39	6.00	3.78	99.48	0.76

Table 14. Effect of varying the value of μ on the average performances of ACOFS for the ionosphere dataset. The value is incremented by a threshold value of 0.005 over 20 individual runs.

Tables 13 and 14 show the average results of our new experiments over 20 independent runs. The significance of the effect of varying μ. can be seen from these results. For example, for the glass dataset (Table 13), the average percentage of the CA improved as the value of μ. increased up to a certain point. Afterwards, the CA degraded as the value of μ. increased. Thus, a subset of features was selected with a large size. A similar scenario can also be seen for the ionosphere dataset (Table 14). It is clear here that the significance of the result of FS in ACOFS depends on the value of μ. Furthermore, the determination of subset size in ACOFS is an important aspect for suitable FS.

7.5. Effect of Hybrid Search

The capability of ACOFS for FS can be seen in Table 3, but the effect of using hybrid search in ACOFS for FS is not clear. Therefore, a new set of experiments was carried out to observe such effects. The setups of these experiments were almost exactly as same as those described before. The only difference was that ACOFS did not use the modified rules of pheromone update and heuristic value for each feature; instead, standard rules were used. In such considerations, we avoided not only the incorporation of the information gain term, but also the concept of random and probabilistic behaviors, during SC for both specific rules. Furthermore, we ignored the exponential term in the heuristic measurement rule.

Dataset	ACOFS without hybrid search				ACOFS			
	n_s	SD	CA (%)	SD	n_s	SD	CA(%)	SD
Glass	4.05	1.35	81.22	1.39	3.30	1.14	82.54	1.44
Credit card	6.15	2.21	87.26	0.66	5.85	1.76	87.99	0.38
Sonar	6.50	2.80	84.42	3.03	6.25	3.03	86.05	2.26
Colon cancer	6.35	4.05	82.18	4.08	5.25	2.48	84.06	3.68

Table 15. Effect of considering hybrid search on average performances of ACOFS. Results were averaged over 20 independent runs.

Table 15 shows the average results of our new experiments for the glass, credit card, sonar, and colon cancer datasets over 20 independent runs. The positive effects of using a hybrid search in ACOFS are clearly visible. For example, for the credit card dataset, the average CAs of ACOFS with and without hybrid search were 87.99% and 87.26%, respectively. A similar classification improvement for ACOFS with hybrid search was also observed for the other datasets. On the other hand, in terms of n_s, for the glass dataset, the average values of n_s of ACOFS and ACOFS without hybrid search were 3.30 and 4.05, respectively. For the other datasets it was also found that ACOFS selected a smaller number of salient features. We used t-test here to determine whether the difference of classification performances between ACOFS and ACOFS without hybrid search was statistically significant. We found that

ACOFS performed significantly better than ACOFS without local search operation at a 95% confidence level for all the datasets, except for the colon cancer dataset. On the other hand, the t-test was also used here to determine whether the difference in performances between the above two approaches with regard to selecting a reduced number of salient features was statistically significant. We found that ACOFS was significantly better than ACOFS without hybrid search at a 95% confidence level for all four datasets.

In order to understand precisely how hybrid search plays an important role in ACOFS for FS tasks, a set of experiments was additionally conducted. The setups of these experiments were similar to those described before, and different initial conditions were maintained constant between these two experiments. Figures 12 and 13 show the CAs of ACOFS without and with hybrid search, respectively. These CAs were produced by local best subsets in different iterations of a single run. The positive role of using hybrid local search in ACOFS can clearly be seen in these figures. In Figure 12, we can see that a better CA was found only in the initial iteration because of the rigorous survey by the ants in finding salient features. For the next iterations, the CAs fluctuated up to a higher iteration, 19, but were not able to reach a best state. This occurred due to the absence of hybrid search, which resulted in a weak search in ACOFS. The opposite scenario can be seen in Figure 13, where the search was sufficiently powerful that by a very low number of iterations, 5, ACOFS was able to achieve the best accuracy (99.42%) of the salient feature subset. Thereafter, ACOFS terminated the searching of salient features. The reason for such a high performance of FS was just the incorporation of the hybrid search.

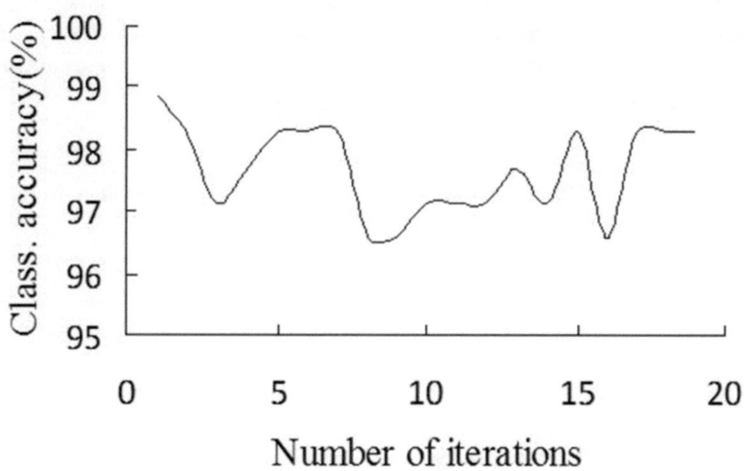

Figure 12. Classification accuracies (CAs) of the cancer dataset without considering hybrid search for a single run. Here, CA is the accuracy of a local best subset.

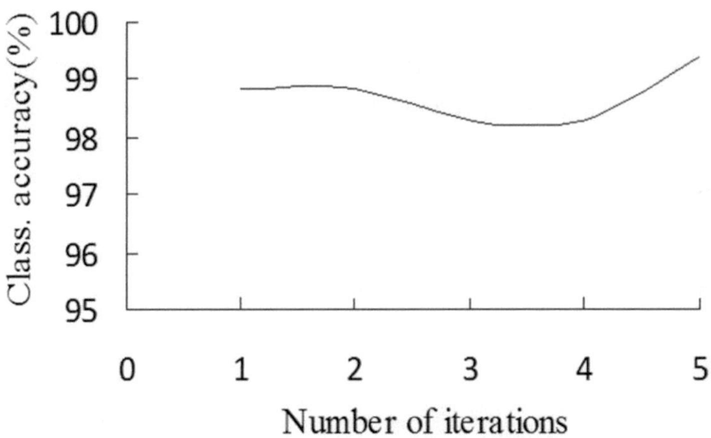

Figure 13. Classification accuracies (CAs) of the cancer dataset in ACOFS for a single run. Here, CA is the accuracy of a local best subset.

7.6. Performance on noisy features

The results presented in Table 3 exhibit the ability of ACOFS to select salient features from real-valued datasets. In this study, we examine the sensitivity of ACOFS to noisy features that have been synthetically inserted into a number of real-valued datasets. In order to generate these noisy features, we followed the process discussed in [32]. Briefly, at first, we considered four features, namely, f_{n1}, f_{n2}, f_{n3}, f_{n4} and the values of these respective features were generated randomly. Specifically, the values of f_{n1} and f_{n2} were bound up to [0, 1] and [-1, +1], respectively. For the domains of f_{n3} and f_{n4}, we first randomly selected two different features from the datasets. Subsequently, the data points of these two selected features were taken as a random basis for use in the domains of f_{n3} and f_{n4}.

Dataset	With all features				With selected features			
	n_s	S.D.	CA (%)	S.D.	n_s	S.D.	CA (%)	S.D.
Cancer	13.00	0.00	97.80	0.89	3.80	1.80	98.74	0.46
Glass	13.00	0.00	73.86	2.81	4.45	1.71	81.69	2.31

Table 16. Performances of ACOFS for noisy datasets. Results were averaged over 20 independent runs.

Table 16 shows the average performances of ACOFS on the real-valued datasets of cancer and glass mixed with noisy features over 20 independent runs. The ability of ACOFS for FS over real-valued datasets can also be found in Table 3. In comparing Tables 3 and 16, the following observations can be made. For the glass dataset, the average CAs with and without noisy features were 81.69% and 82.54%, respectively. On the other hand, in terms of n_s, the average values were 4.45 and 3.30, respectively. A similar scenario can also be found for the cancer dataset. Thus, it is clear that ACOFS has a strong ability to select the salient features from real-valued datasets even with a mixture of noisy features. We can observe that ACOFS selected a slightly higher average number of salient features from the glass dataset with noisy features. The reason is that adding the noisy features created confusion in the feature space. This may assist our ACOFS in selecting a greater number of noiseless features to resolve the confusion in the feature space caused by the noisy features.

7.7. Comparisons

The results of ACOFS obtained on nine real-world benchmark classification datasets are compared here with the results of various existing FS algorithms (i.e., ACO-based and non ACO-based) as well as with a normal ACO-based FS algorithm, as reported in Tables 17-19. The various FS algorithms are as follows: ACO-based hybrid FS ($ACOFS_S$[42]), ACO-based attribute reduction (ACOAR[31]), genetic programming for FS (GPFS[32]), hybrid genetic algorithm for FS (HGAFS[23]), MLP-based FS method (MLPFS[4]), constructive approach for feature selection (CAFS[47]), and artificial neural net input gain measurement approximation (ANNIGMA[26]). The results reported in these tables are over 20 independent runs. In comparing these algorithms, we have mainly used two parameters: classification accuracy (CA) and the number of selected features (n_s).

7.7.1. Comparison with other works

The comparisons between eight FS algorithms represent a wide range of FS techniques. Five of the FS techniques, namely, ACOFS, $ACOFS_S$, ACOAR, GPFS, and HGAFS, use global search strategies for FS. Among them, ACOFS, $ACOFS_S$, and ACOAR use the ant colony optimization algorithm. HGAFS uses a GA in finding salient features, and GPFS uses genetic programming, a variant of GA. For the remaining three FS techniques, namely, MLPFS, ANNIGMA and CAFS; MLPFS and ANNIGMA use backward selection strategy for finding salient features, while CAFS uses forward selection strategy. For evaluating the feature subset, ACOFS, $ACOFS_S$, MLPFS, CAFS, and ANNIGMA use a NN for classifiers, while GPFS and HGAFS use a decision tree and support vector machine, respectively, for classifiers, and ACOAR uses rough set theory by calculating a dependency degree. ACOFS, and CAFS uses a training set, validation set and testing set, while $ACOFS_S$ and ANNIGMA use only a training set and testing set. MLPFS and GPFS use 10-fold cross-validation. A similar method, that is, 5-fold cross-validation, is used in HGAFS, where k refers to a value ranging from 2 to 10, depending on the given dataset scale. The aforementioned algorithms not only use different data partitions, but also employ a different number of independent runs in measuring average performances. For example, ANNIGMA and CAFS use 30 runs, ACOFS uses 20 runs, and MLPFS and GPFS use 10 runs. It is important to note that no further information regarding the number of runs has been mentioned in the literature for $ACOFS_S$ and HGAFS.

Dataset		Comparison		
		ACOFS	$ACOFS_S$	ACOAR
Cancer	n_s	3.50	12.00	
	CA(%)	98.91	95.57	
Thyroid	n_s	3.00	14.00	--
	CA (%)	99.08	94.50	--
Credit card	n_s	5.85	-	8.00
	CA (%)	87.99	-	-
Colon cancer	n_s	5.25	-	8.00
	CA(%)	84.06	-	59.5

Table 17. Comparisons between ACOFS, $ACOFS_S$ [42], ACOAR [31]. Here, "_" means not available.

We can see in Table 17 that ACOFS produced the best solutions in terms of a reduced number of selected features, and the best CA in comparison with the two ACO-based FS algorithms, namely, $ACOFS_S$ and ACOAR, for all four datasets. Furthermore, the results produced by ACOFS shown in Table 18 represented the best CA among the other algorithms for all four datasets. For the remaining three datasets, while HGAFS achieved the best CA for two datasets, GPFS achieved the best CA for one dataset. Note that, ACOFS and ANNIGMA jointly achieved the best CA for the credit card dataset. In terms of n_s, ACOFS selected the smallest number of features for four out of seven datasets, and the second smallest for two dataset; that is to say, CAFS and HGAFS. In a close observation, ACOFS achieved the smallest n_s, which resulted in the best CAs for the glass and ionosphere datasets in comparison with the other five algorithms (see Table 18).

Dataset		Comparison					
		ACOFS	GPFS	HGAFS	MLPFS	CAFS	ANNIGMA
Cancer	n_s	3.50	2.23	3.00	8.00	6.33	5.80
	CA(%)	98.91	96.84	94.24	89.40	98.76	96.50
Glass	n_s	3.30	--	5.00	8.00	4.73	-
	CA (%)	82.54	--	65.51	44.10	76.91	-
Vehicle	n_s	2.90	5.37	11.00	13.00	2.70	-
	CA(%)	75.90	78.45	76.36	74.60	74.56	-
Ionosphere	n_s	4.15	-	6.00	32	6.73	9.00
	CA (%)	99.88	-	92.76	90.60	96.55	90.20
Credit card	n_s	5.85	-	1.00	-	-	6.70
	CA (%)	87.99	-	86.43	-	-	88.00
Sonar	n_s	6.25	9.45	15.00	29.00	-	-
	CA (%)	86.05	86.26	87.02	59.10	-	-
Colon cancer	n_s	5.25	-	6.00	-	-	-
	CA (%)	84.06	-	86.77	-	-	-

Table 18. Comparisons between ACOFS, GPFS [32], HGAFS [23], MLPFS [4], CAFS [47], and ANNIGMA [26]. Here, "_" means not available.

Significantly, it can be said that FS improves the performance of classifiers by ignoring irrelevant features in the original feature set. An important task in such a process is to capture necessary information in selecting salient features; otherwise, the performance of classifiers might be degraded. For example, for the cancer dataset, GPFS selected the smallest feature subset consisting of 2.23 features, but achieved a lower CA. On the other hand, ACOFS selected a slightly larger feature subset that provided a better CA compared to others for the cancer dataset. In fact, the results presented for other algorithms in Table 18 indicate that having the smallest or largest feature subset did not guarantee performing with the best or worst CA.

7.7.2. Comparison with normal ACO based FS algorithm

In this context, a normal ACO algorithm for solving FS is used, considering similar steps as incorporated in ACOFS, except for a number of differences. We call this algorithm "NACOFS". In NACOFS, issues of guiding the ants and forcing the ants during SC were not considered. Instead, the ants followed a process for SC where the size of subsets was fixed for each iteration and increased at a fixed rate for following iterations. On the other hand, hybrid search was not used here; that is to say, the concept of random and probabilistic behavior was not considered, including the incorporation of information gain in designing the pheromone update rule and heuristic information measurement rule.

Dataset	**Comparison**							
	ACOFS				NACOFS			
	n_s	S.D.	CA	S.D.	n_s	S.D.	CA	S.D.
Cancer	3.50	1.36	98.91	0.40	4.50	0.97	98.77	0.37
Glass	3.30	1.14	82.54	1.44	4.60	1.01	80.66	1.44
Ionosphere	4.15	2.53	99.88	0.34	11.45	6.17	99.88	0.34
Credit card	5.85	1.76	87.99	0.38	22.85	6.01	88.19	0.45

Table 19. Comparisons between ACOFS and NACOFS. Here, NACOFS refers to the normal ACO-based FS algorithm.

It is seen in Table 19 that the results produced by ACOFS achieved the best CA compared to NACOFS for three out of four datasets. For the remaining dataset, NACOFS achieved the best result. In terms of n_s, ACOFS selected the smallest number of features for the all four datasets, while NACOFS selected subsets of bulky size. Between these two algorithms, the performances of the CAs seemed to be similar, but the results of the numbers of selected features were very different. The performance of ACOFS was also found to be very consistent, exhibiting a low standard deviation (SD) under different experimental setups.

7.8. Discussions

This section briefly explains the reason that the performance of ACOFS was better than those of the other ACO-based FS algorithms compared in Table 17. There are three major differences that might contribute to the better performance of ACOFS compared to the other algorithms.

The first reason is that ACOFS uses a bounded scheme to determine the subset size, while $ACOFS_S$, ACOAR, and other ACO-based FS algorithms (e.g., [11,49-52]) do not use such a scheme. It is now clear that without a bounded scheme, ants are free to construct subsets of bulky size. Accordingly, there is a high possibility of including a number of irrelevant features in the constructed subsets. Using the bounded scheme with assistance from other techniques, ACOFS includes the most highly salient features in a reduced number, although it functioned upon a wide range of feature spaces. As shown in Table 17, ACOFS selected, on average, 3.00 salient features, while $ACOFS_S$ selected 14.00 features, on average, from the thyroid dataset. For the remaining other three datasets, ACOFS also selected a very small number of salient features. The benefit of using the bounded scheme can also be seen from the results of the selected subsets in ACOFS.

The second reason is the new hybrid search technique integrated in ACOFS. The algorithms $ACOFS_S$, ACOAR and others do not use such a hybrid search technique in performing pheromone update and heuristic information measurement. The benefit of adopting the hybrid search in ACOFS can clearly be seen in Figures 12 and 13. These figures show that ACOFS achieved a powerful and faster searching capability in finding salient features in the feature space. The above advantage can also be seen in Tables 17 and 18. We found that ACOFS had a remarkable capability to produce significant classification performances from different datasets using a reduced number of salient features.

The third reason is that ACOFS used a constructive approach for determining appropriate architectures, that is to say, an appropriate size of the hidden layer for the NN classifiers. The NN then evaluated the subsets constructed by the ants in each iteration during training. The existing ACO-based FS approaches (e.g., [42]) often ignored the above issue of the NN classifiers. Furthermore, a number of other approaches (e.g., [49,50]) often ignored the classifier portions to consider any heuristic methodology by which the activity of the classifiers could be improved for evaluating the subsets effectively. Furthermore, most ACO-based FS approaches performed the pheromone update rule based on classifier performances in evaluating the subsets. In this sense, the evaluation function was one of the most crucial parts in these approaches for FS. However, the most common practice was to choose the number of hidden neurons in the NN randomly. Thus, the random selection of hidden neurons affected the generalization performances of the NNs. Furthermore, the entire FS process was eventually affected, resulting in ineffective solutions in FS. It is also important to say that the performance of any NN was greatly dependent on the architecture [17, 57]. Thus, automatic determination of the number of hidden neurons' lead to providing a better solution for FS in ACOFS.

http://dx.doi.org/10.5772/51707

8. Conclusions

In this chapter, an efficient hybrid ACO-based FS algorithm has been reported. Since ants are the foremost strength of an ACO algorithm, guiding the ants in the correct directions is an urgent requirement for high-quality solutions. Accordingly, ACOFS guides ants during SC by determining the subset size. Furthermore, new sets of pheromone update and heuristic information measurement rules for individual features bring out the potential of the global search capability of ACOFS.

Extensive experiments have been carried out in this chapter to evaluate how well ACOFS has performed in finding salient features on different datasets (see Table 3). It is observed that a set of high-quality solutions for FS was found from small, medium, large, and very large dimensional datasets. The results of the low standard deviations of the average classification accuracies as well as the average number of selected features, showed the robustness of this algorithm. On the other hand, in comparison with seven prominent FS algorithms (see Tables 17 and 18), with only a few exceptions, ACOFS outperformed the others in terms of a reduced number of selected features and best classification performances. Furthermore, the estimated computational complexity of this algorithm reflected that incorporation of several techniques did not increase the computational cost during FS in comparison with other ACO-based FS algorithms (see Section 6.5).

We can see that there are a number of areas, where ACOFS failed to improve performances in terms of number of selected features and classification accuracies. Accordingly, more suitable heuristic schemes are necessary in order to guide the ants appropriately. In the current implementation, ACOFS has a number of user-specified parameters, given in Table 2, which are common in the field of ACO-based algorithms using NNs for FS. Further tuning of the user-specified parameters related to ACO provides some scope for further investigations in future. On the other hand, among these parameters, μ, used in determining the subset size, was sensitive to moderate change, according to our observations. One of the future improvements to ACOFS could be to reduce the number of parameters, or render them adaptive.

Acknowledgements

Supported by grants to K.M. from the Japanese Society for Promotion of Sciences, the Yazaki Memorial Foundation for Science and Technology, and the University of Fukui.

Author details

Monirul Kabir[1], Md Shahjahan[2] and Kazuyuki Murase[3*]

*Address all correspondence to: murase@u-fukui.ac.jp

1 Department of Electrical and Electronic Engineering, Dhaka University of Engineering and Technology (DUET), Bangladesh

2 Department of Electrical and Electronic Engineering, Khulna University of Engineering and Technology (KUET), Bangladesh

3 Department of Human and Artificial Intelligence Systems and Research and Education Program for Life Science, University of Fukui, Japan

References

[1] Abraham, A., Grosan, C., & Ramos, V. (2006). Swarm Intelligence in Data Mining. *Springer-Verlag Press.*

[2] Liu, H., & Lei, Tu. (2004). Toward Integrating Feature Selection Algorithms for Classification and Clustering. *IEEE Transactions on Knowledge and Data Engineering;*, 17(4), 491-502.

[3] Pudil, P., Novovicova, J., & Kittler, J. (1994). Floating Search Methods in Feature Selection. *Pattern Recognition Letters*, 15(11), 1119-1125.

[4] Gasca, E., Sanchez, J. S., & Alonso, R. (2006). Eliminating Redundancy and Irrelevance using a New MLP-based Feature Selection Method. *Pattern Recognition*, 39, 313-315.

[5] Setiono, R., & Liu, H. (1997). Neural Network Feature Selector. *IEEE Trans. on Neural Networks*, 8.

[6] Verikas, A., & Bacauskiene, M. (2002). Feature Selection with Neural Networks. *Pattern Recognition Letters*, 23, 1323-1335.

[7] Guyon, I., & Elisseeff, A. (2003). An Introduction to Variable and Feature Selection. *Journal of Machine Learning Research*, 3-1157.

[8] Photo by Aksoy S. (2012). http://retina.cs.bilkent.edu.tr/papers/patrec_tutorial1.pdf, Accessed 02 July.

[9] Floreano, D., Kato, T., Marocco, D., & Sauser, E. (2004). Coevolution and Active Vision and Feature Selection. *Biological Cybernetics*, 90(3), 218-228.

[10] Dash, M., Kollipakkam, D., & Liu, H. (2006). Automatic View Selection: An Application to Image Mining: proceedings of the International Conference. *PAKDD*, 107-113.

[11] Robbins, K. R., Zhang, W., & Bertrand, J. K. (2008). The Ant Colony Algorithm for Feature Selection in High-Dimension Gene Expression Data for Disease Classification. *Journal of Mathematical Medicine and Biology*, 1-14.

[12] Ooi, C. H., & Tan, P. (2003). Genetic Algorithm Applied to Multi-class Prediction for the Analysis of Gene Expression Data. *Bioinformatics*, 19(1), 37-44.

[13] Chen, J., Huang, H., Tian, S., & Qu, Y. (2009). Feature Selection for Text Classification with Naïve Bayes. *Expert Systems with Applications*, 36, 5432-5435.

[14] Fayyad, U. M., Piatesky-Shapiro, G., Smyth, P., & Uthurusamy, R. (1996). Advances in Knowledge Discovery and Data Mining. *AAAI: MIT Press.*

[15] Newman, D. J., Hettich, S., Blake, C. L., & Merz, C. J. (1998). UCI Repository of Machine Learning Databases. *University of California, Irvine,* http://www.ics.uci.edu/~mlearn/MLRepository.html, Accessed 02 July 2012.

[16] Prechelt, L. (1994). PROBEN1-A set of Neural Network Benchmark Problems and Benchmarking Rules. *Technical Report 21/94, Faculty of Informatics, University of Karlsruhe.*

[17] Yao, X., & Liu, Y. (1997). A New Evolutionary System for Evolving Artificial Neural Networks. *IEEE Trans. on Neural Networks*, 8(3), 694-713.

[18] Alon, U., Barkai, N., Notterman, D. A., Gish, K., Ybarra, S., Mack, D., & Levine, A. J. (1999). Broad Patterns of Gene Expression Revealed by Clustering Analysis of Tumor and Normal Colon Tissues Probed by Oligonucleotide Arrays: proceedings of International Academic Science. *USA*, 96, 6745-6750.

[19] Alizadeh, AA, et al. (2000). Distinct Types of Diffuse Large B-cell Lymphoma Identified by Gene Expression Profiling. *Nature*, 403-503.

[20] Golub, T., et al. (1999). Molecular Classification of Cancer: Class Discovery and Class Prediction by Gene Expression. *Science*, 286(5439), 531-537.

[21] Guyon, I., & Elisseeff, A. An Introduction to Variable and Feature Selection. *Journal of Machine Learning Research*, 3, 1157-1182.

[22] Dash, M., & Liu, H. (1997). Feature Selection for Classification. *Intelligent Data Analysis*, 1, 131-156.

[23] Huang, J, Cai, Y, & Xu, X. (2007). A Hybrid Genetic Algorithm for Feature Selection Wrapper based on Mutual Information. *Pattern Recognition Letters*, 28, 1825-1844.

[24] Guan, S., Liu, J., & Qi, Y. (2004). An Incremental Approach to Contribution-based Feature Selection. *Journal of Intelligence Systems*, 13(1).

[25] Peng, H., Long, F., & Ding, C. (2003). Overfitting in Making Comparisons between Variable Selection Methods. *Journal of Machine Learning Research*, 3, 1371-1382.

[26] Hsu, C., Huang, H., & Schuschel, D. (2002). The ANNIGMA-Wrapper Approach to Fast Feature Selection for Neural Nets. *IEEE Trans. on Systems, Man, and Cybernetics-Part B: Cybernetics*, 32(2), 207-212.

[27] Caruana, R., & Freitag, D. (1994). Greedy Attribute Selection: proceedings of the 11th International Conference of Machine Learning. *USA, Morgan Kaufmann.*

[28] Lai, C., Reinders, M. J. T., & Wessels, L. (2006). Random Subspace Method for Multivariate Feature Selection. *Pattern Recognition Letters*, 27, 1067-1076.

[29] Straceezzi, D J, & Utgoff, P E. (2004). Randomized Variable Elimination. *Journal of Machine Learning Research;*, 5, 1331-1362.

[30] Abe, S. (2005). Modified Backward Feature Selection by Cross Validation. *proceedings of the European Symposium on Artificial Neural Networks*, 163-168.

[31] Ke, L., Feng, Z., & Ren, Z. (2008). An Efficient Ant Colony Optimization Approach to Attribute Reduction in Rough Set Theory. *Pattern Recognition Letters*, 29, 1351-1357.

[32] Muni, D. P., Pal, N. R., & Das, J. (2006). Genetic Programming for Simultaneous Feature Selection and Classifier Design. *IEEE Trans. on Systems, Man, and Cybernetics-Part B: Cybernetics*, 36(1), 106-117.

[33] Oh, I., Lee, J., & Moon, B. (2004). Hybrid Genetic Algorithms for Feature Selection. *IEEE Trans. on Pattern Analysis and Machine Intelligence*, 26(11), 1424-1437.

[34] Wang, X., Yang, J., Teng, X., Xia, W., & Jensen, R. (2007). Feature Selection based on Rough Sets and Particle Swarm Optimization. *Pattern Recognition Letters*, 28(4), 459-471.

[35] Yang, J. H., & Honavar, V. (1998). Feature Subset Selection using a Genetic Algorithm. *IEEE Intelligent Systems*, 13(2), 44-49.

[36] Pal, N. R., & Chintalapudi, K. (1997). A Connectionist System for Feature Selection. *International Journal of Neural, Parallel and Scientific Computation*, 5, 359-361.

[37] Rakotomamonjy, A. (2003). Variable Selection using SVM-based Criteria. *Journal of Machine Learning Research*, 3, 1357-1370.

[38] Wang, L., Zhou, N., & Chu, F. (2008). A General Wrapper Approach to Selection of Class-dependent Features. *IEEE Trans. on Neural Networks*, 19(7), 1267-1278.

[39] Chow, T W S, & Huang, D. (2005). Estimating Optimal Feature Subsets using Efficient Estimation of High-dimensional Mutual Information. *IEEE Trans. Neural Network*, 16(1), 213-224.

[40] Hall, M A. (2000). Correlation-based Feature Selection for Discrete and Numeric Class Machine Learning:. *Proceedings of 17th International Conference on Machine Learning.*

[41] Sindhwani, V., Rakshit, S., Deodhare, D., Erdogmus, D., Principe, J. C., & Niyogi, P. (2004). Feature Selection in MLPs and SVMs based on Maximum Output Information. *IEEE Trans. on Neural Networks*, 15(4), 937-948.

[42] Sivagaminathan, R. K., & Ramakrishnan, S. (2007). A Hybrid Approach for Feature Subset Selection using Neural Networks and Ant Colony Optimization. *Expert Systems with Applications*, 33-49.

[43] Kambhatla, N., & Leen, T. K. (1997). Dimension Reduction by Local Principal Component Analysis. *Neural Computation*, 9(7), 1493-1516.

[44] Back, A D, & Trappenberg, T P. (2001). Selecting Inputs for Modeling using Normalized Higher Order Statistics and Independent Component Analysis. *IEEE Trans. Neural Network*, 12(3), 612-617.

[45] Mao, K Z. (2002). Fast Orthogonal Forward Selection Algorithm for Feature Subset Selection. *IEEE Trans. Neural Network*, 13(5), 1218-1224.

[46] Caruana, R., & De Sa, V. (2003). Benefitting from the Variables that Variable Selection Discards. *Journal of Machine Learning Research*, 3, 1245-1264.

[47] Kabir, M. M., Islam, M. M., & Murase, K. (2010). A New Wrapper Feature Selection Approach using Neural Network. *Neurocomputing*, 73, 3273-3283.

[48] Chakraborty, D., & Pal, N. R. (2004). A Neuro-fuzzy Scheme for Simultaneous Feature Selection and Fuzzy Rule-based Classification. *IEEE Trans. on Neural Networks*, 15(1), 110-123.

[49] Aghdam, M H, Aghaee, N G, & Basiri, M E. (2009). Test Feature Selection using Ant Colony Optimization. *Expert Systems with Applications*, 36, 6843-6853.

[50] Ani, A. (2005). Feature Subset Selection using Ant Colony Optimization. *International Journal of Computational Intelligence*, 2, 53-58.

[51] Kanan, H. R., Faez, K., & Taheri, S. M. (2007). Feature Selection using Ant Colony Optimization (ACO): A New Method and Comparative Study in the Application of Face Recognition System. *Proceedings of International Conference on Data Mining*, 63-76.

[52] Khushaba, R. N., Alsukker, A., Ani, A. A., & Jumaily, A. A. (2008). Enhanced Feature Selection Algorithm using Ant Colony Optimization and Fuzzy Memberships: proceedings of the sixth international conference on biomedical engineering. *IASTED*, 34-39.

[53] Dorigo, M., & Stutzle, T. (2004). Ant Colony Optimization. *MIT Press*.

[54] Filippone, M., Masulli, F., & Rovetta, S. (2006). Supervised Cassification and Gene Selection using Simulated Annealing. *Proceedings of International Joint Conference on Neural Networks*, 3566-3571.

[55] Goldberg, D E. (2004). Genetic Algorithms in Search. *Genetic Algorithms in Search, Optimization and Machine Learning*, Addison-Wesley Press.

[56] Rumelhart, D. E., & Mc Clelland, J. (1986). Parallel Distributed Processing. *MIT Press*.

[57] Reed, R. (1993). Pruning Algorithms-a Survey. *IEEE Trans. on Neural Networks*, 4(5), 740-747.

[58] Girosi, F., Jones, M., & Poggio, T. (1995). Regularization Theory and Neural Networks Architectures. *Neural Computation*, 7(2), 219-269.

[59] Kwok, T Y, & Yeung, D Y. (1997). Constructive Algorithms for Structure Learning in Feed-forward Neural Networks for Regression Problems. *IEEE Trans. on Neural Networks*, 8, 630-645.

[60] Lehtokangas, M. (2000). Modified Cascade-correlation Learning for Classification. *IEEE Transactions on Neural Networks*, 11, 795-798.

[61] Dorigo, M., Caro, G. D., & Gambardella, L. M. (1999). Ant Algorithm for Discrete Optimization. *Artificial Life*, 5(2), 137-172.

[62] Kudo, M., & Sklansky, J. (2000). Comparison of Algorithms that Select Features for Pattern Classifiers. *Pattern Recognition*, 33, 25-41.

[63] Kim, K., & Cho, S. (2004). Prediction of Colon Cancer using an Evolutionary Neural Network. *Neurocomputing*, 61, 61-379.

[64] Kabir, M. M., Shahjahan, M., & Murase, K. (2012). A New Hybrid Ant Colony Optimization Algorithm for Feature Selection. *Expert Systems with Applications*, 39, 3747-3763.

Chapter 2

Parallel Ant Colony Optimization: Algorithmic Models and Hardware Implementations

Pierre Delisle

Additional information is available at the end of the chapter

http://dx.doi.org/10.5772/54252

1. Introduction

The Ant Colony Optimization (ACO) metaheuristic [1] is a constructive population-based approach based on the social behavior of ants. As it is acknowledged as a powerful method to solve academic and industrial combinatorial optimization problems, a considerable amount of research is dedicated to improving its performance. Among the proposed solutions, we find the use of parallel computing to reduce computation time, improve solution quality or both.

Most parallel ACO implementations can be classified into two general approaches. The first one is the parallel execution of the ants construction phase in a single colony. Initiated by Bullnheimer *et al.* [2], it aims to accelerate computations by distributing ants to computing elements. The second one, introduced by Stützle [3], is the execution of multiple ant colonies. In this case, entire ant colonies are attributed to processors in order to speedup computations as well as to potentially improve solution quality by introducing cooperation schemes between colonies.

Recently, a more detailed classification was proposed by Pedemonte *et al.* [4]. It shows that most existing works are based on designing parallel ACO algorithms at a relatively high level of abstraction which may be suitable for conventional parallel computers. However, as research on parallel architectures is rapidly evolving, new types of hardware have recently become available for high performance computing. Among them, we find multicore processors and graphics processing units (GPU) which provide great computing power at an affordable cost but are more difficult to program. In fact, it is not clear that conventional high-level abstraction models are suitable for expressing parallelism in a way that is efficiently implementable and reproducible on these architectures. As academic and industrial combinatorial optimization problems always increase in size and complexity, the field of parallel metaheuristics has to follow this evolution of high performance computing.

The main purpose of this chapter is to complement existing parallel ACO models with a computational design that relates more closely to high performance computing architectures. Emerging from several years of work by the authors on the parallelization of ACO in various computing environments including clusters, symmetric multiprocessors (SMP), multicore processors and graphics processing units (GPU) [5–10], it is based on the concepts of computing entities and memory structures. It provides a conceptual vision of parallel ACO that we believe more balanced between theory and practice. We revisit the existing literature and present various implementations from this viewpoint. Extensive experimental results are presented to validate the proposed approaches across a broad range of computing environments. Key algorithmic, technical and programming issues are also addressed in this context.

2. Literature review on Parallel Ant Colony Optimization

During the past 20 years, the ACO metaheuristic has improved significantly to become one of the most effective combinatorial optimization methods. For about a decade, following this trend, a number of parallelization techniques have been proposed to further enhance its search process. Works on traditional CPU-based parallel ACO can be classified into two general approaches: *parallel ants* and *multiple ant colonies*. These approaches are briefly explained in Sections 2.1 and 2.2. On the other hand, few authors have proposed parallel implementations dedicated to specific architectures. Section 2.3 is dedicated to these *hardware-oriented* approaches. In all cases, a survey of related works is also provided.

2.1. Parallel ants

Works related to the parallel ants approach, which aims to execute the ants tour construction phase on many processing elements, were initiated by Bullnheimer *et al.* [2]. They proposed two parallelization strategies for the Ant System on a message passing and distributed-memory architecture. The first one is a low-level and synchronous strategy that aims to accelerate computations by distributing ants to processors in a master-slave fashion. At each iteration, the master broadcasts the pheromone structure to slaves, which then compute their tours in parallel and send them back to the master. The time needed for these global communications and synchronizations implies a considerable overhead. The second strategy aims to reduce it by letting the algorithm perform a given number of iterations without exchanging information. The authors conclude that this partially asynchronous strategy is preferable due to the considerable reduction of the communication overhead.

The works of Talbi *et al.* [11], Randall and Lewis [12], Islam *et al.* [13], Craus and Rudeanu [14], Stützle [3] and Doerner *et al.* [15] are based on a similar parallelization approach and a distributed memory architecture. Delisle *et al.* [5, 6] implemented this scheme on shared-memory architectures like SMP computers and multi-core processors. They also compared performance between the two types of architectures [7].

2.2. Multiple ant colonies

The multiple ant colonies approach, also based on a message-passing and distributed memory architecture, aims to execute whole ant colonies on available processing elements.

It was introduced by Stützle [3] with the parallel execution of multiple independent copies of the same algorithm. Middendorf *et al.* [16] extended this approach by introducing four information exchange strategies between ant colonies: exchange of globally best solution, circular exchange of locally best solutions, migrants or locally best solutions plus migrants. It is shown that it can be advantageous for ant colonies to avoid communicating too much information and too often. Giving up on the idea of sharing whole pheromone information, they based their strategy on the trade of a single solution at each exchange step.

Chu *et al.* [17], Manfrin *et al.* [18], Ellabib *et al.* [19] and Alba *et al.* [20] have also proposed different information exchange strategies for the multiple ant colony approach. Many parameters are studied like the topology of the links between processors as well as the nature and frequency of information exchanges. These strategies are implemented using MPI on distributed memory architectures. On the other hand, Delisle *et al.* [8] adapted some of them on shared-memory architectures.

2.3. Hardware-oriented parallel ACO

Even though they mostly follow the parallel ants and multiple ant colonies approaches, hardware-oriented approaches are dedicated to specific and untraditional parallel architectures. Scheuermann *et al.* [21, 22] designed parallel implementations of ACO on Field Programmable Gate Arrays (FPGA). Considerable changes to the algorithmic structure of the metaheuristic were needed to take benefit of this particular architecture.

Few authors have tackled the problem of parallelizing ACO on GPU in the form of preliminary work. Catala *et al.* [23] propose an implementation of ACO to solve the Orienteering Problem. Instances of up to a few thousand nodes are solved by building solutions on GPU. Wang *et al.* [24] propose an implementation of the MMAS where the tour construction phase is executed on a GPU to solve a 30 city TSP. Similar implementations are reported by You [25], Zhu and Curry [26], Li *et al.* [27], Cecilia *et al.* [28] and Delévacq *et al.* [9] . Following these works, Delévacq *et al.* [10] have proposed various parallelization strategies for ACO on GPU as well as a comparative study to show the influence of various parameters on search efficiency.

Finally, concerning grid applications, Weis and Lewis [29] implemented an ACO algorithm on an ad-hoc grid for the design of a radio frequency antenna structure. Mocholi *et al.* [30] also proposed a medium grain master-slave algorithm to solve the Orienteering Problem.

In addition to a complete survey, Pedemonte *et al.* [4] proposed a taxonomy for Parallel ACO which is illustrated in Fig. 1. Although it provides a comprehensive view of the field, its relatively high level of abstraction does not capture some important features that are crucial for obtaining efficient implementations on modern high performance computing architectures.

The present work does not seek to replace this taxonomy but rather provides a conceptual view of parallel ACO that relates more closely to real parallel architectures. By bringing together the high-level concepts of parallel ACO and the lower-level parallel computing models, it aims to serve as a methodological framework for the design of efficient ACO implementations.

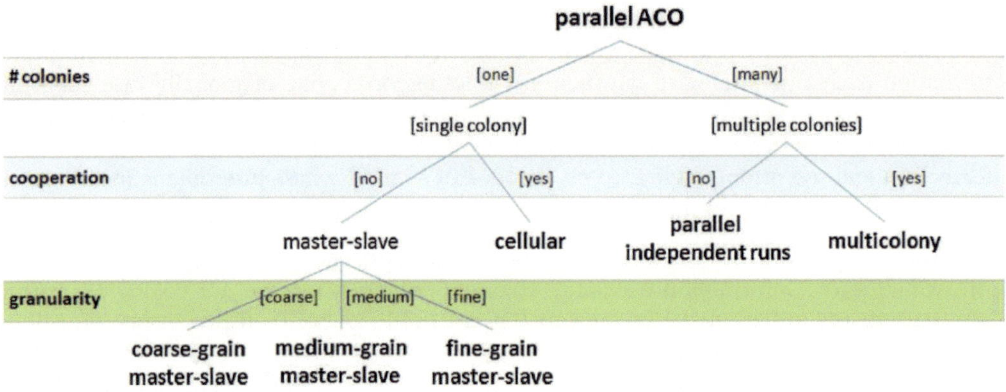

Figure 1. Taxonomy for parallel ACO [4].

3. A new architecture-oriented taxonomy for parallel ACO

The efficient implementation of a parallel metaheuristic in optimization software generally requires the consideration of the underlying architecture. Inspired by Talbi [31], we distinguish the following main parallel architectures: clusters/networks of workstations, symmetric multiprocessors / multicore processors, grids and graphics processing units.

Clusters and Networks of Workstations (COWs/NOWs) are distributed-memory architectures where each processor has its own memory (Fig. 2(a)). Information exchanges between processors require explicit message passing which implies programming efforts and communication costs. NOWs may be seen as an heterogeneous group of computers whereas COWs are homogeneous, unified computing devices.

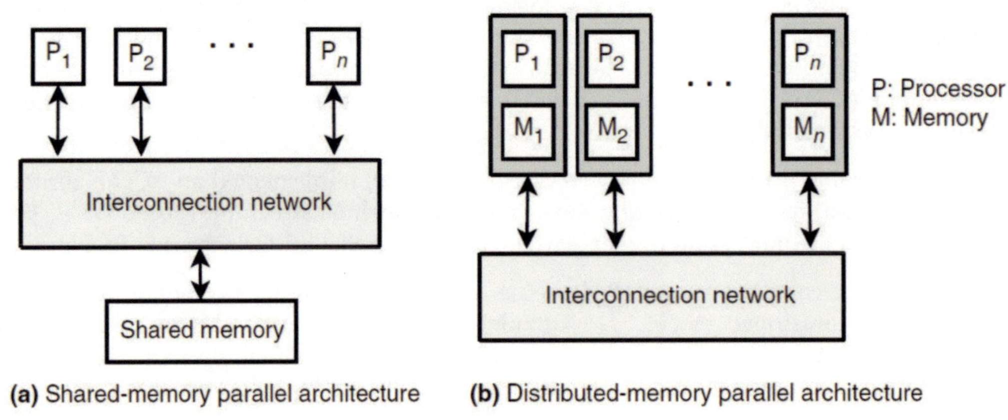

Figure 2. Shared-memory and distributed-memory parallel architectures [31].

Symmetric multiprocessors (SMPs) and multicore processors are shared-memory architectures where the processors are connected to a common memory (Fig. 2(b)). Information exchanges between processors are facilitated by the single address space but synchronizations still have to be managed. SMPs consist of many processors that are linked to a bus network and multicore processors contain many processors on a single chip.

Grids may be considered as pools of heterogeneous and dynamic computing resources geographically distributed across multiple administrative domains and owned by different organizations ([32]). These resources are usually high performance computing platforms connected with a dedicated high-speed network or workstations linked by a nondedicated network such as the Internet. In such volatile systems, security, fault tolerance and resource discovery are important issues to address. Fortunately, middleware usually frees the grid application programmer from much of these issues.

Finally, graphics processing units (GPUs) are devices that are used in computers to manipulate computer graphics. As GPU technology has evolved drastically in the last few years, it has been increasingly used to accelerate general-purpose scientific and engineering applications. As shown in Figure 3, the conventional NVIDIA GPU [33] includes many multiprocessors and processors which execute multiple coordinated threads. Several memories are distinguished on this special hardware, differing in size, latency and access type.

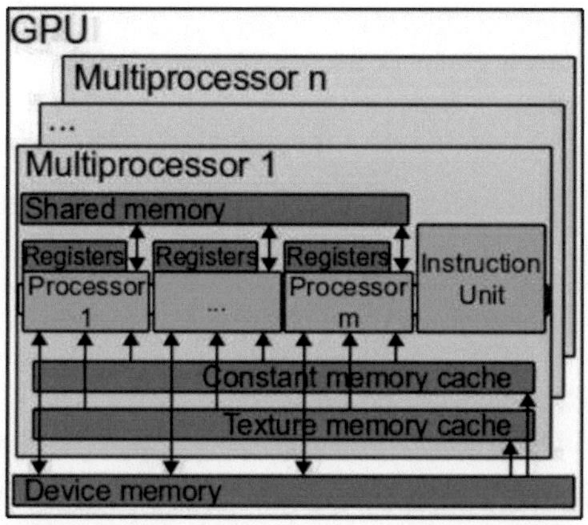

Figure 3. NVIDIA GPU architecture [33].

Considering the variety of architectures currently available in the world of high performance computing, the successful design and implementation of a parallel ACO algorithm on one platform or another may be a significant challenge. Moreover, most computers fall into many categories: a computational cluster may be composed of many distributed nodes which include multicore processors and GPUs. The challenge then becomes two fold: identifying a suitable combination of parallel strategies and implementing it on the target system. In order to make this process simpler, we propose a taxonomy for parallel ACO which takes implementation details into account. It distinguishes three criteria: the ACO granularity level, the "computational entity" associated to that level and the memory structure available at that level.

3.1. ACO granularity level

The decomposition of an ACO algorithm into tasks to be executed by different processors may be performed according to several granularities. One of the main goals of the parallelization process is to find an equitable compromise between the number of tasks and the cost associated to the management of these tasks. Based on the algorithmic structure of

ACO, the proposed classification distinguishes four granularity levels from coarsest to finest: colony, iteration, ant and solution element.

Parallelization at the **colony** level consists in defining the execution of a whole ACO algorithm as a task and assigning it to a processor. The multiple independent colonies and the multiple cooperating colonies approaches, as defined respectively by Stützle [3] and Middendorf *et al.* [16], may be associated to this level. A single colony is typically assigned to a processor but it is possible to assign many with some form of scheduling. At this level, the main factors to consider in the parallelization process are the homogeneity of the colonies as well as their interactions.

Depending on design choices, parallelization at the **iteration** level may be considered as a particular case of either the colony level or the ant level parallelizations. In fact, it may be seen as a hybrid between these two levels instead of a full level. The idea is then to share the iterations of the algorithm between available processors. A first way to implement this strategy is to divide the ants of a single colony into groups and to let each group evolve independently during the algorithm. A second way is to let these groups share their pheromone information after a given number of iterations in a way similar to the partially asynchronous implementation of Bullnheimer *et al.* [2]. At this level, the way the iterations are coordinated between groups will effect the global parallel performance.

Parallelization at the **ant** level implies the distribution of the tasks included in an iteration to available processors. It is mainly the ants construction phase but also operations associated to pheromone update and solution management. This level is related to the typical parallel ants strategy where one or many ants are assigned to each processing element. In that case, special care must be taken to ensure that pheromone updates and general management operations like the identification and update of the best ant do not significantly degrade the performance of the implementation.

Until a few years ago, parallelization at the ant level was generally the finest granularity considered for most optimization problems. However, the emergence of massively parallel architectures like the GPU have resulted in the need for finer approaches. At the **solution element** level, the main operations that are considered for parallelization are the state transition rule and solution evaluation. In the first case, one possible strategy is to evaluate several candidates in parallel to speedup the choice of the next move by an ant. In the second case, the evaluation of the objective function of a particular ant is decomposed among several processors.

The approach proposed in this section sought to determine a parallelization framework taking into account both the main ACO components and the multiple possible granularities. In the next section, it is augmented by considering the underlying computational architecture.

3.2. Computational entity

Nowadays, the typical high performance parallel computer is composed of a hierarchy of several different architectures. For example, it is common to find a computational cluster with multiple distributed SMP nodes, each one of them being composed of multicore processors and GPU cards. Moreover, this type of machine is often found in computational grids. In order to obtain the best possible performance on these platforms, an algorithm has to be implemented according to at least a part of this hierarchy. The proposed classification distinguishes each level of this hierarchy from the parallel programming perspective. This translates into the definition of five computational entities: system, node, process, block and thread.

A **system** defines a parallel computer as a unified computational resource which may be a standard workstation or a cluster. A distinction is made between these single systems and grids which are considered multiple systems.

A **node** is a discernable part of a system to which tasks can be assigned. A system may then be composed of a single node which is the case of the standard workstation, or of multiple nodes which is the case of clusters.

A **process** is a computational entity that manages and executes sequential and parallel programs. As this concept refers to the typical process in operating systems, it can hold one or many threads which may be grouped together or not. When a process executes only sequential code, it is considered as the smallest indivisible entity of an implementation.

A **block** is an intermediate entity between process and thread. This notion comes from the field of GPU computing in which a block is composed of many threads. The standard processor may be seen as a particular case where a single block is executed. A sequential processor then holds one block and one thread whereas a multicore processor holds one block and several threads.

Finally, a **thread** is a sequential flow of instructions that is part of a block. It represents an indivisible entity and the smallest one in the model: it is always sequential and executes instructions on a processor at a given time. Therefore, even though in practice there may be more threads than processors (some threads will be executed while some others will be idle), in this model we consider that these threads may be merged into a smaller number of threads corresponding to the number of available processors.

Complementary to the notion of computational entity, we add the concept of memory that may be relevant to all five levels previously defined.

3.3. Memory

Memory is an important aspect of ACO algorithms. It serves as a container for pheromone information, problem data and various parameters. It also serves as a channel for information exchange in many parallel implementations. Therefore, as accessibility and access speed will have a significant impact on the feasibility and performance of the parallel implementation, three categories are distinguished: local, global and remote.

Local memory refers to a memory space that is directly accessible by the computational entities of a given level and fast in access time relatively to this particular level. For example, the shared memory of one multiprocessor of a GPU (see Figure 3) is considered as local memory for all the threads that are executed by a block on this multiprocessor. The registers of a processor could also be considered as local memory if they were managed directly, although it is usually not the case.

Global memory is a memory space that can also be accessed directly by the computational entities of a given level, but relatively slow in access time. For example, the device memory of a GPU is considered as global memory for the threads of a given block. The shared memory of a SMP node is also considered as global memory for the processors or cores of that node.

Remote memory is a memory space that can not be directly accessed by the entities, but for which the information can be made available by an explicit operation between entities. Obviously, remote memory access is considered to be slower than global memory access. For example, the memory available to a processor located in a specific node of a cluster will be considered as remote for the processors on other nodes.

Table 1 summarizes the proposed taxonomy. According to it, designing a parallel ACO implementation implies to link a computational entity and a memory structure to each ACO granularity level. In the next section, two case studies, extracted from the author's previous works, are proposed and expressed according to this taxonomy. In each case, the parallelization strategy and experimental results are synthesized and discussed in order to illustrate various features of the classification.

ACO granularity	Computational entity	Memory
Colony	System	Local
Iteration	Node	Global
Ant	Process	Remote
Solution element	Block	
	Thread	

Table 1. Architecture-based taxonomy for parallel ACO.

4. Case studies

Two case studies are presented to illustrate how the proposed framework relates to real implementations. In order to cover the two main general parallelization strategies for ACO, both parallel ants and multicolony approaches are proposed. In the first case, SMP and muticore processors are considered as underlying architectures. In the second case, a GPU is used as a coprocessor of a sequential processor. This section is then concluded with a more general discussion about how this taxonomy applies to most other combinations of ACO algorithms and parallel architectures.

4.1. Multi-Colony parallel ACO on a SMP and multicore architecture

This approach deals with the management of multiple colonies which use a global shared memory to exchange information. The whole algorithm executes on a single system and a single node so there is no parallelism at these levels. The colonies are executed in parallel and spawn multiple parallel ants. Therefore, colonies are associated to processes and ants to threads. At the programming level, this can be implemented either with multiple operating system processes and multiple threads or with multiple nested threads. In this implementation, we choose the latter as the available SMP node supports nested threads with a shared memory available to all processors. Therefore, this implementation is defined as $COLONY^{global}_{process}$-$ITERATION^{global}_{process}$-$ANT^{global}_{thread}$. There is no additionnal parallelism at the solution element level so it is not specified here.

The proposed implementation is defined assuming a shared-memory model based on threads in which algorithm execution begins with a single thread called the master thread and executed sequentially. To execute a part of the algorithm in parallel, a parallel region is defined where many threads are created, each one of them executing that part of the algorithm concurrently. All threads have access to the whole shared memory, but we can define private data, which is data that will be accessible only by a single thread. Inside a parallel region, we can define a parallel loop, which is a loop where cycles are divided among existing threads in a work-sharing manner. To manage synchronizations between threads, some form of explicit control must be used. A barrier, as the name implies, is a point in the execution of the algorithm beyond which no thread may execute until all threads have reached that point. Also, a critical region is a part of a parallel region which can be executed only by one thread at a time. It is usually used to avoid concurrent writes to shared data. We can now describe the shared-memory parallelization strategy for ACO.

Two versions of the multicolony strategy are proposed which are related to the author's previous work ([6, 8]). The first one, related to parallel independent runs as defined by Stützle [3], implies multiple threads each executing their own copy of the sequential metaheuristic. For the second strategy, we let the colonies cooperate by using a common global best known solution in the shared memory. In both cases, ants are executed in parallel by many nested threads.

In the first implementation, search processes are independent. There are as many copies of data structures as there are colonies. In particular, even if they all reside in the shared memory, pheromone structures are private and exclusive to each thread. ACO parameters are also private, which means that they could be different even if it will not be experimented in this study. In a theoretical context, this kind of parallelization should imply minimal communication and synchronization overheads, hence maximal efficiency. However, this is not the case in a practical context. Even if the data structures are private, colonies need to simultaneously access them through common system resources. At this point, it is up to the computer system to efficiently manage this concurrency.

Parallelizing ACO in multiple search processes is quite simple: we only need to create a parallel region at the beginning of the sequential algorithm. This way, we can create as many threads as we have colonies. A memory location dedicated to store the global best solution known by all processors is reserved in the shared memory and is accessible by all threads. At the end of the parallel region, a critical section lets each thread verify if the best solution it has found qualifies for replacing the global best one and update the data structure accordingly. The best solution of the parallel independent runs can then be identified after the parallel region as the result of the parallel algorithm.

To illustrate the scheme of multiple interacting colonies in a shared-memory model, the simple case of a common best global solution located in the shared memory is implemented. This relates to the first strategy defined by Middendorf [16], that is, exchange of the globally best solution. The exchange rule of this strategy implies that in each information exchange step, the globally best known solution is broadcast to all colonies where it becomes the locally best solution. Information exchanges are performed at each given number of cycles.

In a shared-memory context, there is no such thing as an explicit broadcast communication step. It is replaced by the use of the global best solution as a dedicated structure in the shared memory. However, it is now used differently and more frequently. At each information exchange step, each thread compare its local value of the best solution with the global best solution. If it has lower cost, it then becomes the new global best known solution. The use of a critical region lets threads do their comparison without risking concurrent writes to the data structure. At this point, the new global best known solution is used by all colonies for the upcoming pheromone update. Since all threads need to have done their comparisons for the new global best solution to be effectively known globally, a synchronization barrier needs to be placed before the pheromone update procedure.

Each colony executes its own ants in parallel by creating a nested group of threads with an additional parallel region. Ants are then distributed to the available processor cores and update the global shared pheromone structure of the colony. Therefore, these updates must be carried out within some form of critical zone to guarantee that unmanaged concurrent writes are avoided. Next subsection shows how these strategies translate into a real computing environment.

4.1.1. Experimental results

The proposed experimentations are based on the Ant Colony System (ACS) applied to the Travelling Salesman Problem ([34]). Both implementations have been experimented on ROMEO II in the Centre de Calcul de Champagne-Ardenne. ROMEO II is a parallel supercomputer of cluster type, consisting of 8 Novascale SMP nodes dedicated to computations. Each node includes 4 Intel Itanium II dual-core processors running at 1.6 GHz with 8MB of cache memory, for a total number of 8 cores, as well as from 16 GB to 128 GB of memory. Each execution is performed on a single node using from 1 to 8 cores. Application code is written in C++ with OpenMP directives for parallelization. The chosen TSP instances range in size from 783 cities to 13 509 cities. For a more detailed version of the experimental setup and results, the reader may consult Delisle *et al.* [8].

Table 2 provides the summary of the experimentations with 1 to 8 independent colonies, each colony residing on a separate core. For each problem and number of cores, the 4 columns provide respectively the speedup, the average tour length, the best tour length and the relative closeness of the average tour length to the optimal solution. For each execution, computed time comes from the last colony that finishes its search and tour length comes from the colony that found the best solution.

We first notice that this implementation is quite scalable. In fact, speedups are relatively close to the number of cores in all configurations. Obviously, there are still some system costs associated to the parallel execution in a shared memory environment, which tend to slightly grow as the number of processors/cores increases. Also, as each core performs the computations associated with a whole ant colony, workload is considerably large in the parallel region. The ratio between parallelism costs and total execution time per core is then greatly reduced.

Table 3 provides results obtained with multiple cooperating colonies. Every 10 iterations, the global best solution is used for the global pheromone update. For the remaining iterations, each colony uses its own best known solution to update its pheromone structure. We first note that the exchange strategy does not significantly hurt the execution time as speedups are still excellent with up to 8 processors. Still, when 4 and 8 processors are used, most efficiency measures are slightly inferior to the ones obtained with independent colonies. This was

http://dx.doi.org/10.5772/54252

Problem	Nb. of cores	Speedup	Avg. tour length	Best tour length	Closeness
rat783	1	-	8,824	8,810	99.80
	2	1.98	8,823	8,806	99.81
	4	3.69	8,820	8,815	99.84
	8	5.93	8,829	8,822	99.74
d2103	1	-	80,511	80,466	99.92
	2	1.97	80,573	80,466	99.85
	4	4.00	80,508	80,477	99.93
	8	6.92	80,501	80,463	99.94
pla7397	1	-	23,365,444	23,353,738	99.55
	2	1.99	23,352,192	23,332,663	99.61
	4	3.80	23,380,613	23,350,736	99.48
	8	7.80	23,425,288	23,396,612	99.29
usa13509	1	-	20,465,969	20,414,755	97.58
	2	1.89	20,376,567	20,250,719	98.03
	4	3.65	20,443,190	20,423,250	97.70
	8	7.30	20,441,068	20,410,519	97.71

Table 2. Multiple independent colonies: number of cores, speedup, average tour length, best tour length and relative closeness of the average tour length to the optimal solution.

Problem	Nb. of cores	Speedup	Avg. tour length	Best tour length	Closeness
rat783	1	-	8,824	8,810	99.80
	2	1.95	8,822	8,810	99.82
	4	3.69	8,819	8,815	99.86
	8	5.72	8,816	8,812	99.89
d2103	1	-	80,511	80,466	99.92
	2	1.95	80,475	80,450	99.97
	4	3.81	80,489	80,450	99.95
	8	6.85	80,484	80,454	99.96
pla7397	1	-	23,365,444	23,353,738	99.55
	2	2.00	23,348,946	23,322,729	99.62
	4	3.89	23,358,733	23,334,364	99.58
	8	7.75	23,356,251	23,350,596	99.59
usa13509	1	-	20,465,969	20,414,755	97.58
	2	2.02	20,456,702	20,392,284	97.63
	4	3.20	20,450,581	20,414,972	97.66
	8	5.55	20,434,287	20,375,145	97.74

Table 3. Multiple cooperating colonies - Global best exchange each 10 cycles: number of cores, speedup, average tour length, best tour length and relative closeness of the average tour length to the optimal solution.

expected as the information exchange steps imply a synchronization cost that grows with the number of colonies used.

Concerning solution quality, the reader may observe that in all cases, the average tour length obtained with multiple cooperating colonies is closer to the optimal solution than with independent colonies or sequential execution. In most cases, the minimum solution found is also better. It shows that the information exchange scheme, while simple, is benefical to solution quality. Overall, results show that a $COLONY_{process}^{global}$-$ITERATION_{process}^{global}$-$ANT_{thread}^{global}$ implementation can be efficiently implemented on a SMP and multi-core computer node containing up to 8 processors.

4.2. Parallel ants on Graphics Processing Units

This approach deals with the execution of a single ant colony on a GPU architecure as defined in the author's previous work ([10]). Ants are associated to blocks and solution elements are associated to threads. As it is shown below, ants may communicate with the relatively slow device memory of the GPU and solution elements may do so with the faster, shared memory of a multiprocessor. As the ACO is not parallelized at the colony and iteration levels, their execution remain sequential and memory structure is not specified. This implementation is then defined as $COLONY_{process}^{-}$-$ITERATION_{process}^{-}$-ANT_{block}^{global}-$SOLUTION\_ELEMENT_{thread}^{local}$. Before providing more details about this implementation, a brief description of the underlying GPU architecture and computational model are given.

As it may be seen in Figure 3, the conventional NVIDIA GPU [33] includes many *Streaming Multiprocessors* (SM), each one of them being composed of *Streaming Processors* (SP). Several memories are distinguished on this special hardware, differing in size, latency and access type (read-only or read/write). *Device memory* is relatively large in size but slow in access time. The *global* and *local* memory spaces are specific regions of the device memory that can be accessed in read and write modes. Data structures of a computer program to be executed on GPU must be created on the CPU and transferred on global memory which is accessible to all SPs of the GPU. On the other hand, local memory stores automatic data structures that consume more registers than available.

Each SM employs an architecture model called *SIMT* (*Single Instruction, Multiple Thread*) which allows the execution of many coordinated threads in a data-parallel fashion. It is composed of a *constant memory cache*, a *texture memory cache*, a *shared memory* and *registers*. Constant and texture caches are linked to the constant and texture memories that are physically located in the device memory. Consequently, they are accessible in read-only mode by the SPs and faster in access time than the rest of the device memory. The constant memory is very limited in size whereas texture memory size can be adjusted in order to occupy the available device memory. All SPs can read and write in their local shared memory, which is fast in access time but small in size. It is divided into memory banks of 32-bits words that can be accessed simultaneously. This implies that parallel requests for memory addresses that fall into the same memory bank cause the serialization of accesses [33]. Registers are the fastest memories available on a GPU but involve the use of slow local memory when too many are used. Moreover, accesses may be delayed due to register read-after-write dependencies and register memory bank conflicts.

http://dx.doi.org/10.5772/54252

GPUs are programmable through different Application Programming Interfaces like CUDA, OpenCL or DirectX. However, as current general-purpose APIs are still closely tied to specific GPU models, we choose CUDA to fully exploit the available state-of-the-art NVIDIA Fermi architecture. In the CUDA programming model [33], the GPU works as a SIMT co-processor of a conventional CPU. It is based on the concept of kernels, which are functions (written in C) executed in parallel by a given number of CUDA threads. These threads are grouped together into *blocks* that are distributed on the GPU SMs to be executed independently of each other. However, the number of blocks that an SM can process at the same time (*active blocks*) is restricted and depends on the quantity of registers and shared memory used by the threads of each block. Threads within a block can cooperate by sharing data through the shared memory and by synchronizing their execution to coordinate memory accesses. In a block, the system groups threads (typically 32) into *warps* which are executed simultaneously on successive clock cycles. The number of threads per block must be a multiple of its size to maximize efficiency. Much of the global memory latency can then be hidden by the thread scheduler if there are sufficient independent arithmetic instructions that can be issued while waiting for the global memory access to complete. Consequently, the more active blocks there are per SM, and also active warps, the more the latency can be hidden.

It is important to note that in the context of GPU execution, flow control instructions (if, switch, do, for, while) can affect the efficiency of an algorithm. In fact, depending on the provided data, these instructions may force threads of a same warp to diverge, in other words, to take different paths in the program. In that case, execution paths must be serialized, increasing the total number of instructions executed by this warp.

In the parallel ants general strategy, ants of a single colony are distributed to processing elements in order to execute tour constructions in parallel. On a conventional CPU architecture, the concept of processing element is usually associated to a single-core processor or to one of the cores of a multi-core processor. On a GPU architecture, the main choices are to associate this concept either to an SP or to an SM. As this case study is concerned with the latter, each ant is associated to a CUDA block and runs its tour construction phase in parallel on a specific SM of the GPU. A dedicated thread of a given block is then in charge of managing the tour construction of an ant, but an additional level of parallelism, the solution element level, may be exploited in the computation of the state transition rule. In fact, an ant evaluates several candidates before selecting the one to add to its current solution. As these evaluations can be done in parallel, they are assigned to the remaining threads of the block.

A simple implementation would then imply keeping ant's private data structures in the global memory. However, as only one ant is assigned to a block and so to an SM, taking advantage of the shared-memory is possible. Data needed to compute the ant state transition rule is then stored in this memory that is faster and accessible by all threads that participate in the computation. Most remaining issues encountered in the GPU implementation of the parallel ants general strategy are related to memory management. More particularly, data transfers between CPU and GPU as well as global memory accesses require considerable time. As it was mentioned before, these accesses may be reduced by storing the related data structures in shared memory. However, in the case of ACO, the three central data structures are the pheromone matrix, the penalty matrix (typically the transition cost between all pairs of solution elements) and the candidates lists, which are needed by all ants of the colony while being too large (typically ranging from $O(n)$ to $O(n^2)$ in size) to fit in shared memory. They are then kept in global memory. On the other hand, as they are not modified during the tour construction phase, it is possible to take benefit of the texture cache to reduce their access times.

4.2.1. *Experimental results*

The proposed GPU strategy is implemented into an MMAS algorithm ([35]) and experimented on various TSPs with sizes varying from 51 to 2103 cities. Minimums and averages are computed from 25 trials for problems with less than 1000 cities and from 10 trials for larger instances. An effort is made to keep the algorithm and parameters as close as possible to the original MMAS. Following the guidelines of Barr and Hickman [36] and Alba [37], the *relative speedup* metric is computed on *mean execution times* to evaluate the performance of the proposed implementation. Speedups are calculated by dividing the sequential CPU time with the parallel time, which is obtained with the same CPU and the GPU acting as a co-processor.

Experiments were made on one GPU of an NVIDIA Fermi C2050 server available at the Centre de Calcul de Champagne-Ardenne. It contains 14 SMs, 32 SPs per SM, 48 KB of shared memory per SM and a warp size of 32. The CPU code runs on one core of a 4-core Xeon E5640 CPUs running at 2.67 Ghz and 24 GB of DDR3 memory. Application code was written in the "C for CUDA V3.1" programming environment.

The implementation uses a number of blocks equal to the number of ants, each one of them being composed of a number of threads equal to the size of candidate lists, in that case 20. Also, the number of iterations is set with the intent of globally keeping the same global number of tour constructions for each experiment. For more details on the experimental setup, the reader may consult Delévacq *et al.* ([10]).

A first step in our experiments is to compare solution quality obtained by sequential and parallel versions of the algorithm. Table 4 presents average tour length, best tour length and closeness to the optimal solution for each problem. The reader may note the similarity between the results obtained by our sequential implementation and the ones provided by the authors of the original MMAS ([35]), as well as their significant closeness to optimal solutions.

A second step is to evaluate and compare the reduction of execution time that is obtained with the GPU parallelization strategy. Table 4 shows the speedups obtained for each problem. The reader may notice that speedups are ranging from 6.84 to 19.47. This shows that distributing ants to blocks and sharing the computation of the state transition rule between several threads of a block is efficient. Also, speedup generally increases with problem size, indicating the good scalabilty of the strategy. However, a slight decrease is encountered with the 2103 cities problem. In that case, the large workload and data structures imply memory access latencies and bank conflicts costs that grow faster than the benefits of parallelizing available work. Associated to the combined effect of the increasing number of blocks required to perform computations and a limited number of active blocks per SM, performance gains become less significative. Overall, results show that a $COLONY_{process}^{-}$-$ITERATION_{process}^{-}$-ANT_{block}^{global}-$SOLUTION\_ELEMENT_{thread}^{local}$ implementation can be efficiently implemented on a state-of-the-art GPU.

Problem		Speedup	Stützle and Hoos	Avg. tour length	Best tour length	Closeness
eil51	Sequential	-	427.80	427.32	426	99.69
	Parallel	6.84	-	427.20	426	99.72
kroA100	Sequential	-	21,336.90	21,314.36	21,282	99.85
	Parallel	8.12	-	21,317.32	21,282	99.83
d198	Sequential	-	15,952.30	15,973.84	15,913	98.77
	Parallel	11.13	-	15,961.64	15,851	98.85
lin318	Sequential	-	42,346.60	42,341.72	42,107	99.26
	Parallel	11.03	-	42,325.32	42,147	99.29
rat783	Sequential	-	-	9,042.44	8,923	97.32
	Parallel	15.58	-	9,002.32	8,899	97.77
fl1577	Sequential	-	-	24,490.30	24,201	89.83
	Parallel	19.47	-	24,287.80	23,938	90.84
d2103	Sequential	-	-	82,754.30	82,378	97.14
	Parallel	17.64	-	82,756.00	82,547	97.13

Table 4. GPU implementation: speedup, average tour length from Stützle and Hoos original MMAS implementation [35], average tour length, best tour length and relative closeness of the average tour length to the optimal solution.

5. Conclusion

The main objective of this chapter was to provide a new algorithmic model to formalize the implementation of Ant Colony Optimization on high performance computing platforms. The proposed taxonomy managed to capture important features related to both the algorithmic structure of ACO and the architecture of parallel computers. Case studies were also presented in order to illustrate how this classification translates into real applications. Finally, with its synthesized literature review and experimental study, this chapter served as an overview of current works on parallel ACO.

Still, as it is the case in the field of parallel metaheuristics in general, much can still be done for the effective use of state-of-the-art parallel computing platforms. For example, maximal exploitation of computing resources often requires algorithmic configurations that do not let ACO perform an effective exploration and exploitation of the search space. On the other hand, parallel performance is strongly influenced by the combined effects of parameters related to the metaheuristic, the hardware technical architecture and the granularity of the parallelization. As it becomes clear that the future of computers no longer relies on increasing the performance on a single computing core but on using many of them in a hybrid system, it becomes desirable to adapt optimization tools for parallel execution on many kinds of architectures. We believe that the global acceptance of parallel computing in optimization systems requires algorithms and software that are not only effective, but also usable by a wide range of academicians and practitioners.

Acknowledgements

This work is supported by the Agence Nationale de la Recherche (ANR) under grant no. ANR-2010-COSI-003-03 and by the Centre de Calcul de Champagne-Ardenne ROMEO which provides the computational resources used for experiments.

Author details

Pierre Delisle

CReSTIC, Université de Reims Champagne-Ardenne, Reims, France

6. References

[1] M. Dorigo and T. Stützle. *Ant Colony Optimization.* MIT Press/Bradford Books, 2004.

[2] B. Bullnheimer, G. Kotsis, and C. Strauss. Parallelization strategies for the ant system. In R. De Leone, A. Murli, P. Pardalos, and G. Toraldo, editors, *High Performance Algorithms and Software in Nonlinear Optimization*, volume 24 of *Applied Optimization*, pages 87–100. Kluwer, Dordrecht, 1997.

[3] T. Stützle. Parallelisation strategies for ant colony optimization. In A.E. Eiben, T. Bäck, H.-P. Schwefel, and M. Schoenauer, editors, *Proceedings of the Fifth International Conference on Parallel Problem Solving from Nature (PPSN V)*, volume 1498, pages 722–731. Springer-Verlag, New York, 1998.

[4] M. Pedemonte, S. Nesmachnow, and H. Cancela. A survey on parallel ant colony optimization. *Applied Soft Computing*, 11:5181–5197, 2011.

[5] P. Delisle, M. Krajecki, M. Gravel, and C. Gagné. Parallel implementation of an ant colony optimization metaheuristic with openmp. In *Proceedings of the International Conference on Parallel Architectures and Compilation Techniques, 3rd European Workshop on OpenMP (EWOMP'01)*, pages 8–12, Barcelona, Spain, 2001.

[6] P. Delisle, M. Gravel, M. Krajecki, C. Gagné, and W. L. Price. A shared memory parallel implementation of ant colony optimization. In *Proceedings of the 6th Metaheuristics International Conference (MIC'2005)*, pages 257–264, Vienna, Autria, 2005.

[7] P. Delisle, M. Gravel, M. Krajecki, C. Gagné, and W. L. Price. Comparing parallelization of an aco: Message passing vs. shared-memory. In M.J. Blesa, C. Blum, A. Roli, and M. Sampels, editors, *Proceedings of the 2nd International Conference on Hybrid Metaheuristics*, volume 3636 of *Lecture Notes in Computer Science*, pages 1–11. Springer-Verlag Berlin Heidelberg, 2005.

[8] P. Delisle, M. Gravel, and M. Krajecki. Multi-colony parallel ant colony optimization on smp and multi-core computers. In *Proceedings of the World Congress on Nature and Biologically Inspired Computing (NaBIC 2009)*, pages 318–323. IEEE, 2009.

[9] A. Delévacq, P. Delisle, M. Gravel, and M. Krajecki. Parallel ant colony optimization on graphics processing units. In H. R. Arabnia, S. C. Chiu, G. A. Gravvanis, M. Ito, K. Joe, H. Nishikawa, and A. M. G. Solo, editors, *Proceedings of the 16th International Conference on Parallel and Distributed Processing Techniques and Applications (PDPTA'10)*, pages 196–202. CSREA Press, 2010.

[10] A. Delévacq, P. Delisle, M. Gravel, and M. Krajecki. Parallel ant colony optimization on graphics processing units. *Journal of Parallel and Distributed Computing*, page doi : 10.1016/j.jpdc.2012.01.003, 2012.

[11] E. Talbi, O. Roux, C. Fonlupt, and D. Robillard. Parallel ant colonies for the quadratic assignment problem. *Future Generation Computer Systems*, 17(4):441–449, 2001.

[12] M. Randall and A. Lewis. A parallel implementation of ant colony optimization. *Journal of Parallel and Distributed Computing*, 62(9):1421–1432, 2002.

[13] M. T. Islam, P. Thulasiraman, and R. K. Thulasiram. A parallel ant colony optimization algorithm for all-pair routing in manets. In *Proceedings of the 17th international Symposium on Parallel and Distributed Processing*. IEEE Computer Society, 2003.

[14] M. Craus and L. Rudeanu. Parallel framework for ant-like algorithms. In *Proceedings of the Third International Symposium on Parallel and Distributed Computing (ISPDC/HeteroPar'04)*, pages 36–41, 2004.

[15] K. Doerner, R. Hartl, S. Benker, and M. Lucka. Parallel cooperative savings based ant colony optimization - multiple search and decomposition approaches. *Parallel Processing Letters*, 16(3):351–370, 2006.

[16] M. Middendorf, F. Reischle, and H. Schmeck. Multi colony ant algorithms. *Journal of Heuristics*, 8(3):305–320, 2002.

[17] D. Chu and A. Y. Zomaya. Parallel ant colony optimization for 3d protein structure prediction using the hp lattice model. In N. Nedjah, L. de Macedo, and E. Alba, editors, *Parallel Evolutionary Computations*, volume 22 of *Studies in Computational Intelligence*, chapter 9, pages 177–198. Springer, 2006.

[18] M. Manfrin, M. Birattari, T. Stützle, and M. Dorigo. Parallel ant colony optimization for the traveling salesman problem. In *Proceedings of the 5th International Workshop on Ant Colony Optimization and Swarm Intelligence*, volume 4150 of *Lecture Notes in Computer Science*, pages 224–234, 2006.

[19] I. Ellabib, P. Calamai, and O. Basir. Exchange strategies for multiple ant colony system. *Information Sciences*, 177(5):1248–1264, 2007.

[20] E. Alba, G. Leguizamon, and G. Ordonez. Two models of parallel aco algorithms for the minimum tardy task problem. *International Journal of High Performance Systems Architecture*, 1(1):50–59, 2007.

[21] B. Scheuermann, K. So, M. Guntsch, M. Middendorf, O. Diessel, H. ElGindy, and H. Schmeck. Fpga implementation of population-based ant colony optimization. *Applied Soft Computing*, 4:303–322, 2004.

[22] B. Scheuermann, S. Janson, and M. Middendorf. Hardware-oriented ant colony optimization. *Journal of Systems Architecture*, 53:386–402, 2007.

[23] A. Catala, J. Jaen, and J. Mocholi. Strategies for accelerating ant colony optimization algorithms on graphical processing units. In *Proceedings of the IEEE Congress on Evolutionary Computation*, pages 492–500. IEEE Press, 2007.

[24] J. Wang, J. Dong, and C. Zhang. Implementation of ant colony algorithm based on gpu. In E. Banissi, M. Sarfraz, J. Zhang, A. Ursyn, W. C. Jeng, M. W. Bannatyne, J. J. Zhang, L. H. San, and M. L. Huang, editors, *Proceedings of the Sixth International Conference on*

Computer Graphics, Imaging and Visualization: New Advances and Trends, pages 50–53. IEEE Computer Society, 2009.

[25] Y. You. Parallel ant system for traveling salesman problem on gpus. In *Proceedings of GECCO 2009 - Genetic and Evolutionary Computation*, pages 1–2, 2009.

[26] W. Zhu and J. Curry. Parallel ant colony for nonlinear function optimization with graphics hardware acceleration. In *Proceedings of the 2009 IEEE international conference on Systems, Man and Cybernetics*, pages 1803–1808. IEEE Press, 2009.

[27] J. Li, X. Hu, Z. Pang, and K. Qian. A parallel ant colony optimization algorithm based on fine-grained model with gpu-acceleration. *International Journal of Innovative Computing, Information and Control*, 5(11(A)):3707–3716, 2009.

[28] J. M. Cecilia, J. M. Garcia, A. Nisbet, M. Amos, and M. Ujaldon.

[29] G. Weis and A. Lewis. Using xmpp for ad-hoc grid computing - an application example using parallel ant colony optimisation. In *Proceedings of the International Symposium on Parallel and Distributed Processing*, pages 1–4, 2009.

[30] J. Mocholí, J. Martínez, and J. Canós. A grid ant colony algorithm for the orienteering problem. In *Proceedings of the IEEE Congress on Evolutionary Computation*, pages 942–949. IEEE Press, 2005.

[31] E. Talbi. *Metaheuristics: From Design to Implementation*. Wiley Publishing, 2009.

[32] I. Foster and C. Kesselman. *The Grid: Blueprint for a New Computing Infrastructure*. Morgan Kaufmann, 1999.

[33] *CUDA : Computer Unified Device Architecture Programming Guide 3.1*, 2010.

[34] M. Dorigo and L. M. Gambardella. Ant colony system: a cooperative learning approach to the traveling salesman problem. *IEEE Transactions on Evolutionary Computation*, 1(1):53–66, 1997.

[35] T. Stützle and H. Hoos. Max-min ant system. *Future Generation Computer Systems*, 16(8):889–914, 2000.

[36] R. S. Barr and B. L. Hickman. Reporting computational experiments with parallel algorithms : Issues, measures and experts' opinions. *ORSA Journal on Computing*, 5(1):2–18, 1993.

[37] E. Alba. Parallel evolutionary algorithms can achieve super-linear performance. *Information Processing Letters*, 82(1):7–13, 2002.

Chapter 3

Strategies for Parallel Ant Colony Optimization on Graphics Processing Units

Jaqueline S. Angelo, Douglas A. Augusto and
Helio J. C. Barbosa

Additional information is available at the end of the chapter

http://dx.doi.org/10.5772/51679

1. Introduction

Ant colony optimization (ACO) is a population-based metaheuristic inspired by the collective behavior of ants which is used for solving optimization problems in general and, in particular, those that can be reduced to finding good paths through graphs. In ACO a set of agents (artificial ants) cooperate in trying to find good solutions to the problem at hand [1].

Ant colony algorithms are known to have a significant ability of finding high-quality solutions in a reasonable time [2]. However, the computational time of these methods is seriously compromised when the current instance of the problem has a high dimension and/or is hard to solve. In this line, a significant amount of research has been done in order to reduce computation time and improve the solution quality of ACO algorithms by using parallel computing. Due to the independence of the artificial ants, which are guided by an indirect communication via their environment (pheromone trail and heuristic information), ACO algorithms are naturally suitable for parallel implementation.

Parallel computing has become attractive during the last decade as an instrument to improve the efficiency of population-based methods. One can highlight different reasons to parallelize an algorithm: to (i) reduce the execution time, (ii) enable to increase the size of the problem, (iii) expand the class of problems computationally treatable, and so on. In the literature one can find many possibilities on how to explore parallelism, and the final performance strongly depends on both the problem they are applied to and the hardware available [3].

In the last years, several works were devoted to the implementation of parallel ACO algorithms [4]. Most of these use clusters of PCs, where the workload is distributed to multiple computers [5]. More recently, the emergence of parallel architectures such as multi-core processors and graphics processing units (GPU) allowed new implementations of parallel ACO algorithms in order to speedup the computational performance.

GPU devices have been traditionally used for graphics processing, which requires a high computational power to process a large number of pixels in a short time-frame. The massively parallel architecture of the GPUs makes them more efficient than general-purpose CPUs when large amount of independent data need to be processed in parallel.

The main type of parallelism in ACO algorithms is the parallel ant approach, which is the parallelism at the level of individual ants. Other steps of the ACO algorithms are also considered for speeding up their performance, such as the tour construction, evaluation of the solution and the pheromone update procedure.

The purpose of this chapter is to present a survey of the recent developments for parallel ant colony algorithms on GPU devices, highlighting and detailing parallelism strategies for each step of an ACO algorithm.

1.1. Ant Colony Optimization

Ant Colony Optimization is a metaheuristic inspired by the observation of real ants' behavior, applied with great success to a large number of difficult optimization problems.

Ant colonies, and other insects that live in colony, present interesting characteristics by the view of the collective behavior of those entities. Some characteristics of social groups in swarm intelligence are widely discussed in [6]. Among them, ant colonies in particular present a highly structured social organization, making them capable of self-organizing, without a centralized controller, in order to accomplish complex tasks for the survival of the entire colony [2]. Those capabilities, such as division of labor, foraging behavior, brood sorting and cooperative transportation, inspired different kinds of ant colony algorithms. The first ACO algorithm was inspired on the capability of ants to find the shortest path between a food source and their nest.

In all those examples ants coordinate their activities via *stigmergy* [7], which is an indirect communication mediated by modifications on the environment. While moving, ants deposit pheromone (chemical substance) on the ground to mark paths that may be followed by other members of the colony, which then reinforce the pheromone on that path. This behavior leads to a self-reinforcing process that results in path marked by high concentration of pheromone while less used paths tend to have a decreasing pheromone level due to evaporation. However, real ants can choose a path that has not the highest concentration of pheromone, so that new sources of food and/or shorter paths can be found.

1.2. Combinatorial problems

In combinatorial optimization problems one wants to find discrete values for solution variables that lead to the optimal solution with respect to a given objective function. An interesting characteristic of combinatorial problems is that they are easy to understand but very difficult to be solved [2].

One of the most extensively studied combinatorial problem is the Traveling Salesman Problem (TSP) [8] and it was the first problem approached by the ACO metaheuristic. The first developed ACO algorithm, called Ant System [1, 9], was initially applied to the TSP, then later improved and applied to many kinds of optimization problems [10].

In the Traveling Salesman Problem (TSP), a salesman, starting from an initial city, wants to travel the shortest path to serve its customers in the neighboring towns, eventually returning to the city where he originally came from, visiting each city once. The representation of the TSP can be done through a fully connected graph $G = (N, A)$, with N being the set of nodes representing cities and A the set of edges fully connecting the nodes. For each arc (i, j) is assigned a value d_{ij}, which may be distance, time, price, or other factor of interest associated with edges $a_{i,j} \in A$. The TSP can be symmetric or asymmetric. Using distances (associated with each arc) as cost values, in the symmetric TSP the distance between cities i and j is the same as between j and i, i.e. $d_{ij} = d_{ji}$; in the asymmetric TSP the direction used for crossing an arc is taken into consideration and so there is at least one arc in which $d_{ij} \neq d_{ji}$. The objective of the problem is to find the minimum Hamiltonian cycle, where a Hamiltonian cycle is a closed tour visiting each of the $n = |N|$ nodes (cities) of G exactly once.

2. Graphics Processing Unit

Until recently the only viable choice as a platform for parallel programming was the conventional CPU processor, be it single- or multi-core. Usually many of them were arranged either tightly as multiprocessors, sharing a single memory space, or loosely as multicomputers, with the communication among them done indirectly due to the isolated memory spaces.

The parallelism provided by the CPU is reasonably efficient and still very attractive, particularly for tasks with low degree of parallelism, but a new trendy platform for parallel computing has emerged in the past few years, the *graphics processing unit*, or simply the GPU architecture.

The beginning of the GPU architecture dates back to a couple of decades ago when some primitive devices were developed to offload certain basic graphics operations from the CPU. Graphics operations, which end up being essentially the task to determine the right color of each individual pixel per frame, are in general both independent and specialized, allowing a high degree of parallelism to be explored. However, doing such operations on conventional CPU processors, which are general-purpose and back then were exclusively sequential, is slow and inefficient. The advantage of parallel devices designed for such particular purpose was then becoming progressively evident, enabling and inviting a new world of graphics applications.

One of those applications was the computer game, which played an important role on the entire development history of the GPU. As with other graphics applications, games involve computing and displaying—possibly in parallel—numerous pixels at a time. But differently from other graphics applications, computer games were always popular among all range of computer users, and thus very attractive from a business perspective. Better and visually appealing games sell more, but they require more computational power. This demand, as a consequence, has been pushing forward the GPU development since the early days, which in turn has been enabling the creation of more and more complex games.

Of course, in the meantime the CPU development had also been advancing, with the processors becoming progressively more complex, particularly due to the addition of cache memory hierarchies and many specific-purpose control units (such as branch prediction, speculative and out-of-order execution, and so on) [11]. Another source of development has been the technological advance in the manufacturing process, which has been allowing the manufactures to systematically increase the transistor density on a microchip. However, all those progresses recently begun to decline with the Moore's Law [12] being threatened by the approaching of the physical limits of the technology on the transistor density and operating frequency. The response from the industry to continually raise the computational power was to migrate from the sequential single-core to the parallel multi-core design.

Although the nowadays multi-core CPU processors perform fairly well, the decades of accumulative architectural optimizations toward sequential tasks have led to big and complex CPU cores, hence restricting the amount of them that could be packed on a single processor—not more than a few cores. As a consequence, the current CPU design cannot take advantage of workloads having high degree of parallelism, in other words, it is inefficient for massive parallelism.

Contrary to the development philosophy of the CPU, because of the requirements of graphics operations the GPU took since its infancy the massive parallelism as a design goal. Filling the processor with numerous ALUs[1] means that there is not much die area left for anything else, such as cache memory and control units. The benefit of this design choice is two-fold: (i) it simplifies the architecture due to the uniformity; and (ii) since there is a high portion of transistors dedicated to actual computation (spread over many ALUs), the theoretical computational power is proportionally high. As one can expect, the GPU reaches its peak of efficiency when the device is fully occupied, that is, when there are enough parallel tasks to utilize each one of the thousands of ALUs, as commonly found on a modern GPU.

Besides being highly parallel, this feature alone would not be enough to establish the GPU architecture as a compelling platform for mainstream high-performance computation. In the early days, the graphics operations were mainly primitive and thus could be more easily and efficiently implemented in hardware through fixed, i.e. specialized, functional units. But again, such operations were becoming increasingly more complex, particularly in visually-rich computer games, that the GPU was forced to switch to a programmable architecture, where it was possible to execute not only strict graphics operations, but also arbitrary instructions. The union of an efficient massively parallel architecture with the general-purpose capability has created one of the most exciting processor, the modern GPU architecture, outstanding in performance with respect to power consumption, price and space occupied.

The following section will introduce the increasingly adopted open standard for heterogeneous programming, including of course the GPU, known as OpenCL.

2.1. Open Computing Language – OpenCL

An interesting fact about the CPU and GPU architectures is that while the CPU started as a general-purpose processor and got more and more parallelism through the multi-core design, the GPU did the opposite path, that is, started as a highly specialized parallel processor and was increasingly endowed with general-purpose capabilities as well. In other words, these architectures have been slowly converging into a common design, although each one still has—and probably will always have due to fundamental architectural differences—divergent strengths: the CPU is optimized for achieving low-latency in sequential tasks whereas the GPU is optimized for maximizing the throughput in highly parallel tasks [13].

[1] *Arithmetic and Logic Unit*, the most basic form of computational unit.

It is in this convergence that OpenCL is situated. In these days, most of the processors are, to some extent, both parallel and general purpose; therefore, it should be possible to come along with a uniform programming interface to target such different but fundamentally related architectures. This is the main idea behind OpenCL, a platform for uniform parallel programming of heterogeneous systems [14].

OpenCL is an open standard managed by a non-profit organization, the Khronos Group [14], that is architecture- and vendor-independent, so it is designed to work across multiple devices from different manufactures. The two main goals of OpenCL are *portability* and *efficiency*. Portability is achieved by the guarantee that every supported device conforms with a common set of functionality defined by the OpenCL specification [15].[2] As for efficiency, it is obtained through the flexible multi-device programming model and a rich set of relatively low-level instructions that allow the programmer to greatly optimize the parallel implementation (possibly targeting a specific architecture if so desirable) without loss of portability.[3]

2.1.1. *Fundamental Concepts and Terminology*

An OpenCL program comprises two distinct types of code: the *host*, which runs sequentially on the CPU, and the *kernel*, which runs in parallel on one or more devices, including CPUs and GPUs. The host code is responsible for managing the OpenCL devices and setting up/controlling the execution of kernels on them, whereas the actual parallel processing is programmed in the kernel code.

2.1.1.1. Host code

The tasks performed by the host portion usually involve: (1) discovering and enumeration of the available compute devices; (2) loading and compilation of the kernels' source code; (3) loading of domain-specific data, such as algorithm's parameters and problem's data; (4) setting up kernels' parameters; (5) launching and coordinating kernel executions; and finally (6) outputting the results. The host code can be written in the C/C++ programming language.[4]

2.1.1.2. Kernel code

Since it implements the parallel decomposition of a given problem—a *parallel strategy*—, the kernel is usually the most critical aspect of an OpenCL program and so care should be taken in its design.

The OpenCL kernel is similar to the concept of a procedure in a programming language, which takes a set of input arguments, performs computation on them, and writes back the result. The main difference is that an OpenCL kernel is a procedure that, when launched, actually multiple instances of them are spawned simultaneously, each one assigned to an individual execution unit of a parallel device.

---

[2] In fact, all the parallel strategies described in Section 4 can be readily applied on a CPU device (or any other OpenCL-supported device, such as DSPs and FPGAs) without modification.

[3] Of course, although OpenCL guarantees the functional portability, i.e. that the code will run on any other supported device, doing optimizations aimed at getting the most out of a specific device or architecture may lead to the loss of what is known as *performance portability*.

[4] C and C++ are the only officially supported languages by the OpenCL specification, but there exist many other third-party languages that could also be used.

An instance of a kernel is formally called a *work-item*. The total number of work-items is referred to as *global size*, and defines the level of decomposition of the problem: the larger the global size, the finer is the granularity, and is always preferred over a coarser granularity when targeting a GPU device in order to maximize its utilization—if that does not imply in a substantial raise of the communication overhead.

The mapping between a work-item and the problem's data is set up through the concept known as *N-dimensional domain range*, or just N-D domain, where N denotes a one-, two-, or three-dimensional domain. In practice, this is the mechanism that connects the work-items execution ("compute domain") with the problem's data ("data domain"). More specifically, the OpenCL runtime assigns to each work-item a unique identifier, a $global_{id}$, which in turn makes it possible to an individual work-item to operate on a subset of the problem's data by somehow indexing these elements through the identifier.

Figure 1 illustrates the concept of a mapping between the compute and data domains. Suppose one is interested in computing in parallel a certain operation over an array of four dimensions ($n = 4$), e.g. computing the square root of each element. A trivial strategy would be to dedicate a work-item per element, but let us assume one wants to limit the number of work-items to just two, that is, $global_{size} = 2$. This means that a single work-item will have to handle two data elements, thus the granularity $g = 2$. So, how could one connect the compute and data domains? There are different ways of doing that, but one way is to, from within the work-item, index the elements of the *input* and *output* by the expression $g \times t + global_{id}$, where $t \in \{0, 1\}$ is the time step (iteration).

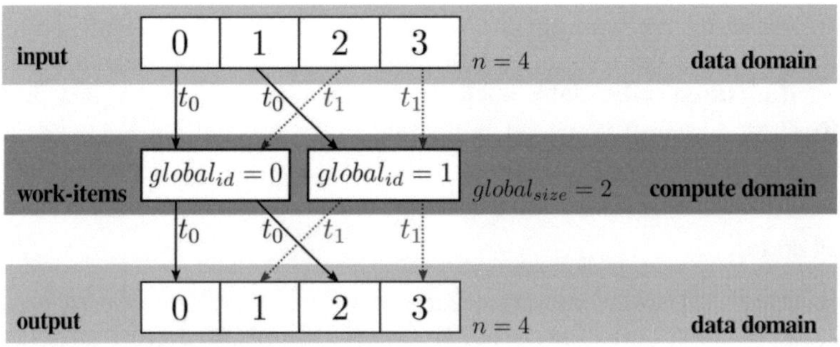

Figure 1. Example of a mapping between the compute and data domains.

A pseudo-OpenCL kernel implementing such strategy is presented in Algorithm 1.[5] At step t_0, the first and second work-items will be accessing, respectively, the indices 0 and 1, and at t_1 they will access the indices 2 and 3.

Algorithm 1: Example of a pseudo-OpenCL kernel

---

for $t \leftarrow 0$ **to** $\frac{n}{global_{size}} - 1$ **do**

$\quad$ output$[g \times t + global_{id}] \leftarrow \sqrt{\text{input}[g \times t + global_{id}]}$;

---

[5] An actual OpenCL kernel is implemented in OpenCL C, which is almost indistinguishable from the C language, but adds a few extensions and also some restrictions [15].

The *N*-D domain range can also be extended to higher dimensions. For instance, in a 2-D domain a work-item would have two identifiers, $global^0_{id}$ and $global^1_{id}$, where the first could be mapped to index the *row* and the second the *column* of a matrix. The reasoning is analogous for a 3-D domain range.

2.1.1.3. Communication and Synchronization

There are situations in which it is desirable or required to allow work-items to *communicate* and *synchronize* among them. For efficiency reasons, such operations are not arbitrarily allowed among work-items across the whole *N*-D domain.[6] For that purpose, though, one can resort to the notion of *work-group*, which in a nutshell is just a collection of work-items. All the work-items within a work-group are free to communicate and synchronize with each other. The number of work-items per work-group is given by the parameter *local size*, which in practice determines how the global domain is partitioned. For example, if $global_{size}$ is 256 and $local_{size}$ is 64, then the computational domain is partitioned into 4 work-groups (256/64) with each work-group having 64 work-items. Again, the OpenCL runtime provides means that allow each work-group and work-item to identify themselves. A work-group is identified with respect to the global *N*-D domain through $group_{id}$, and a work-item is identified locally within its work-group via $local_{id}$.

2.1.2. Compute Device Abstraction

In order to provide a uniform programming interface, OpenCL abstracts the architecture of a parallel compute device, as shown in Figure 2. There are two fundamental concepts in this abstraction, the *compute* and *memory* hierarchies.

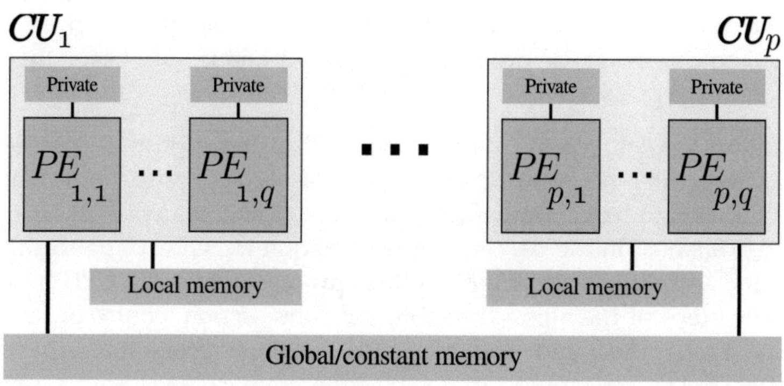

Figure 2. Abstraction of a parallel compute device architecture [16].

OpenCL defines two levels of compute hardware organization, the *compute units* (CU) and *processing elements* (PE). Not coincidentally this partitioning matches the software abstraction of work-groups and work-items. In fact, OpenCL guarantees that a work-group is entirely executed on a single compute unit whereas work-items are executed by processing elements. Nowadays GPUs usually have thousands of processing elements clustered in a dozen of

[6] There are two main reasons why those operations are restricted: (i) to encourage the better programming practice of avoiding dependence on communication as much as possible; and, most importantly, (ii) to allow the OpenCL to support even those rather limited devices that cannot keep—at least not efficiently—the state of all the running work-items as needed to fulfill the requirements to implement the global synchronization.

compute units. Therefore, to fully utilize such devices, there is needed at the very least this same amount of work-items in flight—however, the optimal amount of work-items in execution should be substantially more than that in order to the device have enough room to hide latencies [17, 18].

As for the memories, OpenCL exposes three memory spaces; from the more general to the more specific: the (i) *global/constant* memory, which is the main memory of the device, accessible from all the work-items—the *constant* space is a slightly optimized global memory for read-only access; (ii) the *local* memory, a very fast low-latency memory which is shared only across the work-items within their work-group—normally used as a programmable cache memory or as a means to share data (communicate); and (iii) the *private* memory, also a very fast memory, but only visible to the corresponding work-item.

3. Review of the literature

In the last few years, many works have been devoted to parallel implementations of ACO algorithms in GPU devices, motivated by the powerful massively parallel architecture provided by the GPU.

In reference [19], the authors proposed two parallel ACO implementations to solve the Orienteering Problem (OP). The strategies applied to the GPU were based on the intrinsically data-parallelism provided by the vertex processor and the fragment processor. The first experiments compared a grid implementation with 32 workstations equipped with CPUs Intel Pentium IV at 2.4GHz against one workstation with a GPU NVIDIA GeForce 6600 GT. Both strategies performed similarly with respect to the quality of the obtained solutions. The second experiment compared both the GPU parallel strategies proposed, showing that the strategy applied to the fragment processor performed about 35% faster than the strategy applied to the vertex processor.

In [20], the authors implemented a parallel $\mathcal{MM}$AS using multiple colonies, where each colony is associated with a work-group and ants are associated with work-items within each work-group. The experiments compared a parallel version of $\mathcal{MM}$AS on the GPU, with three serial CPU versions. In the parallel implementation the CPU initializes the pheromone trails, parameters, and also controls the iteration process, while the GPU is responsible for running the main steps of the algorithm: solution construction, choice of the best solution, and pheromone evaporation and updating. Six instances from the Travelling Salesman Problem library (TSPLIB), containing up to 400 cities, were solved using a workstation with a CPU AMD Athlon X2 3600+ running at 1.9GHz and a GPU NVIDIA GeForce GTX 8800 at 1.35GHz with 128 processing elements. The parallel GPU version was 2 to 32 times faster than the sequential version, whereas the solutions quality of the parallel version outperformed all the three $\mathcal{MM}$AS serial versions. In order to accelerate the choice of the iteration-best solution, the authors used a parallel reduction technique that "hangs up" the execution of certain work-items. This technique requires the use of barrier synchronization in order to ensure consistency of memory.

In the work described in [21] the authors implemented a parallel ACO algorithm with a pattern search procedure to solve continuous functions with bound constraints. The parallel method was compared with a serial CPU implementation. Each work-item is responsible for evaluating the solution's costs and constraints, constructing solutions and improving them via a local search procedure, while the CPU controls the initialization process, pheromone evaporation and updating, the sorting of the generated solutions, and the updating of the probability vectors. The experiments were executed on a workstation equipped with a CPU Intel Xeon E5420 at 2.5GHz and a GPU NVIDIA GeForce GTX 280 at 1296MHz and 240 processing elements. The computational experiments showed acceleration values between 128 and almost 404 in the parallel GPU implementation. On the other hand, both the parallel and serial versions obtained satisfactory results. However, regarding the solution quality under a time limit of one second, the parallel version outperformed the sequential one in most of the test problems. As a side note, the results could have been ever better if the authors had generated the random numbers directly on the GPU instead of pre computing them on the CPU.

A parallel $\mathcal{MM}$AS under a MATLAB environment was presented in [22]. The authors proposed an algorithm implementation which arranges the data into large scale matrices, taking advantage of the fact that the integration of MATLAB with the Jacket accelerator handles matrices on the GPU more naturally and efficiently than it could do with other data types. Therefore, auxiliary matrices were created, besides the usual matrices (τ and η) in a standard ACO algorithm. Instances from the TSPLIB were solved using a workstation with a CPU Intel i7 at 3.3GHz and GPU NVIDIA Tesla C1060 at 1.3GHz and 240 processing elements. Given a fixed number of iterations, the experimental evaluation showed that the CPU and GPU implementations obtained similar results, yet with the parallel GPU version much faster than the CPU. The speedup values had been growing with the number of TSP nodes, but when the number of nodes reached 439 the growth could not be sustained and slowed down drastically due to the frequent data-transfer operations between the CPU and GPU.

In [23], the authors make use of the GPU parallel computing power to solve pathfinding in games. The ACO algorithm proposed was implemented on a GPU device, where the parallelism strategies follow a similar strategy to the one presented in [19]. In this strategy, ants works in parallel to obtain a solution to the problem. The author intended to study the algorithm scalability when large size problems are solved, against a corresponding implementation on a CPU. The hardware architecture was not available but the computational experiments showed that the GPU version was 15 times faster than its corresponding CPU implementation.

In [24] an ACO algorithm was proposed for epistasis[7] analysis. In order to tackle large scale problems, the authors proposed a multi-GPU parallel implementation consisting of one, three and six devices. The experiments show that the results generated by the GPU implementation outperformed two other sequential versions in almost all trials and, when the dataset increased, the GPU performed faster than the other implementations.

The Quadratic Assignment Problem (QAP) was solved in [25] by a parallel ACO based algorithm. Besides the initialization process, all the algorithm steps are performed on the GPU, and all data (pheromone matrix, set of solutions, etc.) are located in the global memory of the GPU. Therefore, no data was needed to be transferred between the CPU and GPU, only the best-so-far solution which checks if the termination condition is satisfied. The authors focus on a parallelism strategy for the 2-opt local search procedure since, from previews experiments, this was the most costly step. The experiments were done in a workstation

[7] Phenomenon where the effects of one gene are modified by one or several other genes.

with CPU Intel i7 965 at 3.2GHz and GPU NVIDIA GeForce GTX 480 at 1401MHz and 480 processing elements. Instances from the Quadratic Assignment Problem library (QAPLIB) were solved with the problem size ranging from 50 to 150. The GPU computing performed 24 times faster than the CPU.

An ACO based parallel algorithm was proposed for design validation of circuits [26]. The ACO method is different from the standard ACO implementation, since it does not use pheromones trails to guide the search process. The proposed method explores the maximum occupancy of the GPU, defining the global size as the number of work-groups times the amount of work-items per work-group. A workstation with CPU Intel i7 at 3.33GHz and a GPU NVIDIA GeForce GTX 285 with 240 processing elements were used for the computational experiments. The results showed average speedup values between 7 and 11 regarding all the test problems, and reaching a peak speedup value of 228 in a specific test problem when compared with two other methods.

In [27], the $\mathcal{MM}$AS with a 3-opt local search was implemented in parallel on the GPU. The authors proposed four parallel strategies, two based on parallel ants and two based on multiple ant colonies. In the first parallel-ants strategy, ants are assigned to work-items, each one responsible for all calculation needed in the tour construction process. The second parallel-ants proposal assigned each ant to a work-group, making possible to extract an additional level of parallelism in the computation of the state transition rule. In the multiple colony strategy, a single GPU and multiples GPUs—each one associated to a colony—were used, applying the same parallel-ants strategies proposed. TSP instances varying from 51 to 2103 cities were used as test problems. The experiments were done using two CPUs 4-core Xeon E5640 at 2.67GHz and two GPUs NVIDIA Fermi C2050 with 448 processing elements. Evaluating the parallel ants strategies against the sequential version of the $\mathcal{MM}$AS, the overall experiments showed that the solutions quality were similar, when no local search was used. However, speedup values ranging from 6.84 to 19.47 could be achieved when the ants were associated with work-groups. For the multiple colonies strategies the speedup varied between 16.24 and 23.60.

The authors in [28] proposed parallel strategies for the tour construction and the pheromone updating phases. In the tour construction phase three different aspects were reworked in order to increase parallelism: (i) the choice-info matrix calculation, which combines pheromone and heuristic information; (ii) the *roulette wheel* selection procedure; and (iii) the decomposition granularity, which switched to the parallel processing of both ants and tours. Regarding the pheromone trails updating, the authors applied a *scatter to gather* based design to avoid atomic instructions required for proper updating the pheromone matrix. The hardware used for the computational experiments were composed by a CPU Intel Xeon E5620 running at 2.4Ghz and a GPU NVIDIA Tesla C2050 at 1.15GHz and 448 processing elements. For the phase of the construction of the solution, the parallel version performed up to 21 times faster than the sequential version, while for the pheromone updating the scatter to gather technique performed poorly. However, considering a data-based parallelism with atomic instructions, the authors presented a strategy that was up to 20 times faster than a sequential execution.

The next section will present strategies for the parallel ACO on the GPU for each step of the algorithm.

4. Parallelization strategies

In ACO algorithms, artificial ants cooperate while exploring the search space, searching good solutions for the problem through a communication mediated by artificial pheromone trails. The construction solution process is incremental, where a solution is built by adding solution components to an initially empty solution under construction. The ant's heuristic rule probabilistically decides the next solution component guided by (i) the heuristic information (η), representing a priori information about the problem instance to be solved; and (ii) the pheromone trail (τ), which encodes a memory about the ant colony search process that is continuously updated by the ants.

The main steps of the Ant System (AS) algorithm [1, 9] can be described as: initialization phase, ants' solutions construction, ants' solutions evaluation and pheromone trails updating. In Algorithm 2 a pseudo-code of AS is given. As opposed to the following parallel strategies, this algorithm is meant to be implemented and run as host code, preparing and transferring data to/from the GPU, setting kernels' arguments and managing their executions.

Algorithm 2: Pseudo-code of Ant System.

```
// Initialization phase
Pheromone trails τ;
Heuristic information η;

// Iterative phase
while termination criteria not met do
    Ants' solutions construction;
    Ants' solutions evaluation;
    Pheromone trails updating;

Return the best solution;
```

After setting the parameters, the first step of the algorithm is the initialization procedure, which initializes the heuristic information and the pheromone trails. In ants' solution construction, each ant starts with a randomly chosen node (city) and incrementally builds solutions according to the decision policy of choosing an unvisited node j being at node i, which is guided by the pheromone trails (τ_{ij}) and the heuristic information (η_{ij}) associated with that arc. When all ants construct a complete path (feasible solution), the solutions are evaluated. Then, the pheromone trails are updated considering the quality of the candidate solutions found; also a certain level of evaporation is applied. When the iterative phase is complete, that is, when the termination criteria is met, the algorithm returns the best solution generated.

As showed in the previous section, different parallel techniques for ACO algorithms were proposed, each one adapted to the optimization problem considered and the GPU architecture available. In all cases, researchers tried to extract the maximum efficiency of the parallel computing provided by the GPU.

This section is dedicated to describe, in a pseudo-OpenCL form, parallelization strategies of the ACO algorithm described in Algorithm 2, taking the TSP as an illustrative reference problem.[8] Those strategies, however, should be readily applicable, with minor or no adaptations at all, to all the problems that belong to the same class of the TSP.[9]

4.1. Data initialization

This phase is responsible for defining the stopping criteria, initializing the parameters and allocating all data structures of the algorithm. The list of parameters is: α and β, which regulate the relative importance of the pheromone trails and the heuristic information, respectively; ρ, the pheromone evaporation rate; τ_0, the initial pheromone value; number of ants ($number_{ants}$); and the number of nodes ($number_{nodes}$). The parameters setting is done on the host and then passed as kernel's arguments.

In the following kernels all the data structures, in particular the matrices, are actually allocated and accessed as linear arrays, since OpenCL does not provide abstraction for higher-dimensional data structures. Therefore, the element $a_{ij} \in A$ is indexed in its linear form as $A[i \times n + j]$, where n is the number of columns of matrix A.

4.1.1. Pheromone Trails and Heuristic Information

To initialize the pheromone trails, all connections (i, j) must be set to the same initial value (τ_0), whereas in the heuristic information each connection (i, j) is set as the distance between the nodes i and j of the TSP instance being solved. Since the initialization operation is inherently independent it can be trivially parallelized. Algorithm 3 presents the kernel implementation in which a 2-D domain range[10] is used and defined as

$$\begin{aligned} global^0_{size} &\leftarrow number_{nodes} \\ global^1_{size} &\leftarrow number_{nodes} \end{aligned} \tag{1}$$

Algorithm 3: OpenCL kernel for initializing τ and η

$\tau[global^0_{id} \times global^1_{size} + global^1_{id}] \leftarrow \tau_0$;
$\eta[global^0_{id} \times global^1_{size} + global^1_{id}] \leftarrow$ `Distance(`$x[global^0_{id}]$, $y[global^1_{id}]$`);`

In the kernel, the helper function `Distance`(i, j) returns the distance between nodes i and j. The input data are two arrays with the coordinates x and y of each node. This function should implement the Euclidean, Manhattan or other distance function defined by the problem. The input coordinates must be set on the CPU, by reading the TSP instance, then transferred to the GPU prior to the kernel launch.

---

[8] In this chapter only the key components to the understanding of the parallel strategies—the OpenCL kernels and the corresponding setup of the N-dimensional domains—are presented. For specific details regarding secondary elements, such as the host code and the actual OpenCL kernel, please refer to the appropriated OpenCL literature.

[9] It might be necessary some adaptations concerning the algorithmic structure (data initialization, evaluation of costs, etc.) that might have particular needs with respect to the underlying strategy of parallelism.

[10] The OpenCL kernels presented throughout this chapter are either in a one- or two-dimensional domain range, depending on which one fits more naturally the particular mapping between the data and compute domains.

4.2. Solution construction

For the TSP, this phase is the most costly of the ACO algorithm and needs special attention regarding the parallel strategy.

In this section, a parallel implementation for the solution construction will be presented—the *ant-based* parallelism—which associates an ant with a work-item.

4.2.1. Caching the Pheromone and Heuristic Information

The probability of choosing a node j being at node i is associated with $[\tau_{ij}]^{\alpha}[\eta_{ij}]^{\beta}$. Each of those values need to be computed by all ants, hence, in order to reduce the computation time [2] an additional matrix, $\text{choice}_{info}[\cdot][\cdot]$, is utilized to cache them. For this caching computation, a 2-D domain range is employed and defined as

$$\begin{aligned} global^{0}_{size} &\leftarrow number_{nodes} \\ global^{1}_{size} &\leftarrow number_{nodes}, \end{aligned} \tag{2}$$

with the corresponding kernel described in Algorithm 4.

Algorithm 4: OpenCL kernel for calculating the *choice-info* cache

$\text{choice}_{info}[global^{0}_{id} \times global^{1}_{size} + global^{1}_{id}] \leftarrow$
$\quad \tau[global^{0}_{id} \times global^{1}_{size} + global^{1}_{id}]^{\alpha} \times \eta[global^{0}_{id} \times global^{1}_{size} + global^{1}_{id}]^{\beta};$

Whenever the pheromone trails τ is modified (4.1 and 4.4), the matrix choice_{info} also needs to be updated since it depends on the former. In other words, the caching data is recalculated at each iteration, just before the actual construction of the solution.

4.2.2. Ant-based Parallelism (AP)

In this strategy, each ant is associated with a work-item, each one responsible for constructing a complete solution, managing all data required for this phase (list of visited cities, probabilities calculations, and so on). Algorithm 5 presents a kernel which implements the AS decision rule, where the 1-D domain range is set as

$$global_{size} \leftarrow number_{ants} \tag{3}$$

The matrix of candidate solutions ($\text{solution}[\cdot][\cdot]$) stores the ants' paths, with each row representing a complete ant's solution. The set of visited nodes, $\text{visited}[\cdot]$, keeps track of the current visited nodes for each ant, preventing duplicate selection as forbidden by the TSP: the i-th element is set to *true* when the i-th node is chosen to be part of the ant's solution (initially all elements are set to *false*). At a current node c, $\text{selection}_{prob}[i]$ stores the probability of each node i being selected, which is based on the pheromone trails and heuristic information—such data is cached in $\text{choice}_{info}[c][i]$.

Algorithm 5: OpenCL kernel for the ant-based solution construction

```
// Initialization
visited[·] ← false;

// Selection of the initial node
Initial_node ← Random(0, number_nodes − 1);
solution[global_id × number_nodes + 0] ← Initial_node;
visited[global_id × number_nodes + Initial_node] ← true;

for step ← 1 to number_nodes − 1 do
    sum_prob ← 0.0;
    current_node ← solution[global_id × number_nodes + (step − 1)];

    // Calculation of the nodes' probabilities
    for i ← 0 to number_nodes − 1 do
        if visited[global_id × number_nodes + i] then
            selection_prob[global_id × number_nodes + i] ← 0.0;
        else
            selection_prob[global_id × number_nodes + i] ← choice_info[current_node × number_nodes + i];
            sum_prob ← sum_prob + selection_prob[global_id × number_nodes + i];

    // Node selection via roulette wheel
    r ← Random(0, sum_prob);
    i ← 0;
    p ← selection_prob[global_id × number_nodes + 0];
    while p < r do
        i ← i + 1;
        p ← p + selection_prob[global_id × number_nodes + i];
    solution[global_id × number_nodes + step] ← i;
    visited[global_id × number_nodes + i] ← true;
```

The function `Random(`a, b`)` returns a uniform real-valued pseudo-number between a and b. The random number generator could be easily implemented on the GPU through the simple linear congruential method [29]; the only requirement would be to keep in the device's global memory a *state* information (an integral number) for each work-item that must persist across kernel executions.

There exist data-based parallel strategies for the construction of the solutions, where usually a work-group takes care of an ant and its work-items compute in parallel some portion of the construction procedure. For instance, the ANT_{block} strategy in [27], which in parallel evaluates and chooses the next node (city) from all the possible candidates. However, those strategies are considerably more complex than the ant-based parallelism, and for large-scale problems in which the number of ants is reasonably high—i.e. the class of problems that one would make use of GPUs—the ant-based strategy is enough to saturate the GPU.

4.3. Solution evaluation

When all solutions are constructed, they must be evaluated. The direct approach is to parallelize this step by the number of ants, dedicating a work-item per solution. However, in many problems it is possible to decompose the evaluation of the solution itself, leading to a second level of parallelism: each work-group takes care of an ant, with each work-item within this group in charge of a subset of the solution.

4.3.1. Ant-based Evaluation (AE)

The simplest strategy for evaluating the solutions is to parallelize by the number of ants, assigning each solution evaluation to a work-item. In this case, the kernel could be written as in Algorithm 6, with the 1-D domain range as

$$global_{size} \leftarrow number_{ants} \tag{4}$$

The cost resulting from the evaluation of the complete solution of ant k, which in the kernel

Algorithm 6: OpenCL kernel for the ant-based evaluation

solution$_{value}[global_{id}] \leftarrow 0.0$;

for $i \leftarrow 0$ **to** $number_{nodes} - 2$ **do**
  $j \leftarrow$ solution$[global_{id} \times number_{nodes} + i]$;
  $h \leftarrow$ solution$[global_{id} \times number_{nodes} + (i+1)]$;
  solution$_{value}[global_{id}] \leftarrow$ solution$_{value}[global_{id}] + \eta[j \times number_{nodes} + h]$;

$j \leftarrow$ solution$[global_{id} \times number_{nodes} + (number_{nodes} - 1)]$;
$h \leftarrow$ solution$[global_{id} \times number_{nodes} + 0]$;
solution$_{value}[global_{id}] \leftarrow$ solution$_{value}[global_{id}] + \eta[j \times number_{nodes} + h]$;

is denoted by $global_{id}$, is put into the array solution$_{value}[k]$ of dimension $number_{ants}$.

4.3.2. Data-based Evaluation (DE)

This second strategy adds one more level of parallelism than the one previously presented. In the case of TSP, the costs of traveling from node i to j, j to k and so on can be summed up in parallel. To this end, the parallel primitive known as *prefix sum* is employed [30]. Its idea is illustrated in Figure 3, where $w_0 \dots w_{N-1}$ correspond to the work-items within a work-group. The computational step complexity of the parallel prefix sum is $O(log_2 N)$, meaning that, for instance, the sum of an array of 8 nodes is computed in just 3 iterations.

In order to apply this primitive to a TSP's solution, a preparatory step is required: the cost for each adjacent node must be obtained from the distance matrix and put into an array, let us call it δ.[11] This preprocessing is done in parallel, as shown in Algorithm 7, which also describes the subsequent prefix sum procedure. In the kernel, the helper function `Distance`(k,i) returns the distance between the node i and $i+1$ for ant k; when i is the last node, the function returns the distance from this one to the first node. One can notice the use of the function `Barrier()`. In OpenCL, a barrier is a synchronization point that ensures that a memory region written by other work-items is consistent at that point. The first barrier is necessary because $\delta[local_{id} - s]$ references a memory region that was written by the s-th previous work-item. As for the second barrier, it is needed to prevent $\delta[local_{id}]$ from being updated before the s-th next work-item reads it. Finally, the final sum, which ends up at the last element of δ, is stored in the solution$_{value}$ vector for the ant indexed by $group_{id}$.

[11] To improve efficiency, the array δ could—and frequently is—be allocated directly in the *local* memory (cf. 2.1).

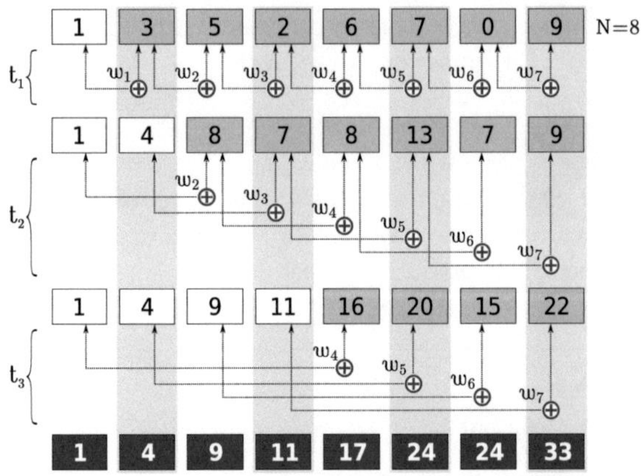

Figure 3. Parallel *prefix sum*: each element of the final array is the sum of all the previous elements, i.e. the partial cost; the last element is the total cost.

Algorithm 7: OpenCL kernel for the data-based evaluation

```
// Preparatory step
δ[local_id] ← Distance(group_id, local_id);
// Prefix sum
tmp ← δ[local_id];
s ← 1;
while s < local_size do
    Barrier();
    if local_id ≥ s then
        tmp ← δ[local_id] + δ[local_id − s];
    Barrier();
    δ[local_id] ← tmp;
    s ← s × 2;
if local_id = group_size − 1 then
    solution_value[group_id] ← δ[group_size − 1];
```

Regarding the *N*-D domain definition, since there are $number_{ants}$ ants and for each ant (solution) there are $number_{nodes}$ distances, the global size is given by

$$global_{size} \leftarrow number_{ants} \times number_{nodes} \tag{5}$$

and the local size, i.e. the amount of work-items devoted to compute the total cost per solution, simply by

$$local_{size} \leftarrow number_{nodes}, \tag{6}$$

resulting in $number_{ants}$ work-groups (one per ant).[12]

[12] For the sake of simplicity, it is assumed that the number of nodes (cities) is such that the resulting local size is less than the device's maximum supported local size, a hardware limit. If this is not the case, then Algorithm 7 should be modified in such a way that each work-item would compute more than just one partial sum.

4.3.3. Finding the Best Solution

It is important at each iteration to keep track of the best-so-far solution. This could be achieved naively by iterating over all the evaluated solutions sequentially. There is though a parallel alternative to that which utilizes a primitive, analogous to the previous one, called *reduction* [30]. The idea of the parallel reduction is visualized in Figure 4. It

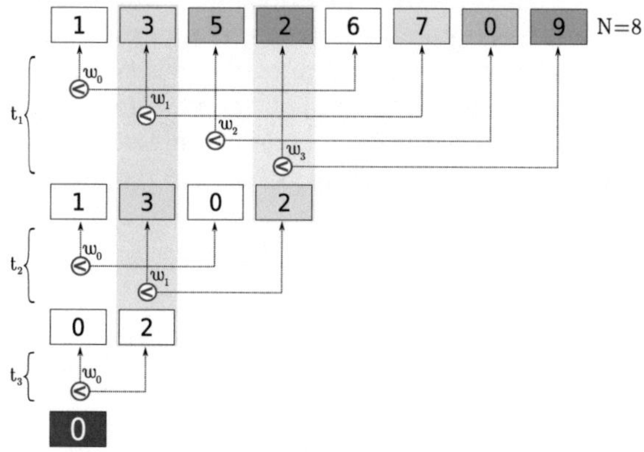

Figure 4. $O(log_2 N)$ parallel reduction: the remaining element is the smallest of the array.

starts by comparing the elements of an array—that is, solution_{value}—by pairs to find the smallest element between each pair. The next iteration finds the smallest values of the previously reduced ones, then the process continues until a single value remains; this is the smallest element—or cost—of the entire array. The implementation is somewhat similar to the prefix sum, and will not be detailed here. The global and local sizes should both be set to $number_{ants}$, meaning that the reduction will occur within one work-group since synchronization is required. The actual implementation will also need a mapping between the cost values (the solution_{value} array) and the corresponding solutions in order to link the smallest cost found with the respective solution.

4.4. Pheromone Trails Updating

After all ants have constructed their tours (solutions), the pheromone trails are updated. In AS, the pheromone update step starts evaporating *all* arcs by a constant factor, followed by a reinforcement on the arcs visited by the ants in their tours.

4.4.1. Pheromone Evaporation

In the pheromone evaporation, each element of the pheromone matrix has its value decreased by a constant factor $\rho \in (0, 1]$. Hence, the parallel implementation can explore parallelism in the order of $number_{nodes} \times number_{nodes}$. For this step, the kernel can be described as in Algorithm 8, with the 2-D domain range given by

$$\begin{aligned} global^0_{size} &\leftarrow number_{nodes} \\ global^1_{size} &\leftarrow number_{nodes} \end{aligned} \tag{7}$$

Algorithm 8: OpenCL kernel for computing the pheromone evaporation

$\tau[global^0_{id} \times global^1_{size} + global^1_{id}] \leftarrow (1 - \rho) \times \tau[global^0_{id} \times global^1_{size} + global^1_{id}]$;

4.4.2. Pheromone Updating

After evaporation, ants deposit different quantities of pheromone on the arcs that they crossed. Therefore, in an ant-based parallel implementation each element of the pheromone matrix may potentially be updated by many ants at the same time, leading of course to memory inconsistency. An alternative is to parallelize on the ant's solution, taking advantage of the fact that in the TSP there is no duplicate node in a given solution. This strategy works on one ant k at a time, but all edges (i, j) are processed in parallel. Hence, the 1-D domain range is given by

$$global_{size} \leftarrow number_{nodes} - 1, \tag{8}$$

with the corresponding kernel described in Algorithm 9. The kernel should be launched $number_{ants}$ times from the host code, each time passing a different $k \in [0, number_{ants})$ as a kernel's argument—the only way of guaranteeing global memory consistency (synchronism) in OpenCL, which is necessary to prevent two or more ants from being processed simultaneously, is when a kernel finishes its execution.

Algorithm 9: OpenCL kernel for updating the pheromone for ant k

$i \leftarrow \text{solution}[k \times number_{nodes} + global_{id}]$;
$j \leftarrow \text{solution}[k \times number_{nodes} + global_{id} + 1]$;

$\tau[i \times number_{nodes} + j] \leftarrow \tau[i \times number_{nodes} + j] + 1.0/\text{solution}_{value}[k]$;
$\tau[j \times number_{nodes} + i] \leftarrow \tau[i \times number_{nodes} + j]$;

5. Conclusions

This chapter has presented and discussed different parallelization strategies for implementing an Ant Colony Optimization algorithm on Graphics Processing Unit, presenting also a list of references on previous works on this area.

The chapter also provided straightforward explanation of the GPU architecture and gave special attention to the Open Computing Language (OpenCL), explaining in details the concepts behind these two topics, which are often just mentioned in references in the literature.

It was shown that each step of an ACO algorithm, from the initialization phase through the return of the final solution, can be parallelized to some degree, at least at the granularity of the number of ants. For complex or large-scale problems—in which numerous ants would be desired—the ant-based parallel strategies should suffice to fully explore the computational power of the GPUs.

Although the chapter has focused on a particular computing architecture, the GPU, all the described kernels can be promptly executed on any other OpenCL parallel device, such as the multi-core CPUs.

http://dx.doi.org/10.5772/51679

Finally, it is expected that this chapter will provide the readers with an extensive view of the existing ACO parallel strategies on the GPU and will assist them in developing new or derived parallel strategies to suit their particular needs.

Acknowledgments

The authors thank the support from the Brazilian agencies CNPq (grants 141519/2010-0 and 308317/2009-2) and FAPERJ (grant E-26/102.025/2009).

Author details

Jaqueline S. Angelo[1,*],
Douglas A. Augusto[1] and Helio J. C. Barbosa[1,2]

* Address all correspondence to: jsangelo@lncc.br; douglas@lncc.br; hcbm@lncc.br

1 Laboratório Nacional de Computação Científica (LNCC/MCTI), Petropólis, RJ, Brazil
2 Universidade Federal de Juiz de Fora (UFJF), MG, Brazil

References

[1] Marco Dorigo. *Optimization, Learning and Natural Algorithms*. PhD thesis, Dipartimento di Elettronica, Politecnico di Milano, Milan, 1992.

[2] Marco Dorigo and Thomas Stutzle. *Ant Colony Optimization*. The MIT Press, 2004.

[3] Thomas Stutzle. Parallelization strategies for ant colony optimization. In *Proc. of PPSN-V, Fifth International Conference on Parallel Problem Solving from Nature*, pages 722–731. Springer-Verlag, 1998.

[4] Martín Pedemonte, Sergio Nesmachnow, and Héctor Cancela. A survey on parallel ant colony optimization. *Appl. Soft Comput.*, 11(8):5181–5197, December 2011.

[5] Stefan Janson, Daniel Merkle, and Martin Middendorf. *Parallel Ant Colony Algorithms*, pages 171–201. John Wiley and Sons, Inc., 2005.

[6] Marco Dorigo, Eric Bonabeau, and Guy Theraulaz. *Swarm Intelligence*. Oxford University Press, Oxford, New York, 1999.

[7] Marco Dorigo, Eric Bonabeau, and Guy Theraulaz. Ant algorithms and stigmergy. *Future Gener. Comput. Syst.*, 16(9):851–871, 2000.

[8] Marco Dorigo, Gianni Di Caro, and Luca M. Gambardella. Ant algorithms for discrete optimization. *Artificial Life*, 5:137–172, 1999.

[9] Marco Dorigo, Vittorio Maniezzo, and Alberto Colorni. Ant system: Optimization by a colony of cooperating agents. *IEEE Trans. on Systems, Man, and Cybernetics–Part B*, 26(1):29–41, 1996.

[10] R.J. Mullen, D. Monekosso, S. Barman, and P. Remagnino. A review of ant algorithms. *Expert Systems with Applications*, 36(6):9608 – 9617, 2009.

[11] J.L. Hennessy and D.A. Patterson. *Computer Architecture: A Quantitative Approach*. The Morgan Kaufmann Series in Computer Architecture and Design. Elsevier Science, 2011.

[12] Ethan Mollick. Establishing Moore's law. *IEEE Ann. Hist. Comput.*, 28:62–75, July 2006.

[13] Michael Garland and David B. Kirk. Understanding throughput-oriented architectures. *Commun. ACM*, 53:58–66, November 2010.

[14] Khronos Group. OpenCL - the open standard for parallel programming of heterogeneous systems.

[15] Khronos OpenCL Working Group. *The OpenCL Specification, version 1.2*, November 2011.

[16] Douglas A. Augusto and Helio J.C. Barbosa. Accelerated parallel genetic programming tree evaluation with opencl. *Journal of Parallel and Distributed Computing*, (0):–, 2012.

[17] Advanced Micro Devices. *AMD Accelerated Parallel Processing Programming Guide - OpenCL*, 12 2010.

[18] NVIDIA Corporation. *OpenCL Best Practices Guide*, 2010.

[19] A. Catala, J. Jaen, and J.A. Modioli. Strategies for accelerating ant colony optimization algorithms on graphical processing units. In *Evolutionary Computation, 2007. CEC 2007. IEEE Congress on*, pages 492 –500, 2007.

[20] Hongtao Bai, Dantong OuYanga, Ximing Li, Lili He, and Haihong Yu. MAX-MIN ant system on GPU with CUDA. In *Fourth International Conference on Innovative Computing, Information and Control*, pages 801–804, 2009.

[21] Weihang Zhu and James Curry. Parallel ant colony for nonlinear function optimization with graphics hardware acceleration. In *Proceedings of the 2009 IEEE international conference on Systems, Man and Cybernetics*, SMC'09, pages 1803–1808. IEEE Press, 2009.

[22] Jie Fu, Lin Lei, and Guohua Zhou. A parallel ant colony optimization algorithm with gpu-acceleration based on all-in-roulette selection. In *Advanced Computational Intelligence (IWACI), 2010 Third International Workshop on*, pages 260–264, 2010.

[23] Jose A. Mocholi, Javier Jaen, Alejandro Catala, and Elena Navarro. An emotionally biased ant colony algorithm for pathfinding in games. *Expert Systems with Applications*, 37:4921–4927, 2010.

[24] Nicholas A. Sinnott-Armstrong, Casey S. Greene, and Jason H. Moore. Fast genome-wide epistasis analysis using ant colony optimization for multifactor dimensionality reduction analysis on graphics processing units. In *Proceedings of the 12th annual conference on Genetic and evolutionary computation*, GECCO 2010, pages 215–216, New York, NY, USA, 2010. ACM.

[25] S. Tsutsui and N. Fujimoto. Fast qap solving by aco with 2-opt local search on a gpu. pages 812 –819, june 2011.

[26] Min Li, Kelson Gent, and Michael S. Hsiao. Utilizing gpgpus for design validation with a modified ant colony optimization. *High-Level Design, Validation, and Test Workshop, IEEE International*, 0:128–135, 2011.

[27] A. Delévacq, P. Delisle, M. Gravel, and M. Krajecki. Parallel ant colony optimization on graphics processing units. *J. Parallel Distrib. Comput.*, 2012.

[28] José M. Cecilia, José M. García, Andy Nisbet, Martyn Amos, and Manuel Ujaldón. Enhancing data parallelism for ant colony optimization on gpus. *Journal of Parallel and Distributed Computing*, 2012.

[29] Donald E. Knuth. *Art of Computer Programming, Volume 2: Seminumerical Algorithms (3rd Edition)*. Addison-Wesley Professional, 3 edition, November 1997.

[30] W. Daniel Hillis and Guy L. Steele, Jr. Data parallel algorithms. *Commun. ACM*, 29(12):1170–1183, December 1986.

Section 2

Applications

Chapter 4

An Ant Colony Optimization Algorithm for Area Traffic Control

Soner Haldenbilen, Ozgur Baskan and Cenk Ozan

Additional information is available at the end of the chapter

http://dx.doi.org/10.5772/51695

1. Introduction

The optimization of traffic signal control is at the heart of urban traffic control. Traffic signal control which encloses delay, queuing, pollution, fuel consumption is a multi-objective optimization. For a signal-controlled road network, using the optimization techniques in determining signal timings has been discussed greatly for decades. Due to complexity of the Area Traffic Control (ATC) problem, new methods and approaches are needed to improve efficiency of signal control in a signalized road network. In urban networks, traffic signals are used to control vehicle movements so as to reduce congestion, improve safety, and enable specific strategies such as minimizing delays, improving environmental pollution, etc. [1]. Signal systems that control road junctions are operated according to the type of junction. Although the optimization of signal timings for an isolated junction is relatively easy, the optimization of signal timings in coordinated road networks requires further research due to the "*offset*" term. Early methods such as that of [2] only considered an isolated signalized junction. Later, fixed time strategies were developed that optimizing a group of signalized junctions using historical flow data [3]. For the ATC, TRANSYT-7F is one of the most useful network study software tools for optimizing signal timing and also the most widely used program of its type. It consists of two main parts: A traffic flow model and a signal timing optimizer. Traffic model utilizes a platoon dispersion algorithm that simulates the normal dispersion of platoons as they travel downstream. It simulates traffic in a network of signalized intersections to produce a cyclic flow profile of arrivals at each intersection that is used to compute a Performance Index (*PI*) for a given signal timing and staging plan. The *PI* in TRANSYT-7F may be defined in a number of ways. One of the TRANSYT-7F's *PI* is the Disutility Index (*DI*). The *DI* is a measure of disadvantageous operation; that is stops, delay, fuel consumption, etc. Optimization in TRANSYT-7F consists of a series of trial simulation runs, using the TRANSYT-7F simulation engine. Each simulation run is assigned a unique signal timing plan by the optimization processor. The optimizer applies the Hill-Climbing (HC) or Genetic Algorithm (GA) searching strategies. The trial simulation run resulting in the best performance is reported as optimal. Although the GA is mathematically better suited for determining the absolute or global optimal solution, relative to HC optimization, it generally requires longer program running times, relative to HC optimization [4].

This chapter proposes Ant Colony Optimization (ACO) based algorithm called ACORSES proposed by [5] for finding optimum signal parameters in coordinated signalized networks for given fixed set of link flows. The ACO is the one of the most recent techniques for approximate optimization methods. The main idea is that it is indirect local communication among the individuals of a population of artificial ants. The core of ant's behaviour is the communication between the ants by means of chemical pheromone trails, which enables them to find shortest paths between their nest and food sources. This behaviour of real ant colonies is exploited to solve optimization problems. The proposed algorithm is based on each ant searches only around the best solution of the previous iteration with reduced search space. It is proposed for improving ACO's solution performance to reach global optimum fairly quickly. In this study, for solving the ATC problem, Ant Colony Optimization TRANSYT (ACOTRANS) model is developed. TRANSYT-7F traffic model is used to estimate total network *PI*.

Wong (1995) proposed group-based optimization of signal timings for area traffic control. In addition, the optimization of signal timings for ATC using group-based control variables was proposed by [7]. However, it was reported that obtaining the derivations of the *PI* for each of the control variable was mathematically difficult. Heydecker (1996) decomposed the optimization of traffic signal timings into two levels; first, optimizing the signal timings at the individual junction level using the group-based approach, and second, combining the results from individual junction level with network level decision variables such as offset and common cycle time. Wong et al. (2000) developed a time-dependent TRANSYT traffic model for the evaluation of *PI*. It was found that the time-dependent model produces a reasonable estimate of *PI* for under saturated to moderately oversaturated conditions. Wong et al. (2002) developed a time-dependent TRANSYT traffic model which is a weighted combination of the estimated delay and number of stops. A remarkable improvement over the average flow scenario was obtained and when compared with the signal plans from independent analyses, a good improvement was found. Girianna and Benekohal (2002) presented two different GA techniques which are applied on signal coordination for oversaturated networks. Signal coordination was formulated as a dynamic optimization problem and is solved using GA for the entire duration of congestion.

Similarly, Ceylan (2006) developed a GA with TRANSYT-HC optimization routine, and proposed a method for decreasing the search space to solve the ATC problem. Proposed approach is better than signal timing optimization regarding optimal values of timings and *PI* when it is compared with TRANSYT. Chen and Xu (2006) investigated the application of Particle Swarm Optimization (PSO) algorithm to solve signal timing optimization problem. Their results showed that PSO can be applied to the traffic signal timing optimization problem under different traffic demands. A hybrid optimization algorithm for simultaneously solving delay-minimizing and capacity-maximizing ATC was presented by [14]. Numerical computations and comparisons were conducted on a variety of road networks. Numerical tests showed that the effectiveness and robustness of this hybrid heuristic algorithm. Similarly, Chiou (2007) presented a computation algorithm based on the projected Quasi-Newton method to effectively solve the ATC problem. The proposed method combining the locally optimal search and global search heuristic achieved substantially better performance than did traditional approaches in solving the ATC problem with expansions of link capacity.

Dan and Xiaohong (2008) developed a real-coded improved GA with microscopic traffic simulation model to find optimal signal plans for ATC problem, which takes the coordination of signals timing for all signal-controlled junction into account. The results showed that the method based on GA could minimize delay time and improve capacity of network. Li (2011) presented an arterial signal optimization model that consider queue blockage among intersection lane groups under oversaturated conditions. The proposed model captures traffic dynamics with the cell transmission concept, which takes into account complex flow interactions among different lane groups. Through comparisons with signal-timing plans from TRANSYT-7F, the model was successful for signal-timing optimization particularly under congested conditions. The optimization of signal timings on coordinated signalized road network, which includes a set of non-linear mathematical formulations, is very difficult. Therefore, new methods and approaches are needed to improve efficiency of signal control in a road network due to complexity of the ATC problem. Although there are many studies in literature with different heuristic methods to optimize traffic signal timings, there is no application of ACO to this area. Thus, this study proposes Ant Colony Optimization TRANSYT-7F (ACOTRANS) model in which ACO and TRANSYT-7F are combined for solving the ATC problem. The remaining content of this chapter is organized as follows. ACO algorithm and its solution process are given in Section 2, and definition of the ACOTRANS model is provided in Section 3. Numerical application is presented in Section 4. Last section is about the conclusions.

2. Ant Colony Optimization

Ant algorithms were inspired by the observation of real ant colonies. Ants are social insects that live in colonies and whose behaviour is directed more to the survival of the colony as a whole than to that of a single individual component of the colony. Social insects have captured the attention of many scientists because of the high structuration level their colonies can achieve, especially when compared to the relative simplicity of the colony's individuals. An important and interesting behaviour of ant colonies is their foraging behaviour, and, in particular, how ants can find shortest paths between food sources and their nest [18]. Ants are capable of finding the shortest path from food source to their nest or vice versa by smelling pheromones which are chemical substances they leave on the ground while walking. Each ant probabilistically prefers to follow a direction rich in pheromone. This behaviour of real ants can be used to explain how they can find a shortest path [19]. The main idea is that it is indirect local communication among the individuals of a population of artificial ants. The core of ant's behavior is the communication between the ants by means of chemical pheromone trails, which enables them to find shortest paths between their nest and food sources. This behaviour of real ant colonies is exploited to solve optimization problems [20]. The general ACO algorithm is illustrated in Fig. 1. The first step consists mainly on the initialization of the pheromone trail. At beginning, each ant builds a complete solution to the problem according to a probabilistic state transition rules. They depend mainly on the state of the pheromone.

Step 1:	Initialize Pheromone trail

Step 2:	Iteration
	Repeat for each ant
	  Solution construction using pheromone trail
	  Update the pheromone trail
	Until stopping criteria

Figure 1. A generic ant algorithm.

Once all ants generate a solution, then global pheromone updating rule is applied in two phases; an evaporation phase, where a fraction of the pheromone evaporates, and a reinforcement phase, where each ant deposits an amount of pheromone which is proportional to the fitness. This process is repeated until stopping criteria is met. The ACORSES proposed by [5] is consisted of three main phases; Initialization, pheromone update and solution phase. All of these phases build a complete search to the global optimum as can be seen in Fig. 2.

As shown in Figure 2, pheromone update phase is located after the initialization phase, means that quantity of pheromone intensifies at each iteration within the reduced search space. Thus, global optimum is searched within the reduced search space using best values obtained from new ant colony in the previous iteration. Main advantageous of the ACORSES is that Feasible Search Space (FSS) is reduced with β and it uses the information taken from previous iteration.

At the beginning of the first cycle, all ants search randomly to the best solution of a given problem within the FSS, and old ant colony is created at initialization phase. After that, quantity of pheromone is updated. In the solution phase, new ant colony is created based on the best solution from the old ant colony using Equation (1) and (2). Then, the best solutions of two colonies are compared. At the end of the first cycle, FSS is reduced by β and best solution obtained from the previous iteration is kept. Global or near global optimum solution is then searched in the reduced search space during the solution progress. The ACORSES reaches to the global or near global optimum as ants find their routes in the limited space [5].

Initialization
for i=1 to I (I=cycle number)
if i=1 then generate m random ants within FSS
else reduce FSS with range $[x_{t-1}^{best}+\beta; x_{t-1}^{best}-\beta]$
end if
for i=1 to m
Determine $f(x_t^{best})$
Save x_t^{best}
end
Pheromone update
Pheromone evaporation
Update pheromone trail
Solution phase
Determine search direction
Generate the values of α vector
for i=1 to m
Determine the values of new colony
Determine new $f(x_t^{best})$
Save x_t^{best}
end
if $f(x_t^{best})^{new} \leq f(x_t^{best})^{old}$ then $x^{global\min} = (x_t^{best})^{new}$
else $x^{global\min} = (x_t^{best})^{old}$
end if
$\alpha_t = \alpha_{t-1} * 0.99$
$\beta_t = \beta_{t-1} * 0.99$
end

Figure 2. Steps of ACORSES [5].

Let number of m ants being associated with m random initial vectors(x^k, k=1, 2, 3, ...m). The solution vector of each ant is updated using following expression:

$$x_t^{k(new)} = x_t^{k(old)} \pm \alpha$$
$$(t = 1, 2, \ldots\ldots, I) \qquad (1)$$

where $x_t^{k(new)}$is the solution vector of the k th ant at cycle t, $x_t^{k(old)}$is the solution obtained from the previous step at cycle t, and $\alpha$is a vector generated randomly to determine the length of jump. αcontrols the global optimum search direction not being trapped at bad local optimum. Ant vector $x_t^{k(new)}$obtained at t th cycle in (1) is determined using the value of same ant obtained from previous step. Furthermore, in expression (1), (+) sign is used when point $x_t^k$is on the left of the best solution on the x coordinate axis. (-) sign is used when point $x_t^k$is on the right of the best solution on the same axis. The direction of search is defined by expression (2).

$$\bar{x}_t^{best} = x_t^{best} + (x_t^{best} * 0.01) \tag{2}$$

If $f(\bar{x}_t^{best}) \leq f(x_t^{best})$, (+) sign is used in (1). Otherwise, (-) sign is used. ($\pm$)sign defines the search direction to reach to the global optimum. α value is used to define the length of jump, and it will be gradually decreased in order not to pass over global optimum, as shown in Fig. 2. At the end of each cycle, a new ant colony is developed as the number of ants generated in old colony. Quantity of pheromone (τ_t) is reduced to simulate the evaporation process of real ant colonies using (3) in the pheromone update phase. After reducing of the number of pheromone, it is updated using (4). Quantity of pheromone only intensifies around the best objective function value. This process is repeated until the given number of cycle, *I*, is completed. Initial pheromone intensity is set to the value of 100.

$$\tau_t = 0.1 * \tau_{t-1} \tag{3}$$

$$\tau_t = \tau_{t-1} + 0.01 * f(x_{t-1}^{best}) \tag{4}$$

ACO uses real numbers instead of coding them as in GA to optimise any given objective function. This is one of the main advantage of ACO that it provides to optimise the signal timings with less mathematically lengthy. Moreover, ACORSES algorithm has ability to reach to the global optimum quickly without being trapped in bad local optimum because it uses the reduced search space and the values of optimum signal timings are then searched in the reduced search space during the algorithm progress. The ACORSES reaches to the global optimum or near global optimum as ants find their routes in the limited space. For better understanding, consider a problem of five ants represents the formulation of the problem.

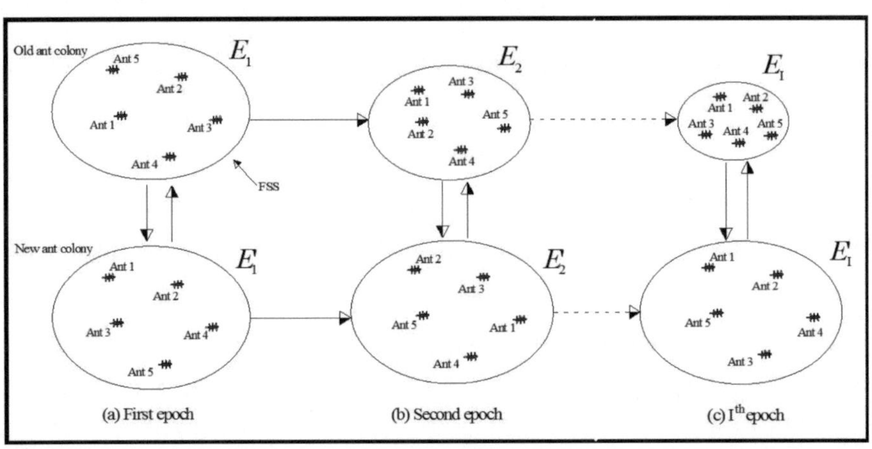

Figure 3. Main idea of the ACORSES [5].

As shown in Fig.3, five ants being associated five random initial vectors. At the beginning of the first cycle (Fig. 3a), old ant colony is randomly created within the feasible search space for any given problem. After pheromone update phase, new ant colony is created at the last phase of the first cycle according to old ant colony using Equation (1) and (2). After that, the best values of the two colonies are compared. According to the best value obtained so far by comparing the old and new colonies and β, the FSS is reduced at the beginning of the second cycle and once again old ant colony is created, as can be seen in Fig. 3b. The new ant colony is created at the last phase of the second cycle according to randomly generated α value using Equation (1). Any of the newly created solution vectors may be outside the reduced search space that is created at the beginning of the second cycle. Therefore, created new ant colony prevents being trapped in bad local optimum [5].

3. ACOTRANS for area traffic control

The ACOTRANS consists of two main parts namely ACO based algorithm and TRANSYT-7F traffic model. ACO algorithm optimizes traffic signal timings under fixed set of link flows. TRANSYT-7F traffic model is used to compute *PI*, which is called objective function, for a given signal timing and staging plan in network. The network Disutility Index (*DI*), one of the TRANSYT-7F's *PI*, is used as objective function. The *DI* is a measure of disadvantageous operation; that is stops, delay, fuel consumption, etc. The standard TRANSYT-7F's *DI* is linear combination of delay and stops. The objective function and corresponding constraints are given in Eq. (5).

$$PI = \underset{\psi,q=fixed}{Min}\ DI = \sum_{a\in L}\left[w_{d_a} \cdot d_a(\psi) + K \cdot w_{s_a} \cdot S_a(\psi) \right] \tag{5}$$

$$\text{Subject to}\quad \psi(c,\theta,\varphi)\in\Omega_0;\ \left\{\begin{array}{ll} c_{\min}\le c\le c_{\max} & \text{cycle time constraints}\\ 0\le\theta\le c & \text{values of offset constraints}\\ \varphi_{\min}\le\varphi\le c & \text{green time constraints}\\ \sum_{i=1}^{z}(\varphi+I)_i=c & \end{array}\right\}$$

where d_a is delay on link a (L set of links), w_{d_a} is link-specific weighting factor for delay d, K is stop penalty factor to express the importance of stops relative to delay, S_a is stop on link a per second, w_{s_a} is link-specific weighting factor for stops S on link a, q is fixed set of link flows, ψ is signal setting parameters, c is common cycle time (sec), θ is offset time (sec), φ is green time (sec), Ω_0 is feasible region for signal timings, I is intergreen time (sec), and z is number of stages at each signalized intersection in a given road network.

The green timings can be distributed to all signal stages in a road network according to Eq. (6) in order to provide the cycle time constraint [21].

$$\varphi_i = \varphi_{\min,i} + \frac{p_i}{\sum_{k=1}^{z} p_i}(c - \sum_{k=1}^{z} I_k - \sum_{k=1}^{z} \varphi_{\min,k}) \tag{6}$$

$$i = 1, 2, \ldots z$$

where φ_i is the green time (sec) for stage i, $\varphi_{\min,i}$is minimum green time (sec) for stage i, p_i is generated randomly green timings (sec) for stage i, z is the number of stages and I is inter-green time (sec) between signal stages and c is the common cycle time of the network (sec).

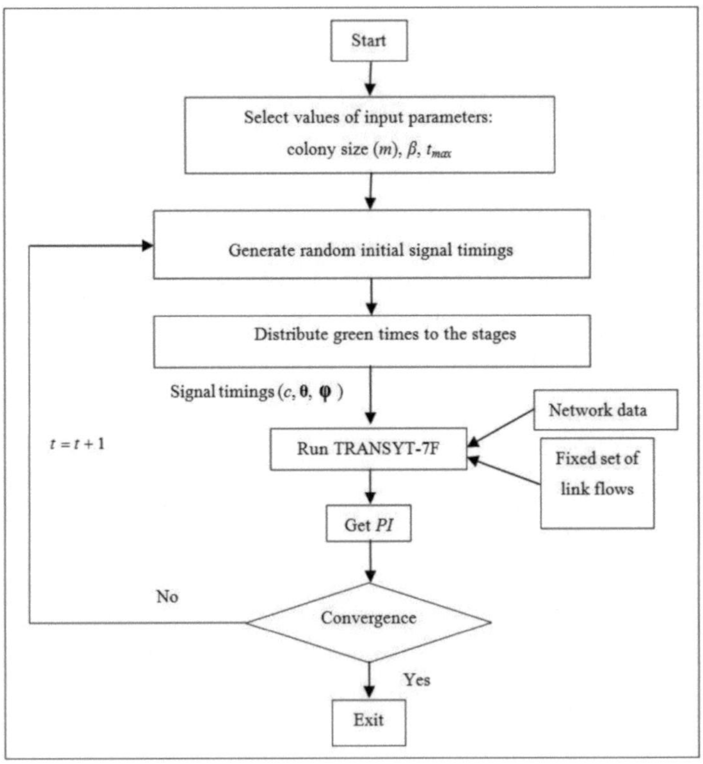

Figure 4. The flowchart of the ACOTRANS.

In the ACOTRANS, optimization steps can be given in the following way:

Step 0: Initialization. Define the user specified parameters; the number of decision variables (n) (this number is sum of the number of green times as stage numbers at each intersection, the number of offset times as intersection numbers and common cycle time), the constraints for each decision variable, the size of ant colony (m), search space value (β) for each decision variable.

Step 1: Set $t = 1$.

Step 2: Generate the random initial signal timings, $\psi(c, \theta, \varphi)$within the constraints of decision variables.

Step 3: Distribute to the initial green timings to the stages according to distribution rule as mentioned above. At this step, randomly generated green timings at Step 2 are distributed to the stages according to generated cycle time at the same step, minimum green and intergreen time.

Step 4: Get the network data and fixed set of link flows for TRANSYT-7F traffic model.

Step 5: Run TRANSYT-7F.

Step 6: Get the network *PI*. At this step, the *PI* is determined using TRANSYT-7F traffic model.

Step 7: If $t = t_{max}$ then terminate the algorithm; otherwise, $t = t + 1$and go to Step 2.

The flowchart of the ACOTRANS can be seen in Fig. (4).

4. Numerical Application

The ACOTRANS is tested on two example networks taken from literature. First, it is applied to two junction road network. The network contains one origin destination pair, eight links and six signal setting variables. The network and its representation of signal stages can be seen in Fig. (5a) and (5b). The fixed set of link flows, taken from [22] is given in Table 1.

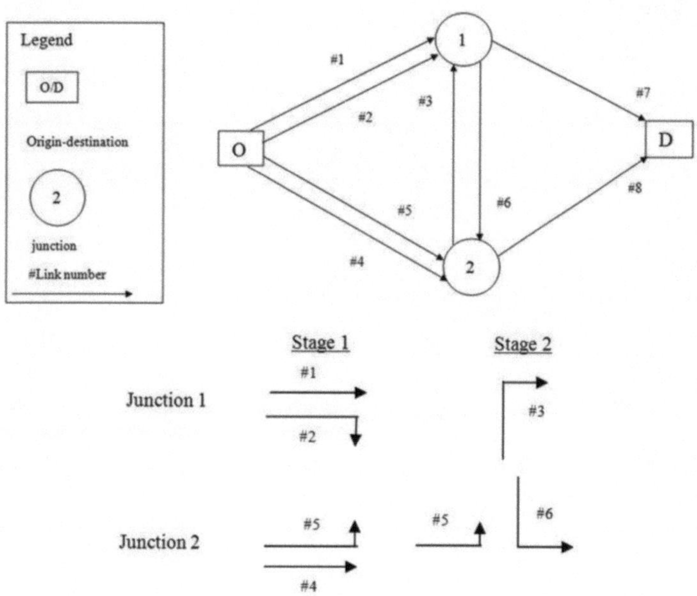

Figure 5. a) Two junction network ; b) Representation of signal stages of two-junction network.

Link number	Link flow (veh/h)	Saturation flow (veh/h)	Free-flow travel time (sec)
1	615	1800	20
2	45	1800	20
3	225	1800	20
4	615	1800	20
5	225	1800	20
6	45	1800	20

Table 1. Fixed set of link flows on two junction network.

The constraints on signal timings are set as follows:

$36 \le c \le 90$cycle time constraint

$0 \le \theta \le c$ offsets

$7 \le \varphi \le c$green split

$I_{1-2} = I_{2-1} = 5$seconds intergreen time

The ACOTRANS model was coded by the MATLAB software. It is performed with the following user-specified parameters: colony size is 20, and maximum number of cycle (t_{max}) is 75. The convergence of the model can be seen in Fig. (6).

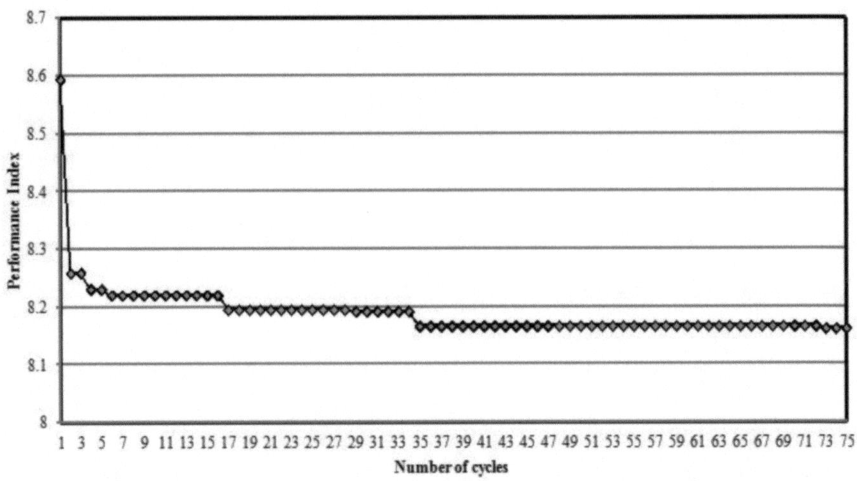

Figure 6. The convergence of the ACOTRANS for small sized network.

In 75th cycle, ACOTRANS is reached to *PI* value of 8.16. The common network cycle time obtained from the ACOTRANS is 76 sec. In addition, two junction road network is optimized using TRANSYT-7F which included GA and HC optimization tools. In GA parameters, population size and maximum number of cycle are chosen 20 and 300, respectively. In HC optimization tool in TRANSYT-7F, the default optimization parameters used by program are effective and system is simulated for every integer cycle length between minimum and maximum cycle length. Therefore, HC optimization parameters are not being manipulated. For two junction road network, the ACOTRANS model and TRANSYT-7F optimizers' results are given in Table 2.

	Performance Index	Cycle Time c (s)	Junction number i	Duration of stages (s) Stage 1 θ_i	Stage 2 $\varphi_{i,1}$	Offsets (s) $l_{1-2}=l_{2-1}=5$
ACOTRANS	8.16	76	1	55	21	0
			2	66	10	36
TRANSYT-7F with HC	8.18	78	1	55	23	0
			2	68	10	0
TRANSYT-7F with GA	8.17	79	1	58	21	0
			2	69	10	6

Table 2. The best *PI* and signal timings for two junction road network

While the best *PI* is 8.18 in TRANSYT-7F with HC, the best *PI* is 8.17 in TRANSYT-7F with GA. The common network cycle time is 79 sec and 78 sec in TRANSYT-7F with GA and HC. As can be seen in Table 2, the *PI* obtained from the ACOTRANS model is slightly better than the values obtained from the TRANSYT-7F with GA and HC. These results indicate that the ACOTRANS produces comparable results to the in TRANSYT-7F with GA and HC. Hence, the proposed ACOTRANS model provides an alternative to the HC and GA optimization algorithm in TRANSYT-7F that could produce better results in terms of the *PI* for this small sized network.

In order to test the ACOTRANS model's effectiveness and robustness, it is also applied to medium sized road network. The network is illustrated based upon the one used by [23]. Basic layouts of the network and stage configurations are given in Fig. (7) and (8). This network includes 23 links and 21 signal setting variables at six signal-controlled junctions.

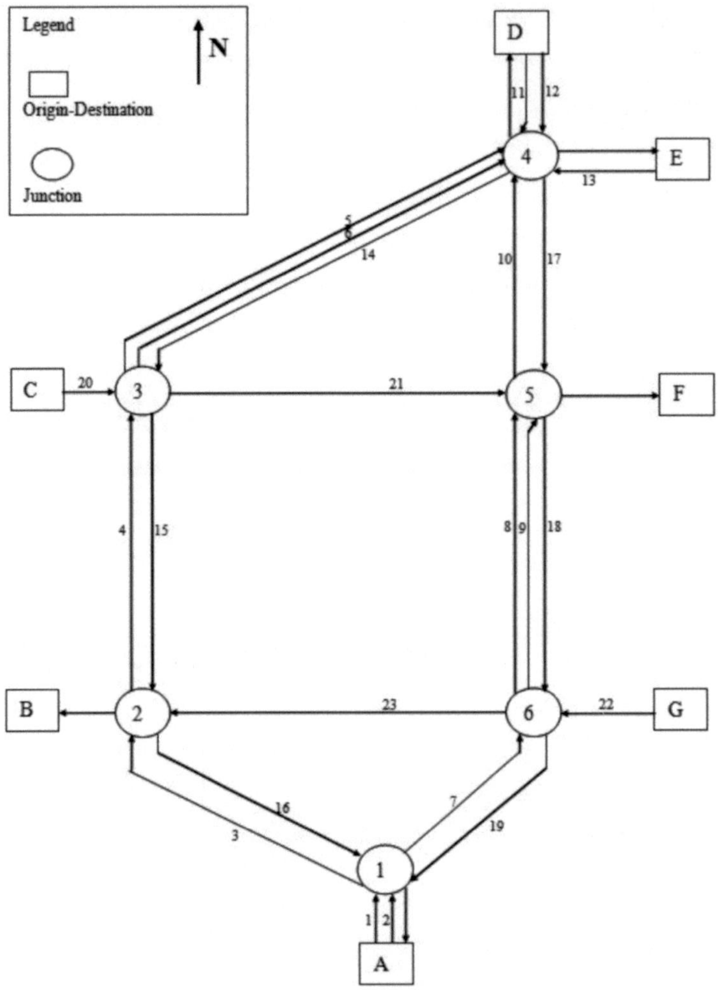

Figure 7. Layout for medium sized network

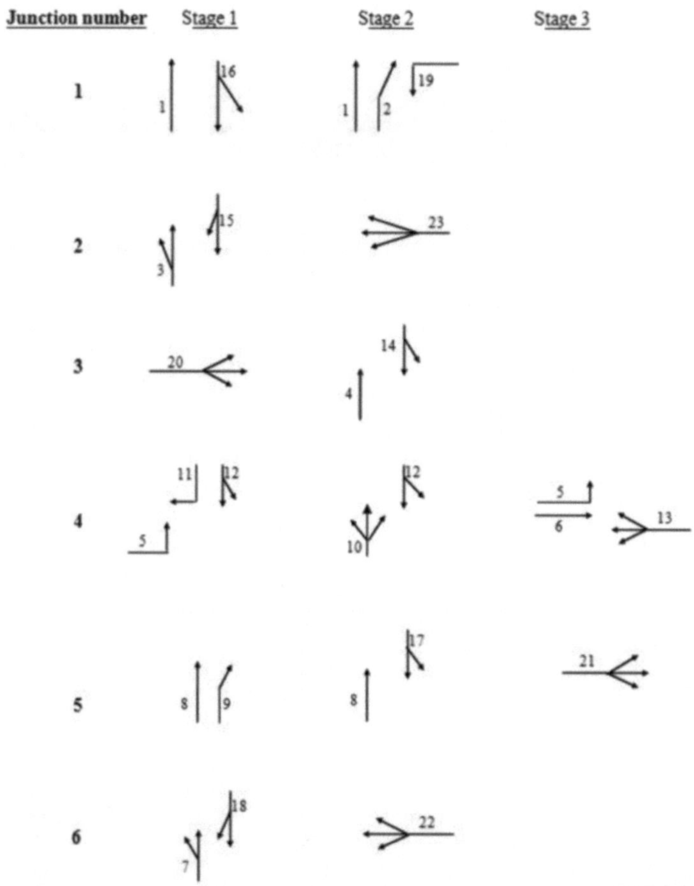

Figure 8. Stage configurations for medium sized network

The fixed set of link flows, taken from [22], is given in Table 3.

Link number	Link flow (veh/h)	Saturation flow (veh/h)	Free-flow travel time (sec)
1	716	2000	1
2	463	1600	1
3	716	3200	10
4	569	3200	15
5	636	1800	20
6	173	1850	20
7	462	1800	10

Link number	Link flow (veh/h)	Saturation flow (veh/h)	Free-flow travel time (sec)
8	478	1850	15
9	120	1700	15
10	479	2200	10
11	499	2000	1
12	250	1800	1
13	450	2200	1
14	789	3200	20
15	790	2600	15
16	663	2900	10
17	409	1700	10
18	350	1700	15
19	625	1500	10
20	1290	2800	1
21	1057	3200	15
22	1250	3600	1
23	837	3200	15

Table 3. Fixed set of link flows on medium sized network

The constraints on signal timings are set as follows:

$36 \leq c \leq 140$cycle time constraint

$0 \leq \theta \leq c$ offsets

$7 \leq \varphi \leq c$green split

$I_{1-2} = I_{2-1} = 5$seconds intergreen time

In Fig. (9), the convergence of the ACOTRANS for medium sized network can be seen. The best signal timings obtained from the previous cycle are stored in order not to being bad local optimum. By means of the generated new ant colony, global optimum is searched around the best signal setting parameters using reduced search space during the algorithm process. As shown Fig. 9, the ACORSES starts the solution process according to random generated signal timings and it was found that the value of *PI* is about 551. The ACORSES keeps the best solution and then it uses the best solution to the optimum in the reduced search space. Optimum solution is then searched in the reduced search space during the algorithm progress. The significant improvement on the objective function takes place in the first few cycle because the ACORSES starts with randomly generated ants in a large colony size. After that, small improvements to the objective function takes place since the pheromone updating rule and new created ant colony provide new solution vectors on the different search directions. Finally, the minimum number of *PI* reached to the value of about 362 after 150 cycles.

This numerical test shows that the ACORSES is able to prevent being trapped in bad local optimum for solving ATC problem. In order to overcome non-convexity, the ACORSES starts with a large base of solutions, each of which provided that the solution converges to the optimum and it also uses the reduced search space technique. In ACORSES, new ant colony is created according to randomly generated α value. For this reason, any of the newly created solution vectors may be outside the reduced search space. Therefore, created new ant colony prevents being trapped in bad local optimum. The ACORSES is able to achieve global optimum or near global optimum to optimise signal timings because it uses concurrently the reduce search technique and the orientation of all ants to the global optimum.

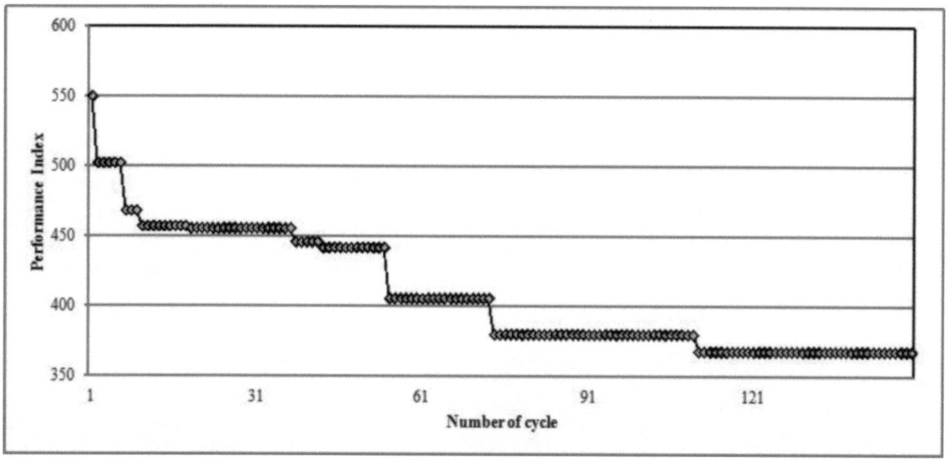

Figure 9. The convergence of the ACOTRANS for medium sized network

The common network cycle time obtained from the ACOTRANS is 106 sec. Moreover, medium sized network is optimized using TRANSYT-7F, which are GA and HC optimization tools. For studied network, the ACOTRANS and TRANSYT-7F optimizers' results are given in Table 4. The best *PI* is found as 410.0 in TRANSYT-7F with GA while its value is obtained as 420.5 in TRANSYT-7F with HC. The common network cycle time is 114 sec and 120 sec in TRANSYT-7F with HC and GA, respectively. The ACOTRANS improves network's *PI* 11.7% and 13.9 % when it is compared with TRANSYT-7F with GA and HC. It also decreases common cycle time 11.5% and 7% when it is compared with the cycle times produced TRANSYT-7F with GA and HC. These results showed that the ACOTRANS model illustrates good performance for optimizing traffic signal timings in coordinated networks with fixed set of link flows. Hence, the ACOTRANS provides an alternative to the HC and GA optimization tools in TRANSYT-7F that could produce better results in terms of *PI*.

	PI	Cycle Time c (s)	Junction number *i*	Duration of stages (s) Stage 1 $I_{1-2}=I_{2-1}=5$	Stage 2 θ_i	Stage 3 $\varphi_{i,1}$	Offsets (s) $7 \le \varphi \le c$
ACOTRANS	361.9	106	1	46	60	-	0
			2	64	42	-	96
			3	62	44	-	10
			4	38	34	34	36
			5	15	33	58	38
			6	34	72	-	74
TRANSYT-7F with HC	420.5	114	1	44	70	-	0
			2	56	58	-	98
			3	69	45	-	98
			4	43	36	35	98
			5	15	36	63	98
			6	39	75	-	98
TRANSYT-7F with GA	410.0	120	1	60	60	-	0
			2	74	46	-	89
			3	71	49	-	37
			4	44	38	38	106
			5	15	38	67	75
			6	60	60	-	55

Table 4. The results for medium sized network

5. Conclusions

This study deals with the area traffic control problem using the ACOTRANS. For this purpose, ACO based algorithm called ACORSES was used. The ACORSES algorithm for solving ATC problem differs from approaches in that new ant colony is generated at each cycle with the assistance of the best solution of the previous information. Moreover, the best solution that is obtained from the previous evaluation is saved to prevent being trapped in bad local optimum. The ACOTRANS is introduced to optimize traffic signal timings at coordinated signalized network. TRANSYT-7F is used to compute *PI* for a given set of signal timing and staging plan in network. The ACOTRANS is tested on two road networks in order to show its robustness and effectiveness. For first test network which contains two junctions, results showed that the ACOTRANS produces slightly better results than TRANSYT-7F with GA and HC. Proposed algorithm was also applied to medium sized network which

http://dx.doi.org/10.5772/51695

contains six junctions. Results also showed that the ACOTRANS improves network's *PI* by 11.7 % and 13.9 % according to TRANSYT-7F with GA and HC. The ACOTRANS provides an alternative to the HC and GA optimization tools in TRANSYT-7F that could produce better results in terms of the *PI*. As a result, the ACOTRANS may be used to optimize traffic signal timings at coordinated signalized network. In future works, the ACOTRANS will be applied to a real-sized network in order to demonstrate the applicability and the effectiveness of the proposed model.

Author details

Soner Haldenbilen*, Ozgur Baskan and Cenk Ozan

*Address all correspondence to: shaldenbilen@pau.edu.tr

Pamukkale University, Engineering Faculty, Department of Civil Engineering, Transportation Division, Turkey

References

[1] Teklu, F., Sumalee, A., & Watling, D. (2007). A genetic algorithm approach for optimizing traffic control signals considering routing. *Computer-Aided Civil and Infrastructure Engineering*, 22, 31-43.

[2] Webster, F. V. (1958). Traffic Signal Settings Road Research Technical Paper. *HMSO London* [39].

[3] Robertson, DI. (1969). TRANSYT' method for area traffic control. *Traffic Engineering and Control*, 10, 276-81.

[4] TRANSYT-7F Release 11.3 Users Guide,. (2008). McTrans Center, University of Florida, Gaineville, Florida.

[5] Baskan, O., Haldenbilen, S., Ceylan, H., & Ceylan, H. (2009). A new solution algorithm for improving performance of ant colony optimization. *Applied Mathematics and Computation*, 211(1), 75-84.

[6] Wong, SC. (1995). Derivatives of the performance index for the traffic model from TRANSYT. *Transportation Research Part B*, 29(5), 303-327.

[7] Wong, SC. (1996). Group-based optimisation of signal timings using the TRANSYT traffic model. *Transportation Research Part B*, 30(3), 217-244.

[8] Heydecker, BG. (1996). A decomposed approach for signal optimization in road networks. *Transportation Research Part B*, 30(2), 99-114.

[9] Wong, S. C., Wong, W. T., Xu, J., & Tong, C. O. (2000). A Time-dependent TRANSYT Traffic Model for Area Traffic Control. *Proceedings of the Second International Conference on Transportation and Traffic Studies. ICTTS*, 578-585.

[10] Wong, S. C., Wong, W. T., Leung, C. M., & Tong, C. O. (2002). Group-based optimization of a time-dependent TRANSYT traffic model for area traffic control. *Transportation Research Part B*, 36, 291-312.

[11] Girianna, M., & Benekohal, R. F. (2002). Application of Genetic Algorithms to Generate Optimum Signal Coordination for Congested Networks. *Proceedings of the Seventh International Conference on Applications of Advanced Technologies in Transportation*, 762-769.

[12] Ceylan, H. (2006). Developing Combined Genetic Algorithm-Hill-Climbing Optimization Method for Area Traffic Control. *Journal of Transportation Engineering*, 132(8), 663-671.

[13] Chen, J., & Xu, L. (2006). Road-Junction Traffic Signal Timing Optimization by an adaptive Particle Swarm Algorithm. *9th International Conference On Control, Automation, Robotics And Vision*, 1- 5, 1103-1109.

[14] Chiou, S-W. (2007). A hybrid optimization algorithm for area traffic control problem. *Journal of the Operational Research Society*, 58, 816-823.

[15] Chiou, S. W. (2007). An efficient computation algorithm for area traffic control problem with link capacity expansions. *Applied Mathematics and Computation*, 188, 1094-1102.

[16] Dan, C., & Xiaohong, G. (2008). Study on Intelligent Control of Traffic Signal of Urban Area and Microscopic Simulation. *Proceedings of the Eighth International Conference of Chinese Logistics and Transportation Professionals*, Logistics: The Emerging Frontiers of Transportation and Development in China, 4597-4604.

[17] Li, Z. (2011). Modeling Arterial Signal Optimization with Enhanced Cell Transmission Formulations. *Journal of Transportation Engineering*, 137(7), 445-454.

[18] Dorigo, M., Di Caro, G., & Gambardella, L. M. (1999). Ant Algorithms for Discrete Optimization. *Artificial Life, MIT press*.

[19] Eshghi, K., & Kazemi, M. (1999). Ant colony algorithm for the shortest loop design problem. *Computers & Industrial Engineering*, 50, 358-366.

[20] Baskan, O., & Haldenbilen, S. (2011). Ant Colony Optimization Approach for Optimizing Traffic Signal Timings. *Ant Colony Optimization- Methods and Applications*, InTech, 205-220.

[21] Ceylan, H., & Bell, M. G. H. (2004). Traffic signal timing optimisation based on genetic algorithm approach, including drivers' routing. *Transportation Research Part B*, 38(4), 329-342.

[22] Ceylan, H. (2002). A genetic algorithm approach to the equilibrium network design problem. Ph.D. Thesis, University of Newcastle upon Tyne, UK.

[23] Allsop, R. E., & Charlesworth, J. A. (1977). Traffic in a signal-controlled road network: an example of different signal timings including different routings. *Traffic Engineering Control*, 18(5), 262-264.

Chapter 5

ANGEL: A Simplified Hybrid Metaheuristic for Structural Optimization

Anikó Csébfalvi

Additional information is available at the end of the chapter

http://dx.doi.org/10.5772/52188

1. Introduction

The weight minimization of the shallow truss structures is a challenging but sometimes frustrating engineering optimization problem. Theoretically, the optimal design searching process can be formulated as an implicit nonlinear mixed integer optimization problem with a huge number of variables. The flexibility of the shallow truss structures might cause different types of structural instability. According to the nonlinear behavior of the resulted lightweight truss structures, a special treatment is required in order to tackle the "hidden" global stability problems during the optimization process. Therefore, we have to replace the traditional "design variables → response variables" like approach with a more time-consuming "design variables → response functions" like approach, where the response functions describe the structural response history of the loading process up to the maximal load intensity without constraint violation.

In this study, a higher order path-following method [1] is embedded into a hybrid heuristic optimization method in order to tackle the structural stability constraints within the truss optimization. The proposed path-following method is based on the perturbation technique of the stability theory and a non-linear modification of the classical linear homotopy method.

The nonlinear function of the total potential energy for conservative systems can be expressed in terms of nodal displacements and the load parameter. The equilibrium equations are given from the principle of stationary value of total potential energy. The stability investigation is based on the eigenvalue computation of the Hessian matrix. In each step of the path-following process, we get information about the displacement, stresses, local, and global stability of the structure.

With the help of the higher-order predictor-corrector algorithm, we are able to follow the load-response path and detect the hidden bifurcation points along the path in time. During the optimization process, the optimal design is characterized by the maximal load intensity factor along the equilibrium path. Consequently, all the structural constraints are controlled by a fitness function in terms of the maximal feasible load intensity factor. Because the function evaluation is very expensive (for example, we have to call a professional system like ANSYS to carry out an "eigenvalue buckling analysis") we have to select the appropriate population-based metaheuristic frame very carefully. In everyday language, a population-based metaheuristic means a good tale usually inspired by the nature, a set of operators, which describes the daily life of the population, and a set of rules which controls the life or death of individuals. In the heuristic frame developing process we applied a "minimal art" like approach to reach the "good quality solution within reasonable time" goal. According to our approach, we decreased the number of operators and tunable-parameters, and simplified the significant operators and rules coming from different tales as much as possible.

In this chapter we present the result, which is a simple but very efficient hybrid metaheuristic for truss weight minimization with continuous and discrete design variables, and global and local stability constraints.

The presented "supernatural" ANGEL method [2-6] combines ant colony optimization (AN), genetic algorithm (GE) and gradient-based local search (L) strategy. In the algorithm, AN and GE search alternately and cooperatively in the design space. The powerful L algorithm, which is based on the local linearization of the constraint set, is applied to yield a more feasible or less unfeasible solution, when AN or GE obtains a solution.

The highly nonlinear and non-convex large-span and large-scale shallow truss examples with continuous and discrete design variables and response curves show that ANGEL may be more efficient and robust than the conventional gradient based deterministic or the traditional population based heuristic (metaheuristic) methods in solving explicit (implicit) optimization problems. ANGEL produces highly competitive results [16-18] in significantly shorter run-times than the previously described pure approaches.

The benefit of synergy can be demonstrated by standard statistical tests. To the best of our knowledge, no such work has been done in the literature for truss weight minimization with response curves. The reason is simple: the question of the global stability loss (the collapse of the structure as a whole) was not investigated very carefully in the truss optimization literature so far, according to a popular but totally misleading "assumption" of the truss optimization community that the local stability loss (local buckling) always precedes the global stability loss (the collapse), therefore the time-consuming investigation of the global stability is meaningless (see in Hanahara and Tada [20]).

2. Structural optimization

Generally, the traditional implicit “design variables → response variables” weight minimization problem with continuous and discrete design variables can be written as follows:

$$W(Z) \rightarrow \min \quad (1)$$

$$G_j(Z) \in \left[\underline{G}_i, \bar{G}_i \right], j \in \{ 1,2,\ldots,M \} \quad (2)$$

$$X_i \in \left[\underline{X}_i, \bar{X}_i \right], i \in \{ 1,2,\ldots,N \} \quad (3)$$

$$Y_g \in \{ C_1, C_2, \ldots, C_C \}, g \in \{ 1,2,\ldots,G \} \quad (4)$$

where$W(\boldsymbol{X})$ is the weight of the structure, G_j, $j \in \{1, 2, \ldots, M\}$are the implicit response variables, and$Z = \{ X = \{ X_1, X_2 \ldots, X_N \}, \ Y = \{ Y_1, Y_2 \ldots, Y_G \} \}$is the set of continuous and discrete design variable sets.

The investigated new "design variables → response functions" weight minimization approach can be described as follows:

$$W(Z) \rightarrow \min \quad (5)$$

$$G_j(Z, \lambda) \in \left[\underline{G}_i, \bar{G}_i \right], j \in \{ 1,2,\ldots,M \}, 0 \le \lambda \le 1 \quad (6)$$

$$X_i \in \left[\underline{X}_i, \bar{X}_i \right], i \in \{ 1,2,\ldots,N \} \quad (7)$$

$$Y_g \in \{ C_1, C_2, \ldots, C_C \}, g \in \{ 1,2,\ldots,G \} \quad (8)$$

where$\lambda = \lambda(Z)$ the load intensity factor and constraint $0 \le \lambda \le 1$ means that loading process reached the maximal load intensity level without constraint violation.

In the path-following algorithm (details of the nonlinear structural investigation see in [1]), a design is represented by the set of$\{ W, \lambda, \ Z, \ \Phi \}$, where W is the weight of the structure, λ is the maximal load intensity factor without constraint violation, and $Z = \{ X, \ Y \}$ is the set of design variables. In our study, we used a problem-specific fitness function $\Phi = \Phi(Z)$ $(0 \le \Phi \le 2)$ which is defined as following:

$$\Phi = \begin{cases} 2 - \dfrac{W - W^L}{W^U - W^L} & \text{if } \lambda = 1 \\ \lambda & \lambda < 1 \end{cases} \qquad (9)$$

where W^L (W^U) is the minimal (maximal) weight of the structure, according to the given design space.

Our feasibility-oriented fitness function is based on the following set of criteria:

- Any feasible solution is preferred to any infeasible solution,
- Between two feasible solutions, the one having a smaller weight is preferred,
- Between two infeasible solutions, the one having a larger load intensity factor is preferred.

The minimal weight design problem can be formulated in terms of member cross-sections (a member cross-section may be a continuous variable or discrete value taken from a given catalogue) and nodal point shifts (to modify the shape), and may be constrained by the allowable nodal-point displacements, element stresses and the global stability requirement which simple means a non-singular Hessian on the load-response path.

We have to mention, that in our study we investigated only truss structures therefore the applied structural model was a large deflection truss model without simplifications. To avoid any type of stability loss even a structural collapse, a path-following approach was used to compute the structural response.

The applied measure of design infeasibility was defined as the maximal load intensity factor subject to all of the structural constraints. Naturally, ANGEL which is presented in the next section can be used in the traditional "design variables → response variables" approach and may be easily adopted for other types of optimization problems including the traditional explicit function minimization problems.

3. ANGEL

First, we have to note, that ANGEL as a name of a combined population-based metaheuristic for the resource-constrained project scheduling problem was introduced by Tseng and Chen [15]. We use this name in a different context with a different content. Our ANGEL algorithm, according to the systematic simplification, is based only three operators: random selection (RS), random perturbation (RP), and random combination (RC). In ANGEL the traditional mutation operator was replaced by the local search procedure (L) as a "locally best" form of mutation. That is, rather than introducing small random perturbations into the offspring solution, a gradient-based local search is applied to improve the solution until a local optimum is reached. The first result of our systematic simplification work is trivial: hard to imagine a population-based heuristic without an RS operator. The RS operator is in a special position in the heuristic community therefore the population-based heuristic literature is full with many general and problem-specific selection mechanisms (a good overview can be found in the work of Sivaraj and Ravichandran [13]). When we imagine the population as a matrix in which the rows are individuals and the columns are variables and the fitness function values of the individuals form a corresponding column vector, then very easy to identify the two basic selection possibilities: the column-wise (AN like) and the row-wise (GE like) selection mechanisms (see Figure 1). In Figure 1 we used a grey-scale to show the fitness of individuals (the lighter the grey color the better the individual) and we assumed that the individuals are ordered according to their fitness values. To demonstrate the possibilities we presented two similar cases (two parents (P2) → one child (C1)).

The AN mechanism selects at least one "more or less good parent" from each column step by step and after that applies the RP or RC operator procedure for each selected variable or variable set independently to get a child, from which L try to make a "better child".

The GE mechanism selects at least one "more or less good parent" in exactly one step for each case. In other words, GE selects at least one complete row. After that the algorithm repeats the previous steps to generate the child by applying the RP or RC operator for each variable or variable set of the selected parent or parents and after that L try to improve the quality of the child to get a "locally best" child.

In AN approach, by definition, the RS means a set of randomly selected "more or less good" element or elements according to the tale-dependent fitness function. This approach always imitates a "route" independently from its reality. When we imagine a bee flying from flower to flower or a salesperson travelling from city to city, the reality of the abstraction is trivial. But when we have to solve an optimal truss design problem minimizing its total weight on the set of element cross-sections as design variables, subject to the displacement and stress constraints, the local and global stability requirements and load conditions and imagine the construction as a whole, then the "from cross-section to cross-section" route may be totally meaningless and misleading abstraction. We may become the slave of the tale, which may yield a "brutal-force-search" like efficiency, because in our case the function evaluation is very expensive and time-consuming according to the implicit dependency between the design variables (element cross-sections) and the response variables (for example: global stability loss).

According to the optimal structural design problem, it is very easy to imagine the GE selection strategy, in which we select randomly at least one "more or less good design" and after that, according to the other operators of the tale, we try to make a better one (less unfeasible or lighter feasible) by RP or RC.

Easy to imagine, that the combination of the two selection mechanisms may increase the variability of the searching process as a synergism. The two selection mechanisms are very general: from single-parent to multi-parents they are able to manage every case using only the RP and RC operators. In this study, "tradition is a tradition" we used the generally accepted operator types. Namely we used the AN-P1-C1 and GE-P2-C1 operators alternately and cooperatively using only the RP, RC, and L operators, which are invariant to the selection direction.

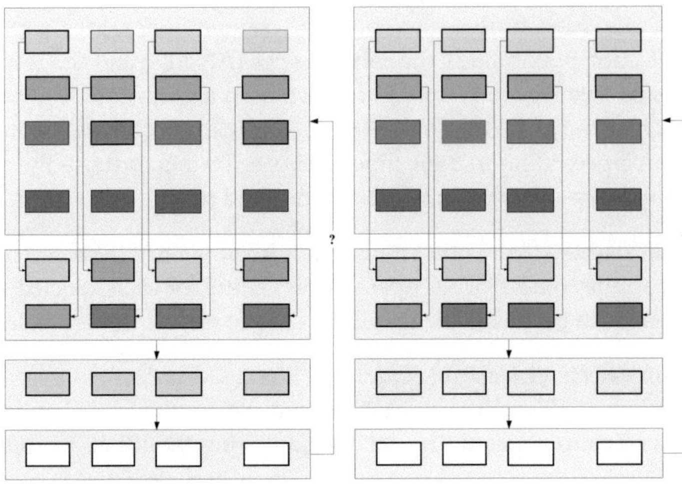

Figure 1. AN-P2-C1 + L and GE-P2-C1 + L

In the ANGEL developing process, we tried to simplify the three operators (RS, RP, and RC) and decrease the number of tunable-parameters, namely the size of the problem-specific "golden-number" set, as much as possible, to minimize the time requirement of the so-called "preliminary investigation". In our case, the preliminary investigation may be an "experimental design and analysis" like problem in the problem with terrible large computational cost which yields only 'good" problem-specific golden-number-set after several "try-and-error" iterations.

The flowchart of the proposed simplified heuristic ANGEL method is presented in Figure 2.The main procedure of the proposed hybrid metaheuristic follows the repetition of these two steps:

1. AN with LS and
2. GE with LS.

According to the systematic simplification, the hybrid algorithm is based only three operators:

1. random selection (AN+GE),
2. random perturbation (AN), and
3. random combination (GE).

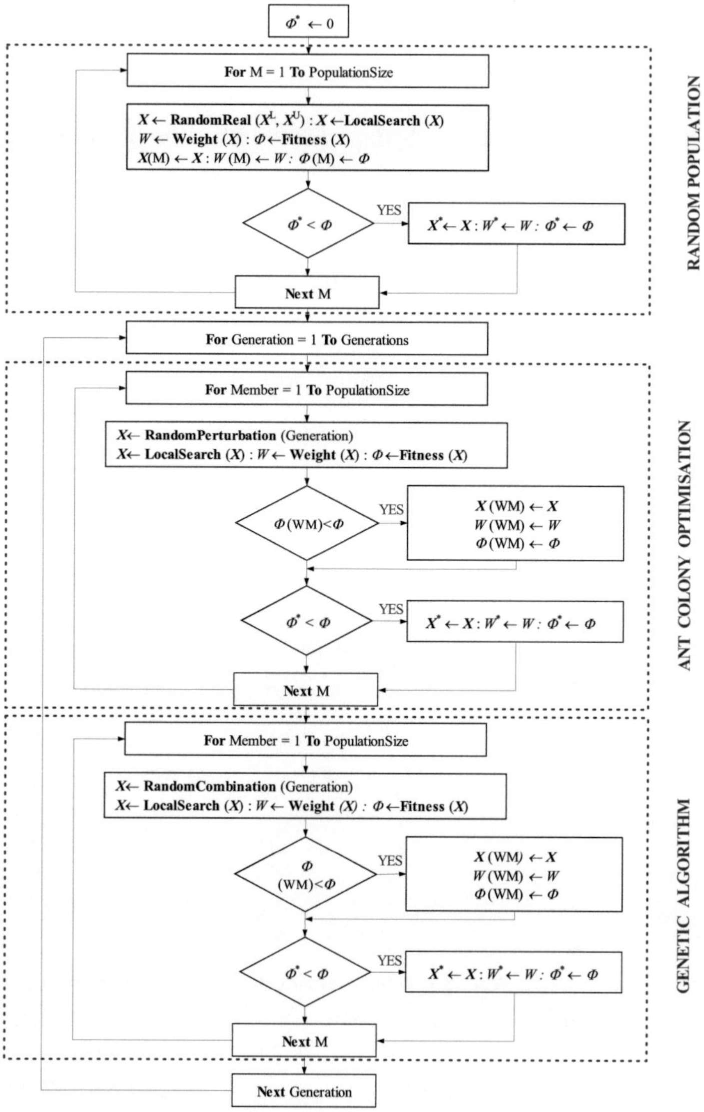

Figure 2. Flowchart of ANGEL

In the presented form, the population-based ANGEL has only three "tunable" parameters $\{ PS, \ NG, \ MI \}$, where PS is the size of the population, NG is the number of generations, MI is the maximal number of gradient-based local search iterations $(0 \le MI \le 100)$, and an additional parameter pair $\left\{ \bar{S}, \ \underline{S} \right\}$ which defines a exponentially decreasing multiplier in the function of generation gen, $gen \in \{ 1, \ 2, \ \ldots, \ NG \}$:

$$S(gen) = \bar{S} * \exp\left(\log\left(\frac{\underline{S}}{\bar{S}}\right) * \frac{gen-1}{NG-1}\right) \tag{10}$$

The parameter pair $\left\{\bar{S}, \underline{S}\right\}$, which controls the smooth transition from diversity to intensity, can be kept "frozen" in the algorithm:

$$\left\{\bar{S}, \underline{S}\right\} = \left\{1.0,\ 0.01\right\} \tag{11}$$

which means, that ANGEL is practically a "tuning-free" algorithm.

The monotonically decreasing standard deviation function for each continuous design variable can be defined in the following way:

$$S_i^{gen} = S(gen) * \left(\bar{X}_i - \underline{X}_i\right), gen \in \left\{1,2,\ldots,NG\right\}, i \in \left\{1,2,\ldots,N\right\} \tag{12}$$

In our approach, the case of the discrete design variables can be managed in a similar way. The only difference is that we replace the value set with the equivalent index set and carry out all the operations on the index set.

The main procedure of the proposed meta-heuristic method follows the repetition of these two steps:

1. AN with L and

2. GE with L.

In other words, meta-heuristic ANGEL firstly generates an initial population, after that, in an iterative process AN and GE search alternately and cooperatively on the current design set. The initial population is a totally random set. The random perturbation and random combination procedures which are based on the normal distribution, call therandom selection function which uses the discrete inverse method, to select a "more or less good" design (GE) or a set of "more or less good" design variable values from the current population. The higher the fitness values of a design (a design variable value) the higher the chance is that it will be selected by the function (see Figure 3).

The random perturbation procedure uses the continuous inverse method to generate a new solution from the old one (see Figure 4). The random combination procedure generates an offspring solution from the selected mother and father solutions (see Figure 5). The offspring solution is generated from the combined distribution, where the combined distribution is the weighted sum of the parent's distributions. The two procedures are controlled by the standard deviation, which is decreasing exponentially from generation to generation.

In our algorithm an offspring will not necessarily be the member of the current population, and a parent will not necessarily die after mating. The reason is straightforward, because our algorithm uses very simple rule without explicit pheromone evaporation handling: If the current design is better than the worst solution of the current population than the worst one will be replaced by the better one.

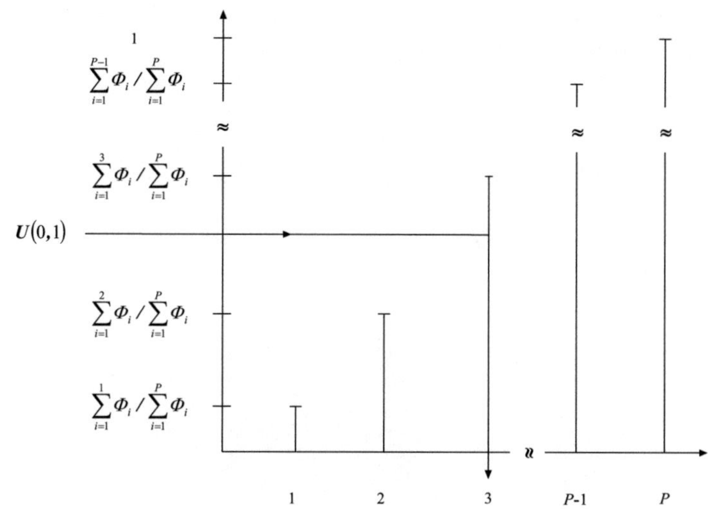

Figure 3. Random selection

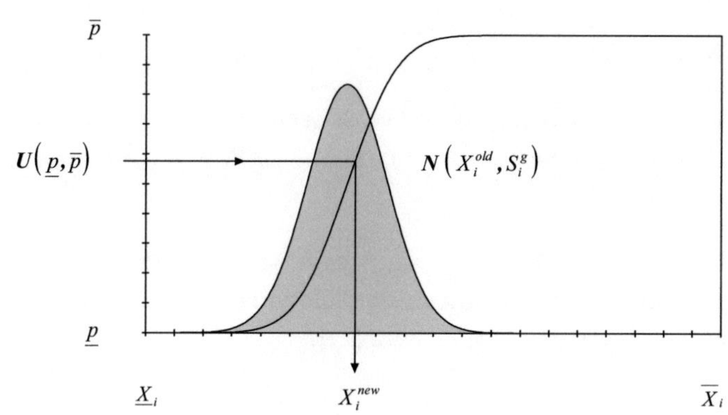

Figure 4. Random perturbation

In this work, without loss of generality, we only deal with the two fundamental cases when the design variables are only element (element-group) cross-section areas. In the continuous case a cross-section area may be any value from a given interval and in the discrete case a cross-section area has to be taken from a discrete catalogue. Additionally, also without loss of generality, it is assumed that we are interested only in the local and global stability investigation without displacement constraints. We assume that the allowed maximal positive (stretching) stress defined by a constant, and the allowed minimal negative (compressive) stress is constrained by a local buckling function, which is a function of the material properties, the element length, and the element cross-sectional area. The global stability investigation is based on the load-eigenvalue curves. From the global stability point of view a truss design is feasible, when during the loading process each load-eigenvalue curve remains in the positive segments up to the end of the process.

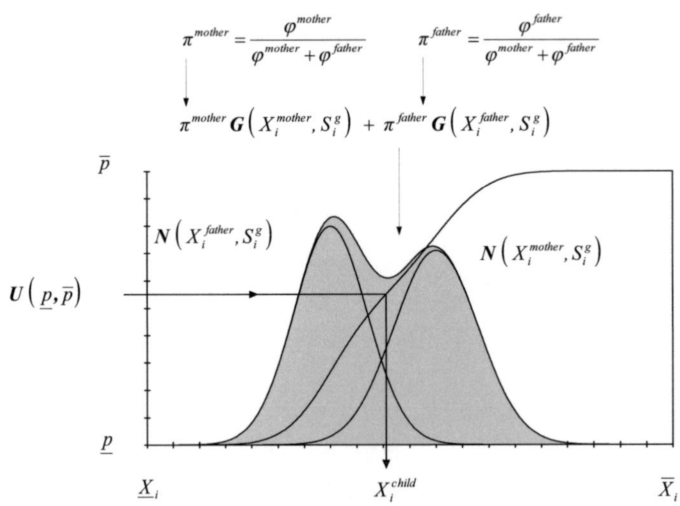

Figure 5. Random combination

In the pure continuous case (when only the cross-section range is fixed) the iterative local search procedure (L) alternates two approaches according to the current feasibility indicator value.

If the current design is feasible, namely:$\lambda = 1$, then it solves the following linear programming problem to get a lighter but feasible design allowing only a limited weight decrement in each iteration (see Lamberti and Pappalettere [11]):

$$\Delta W(\Delta X_1, \ldots, \Delta X_i, \ldots, \Delta X_N) \rightarrow \max \tag{13}$$

$$G_j(X) + \sum_{i=1}^{N} \frac{\partial G_j(X)}{\partial X_i} * \Delta X_i \in [\underline{G}_j, \overline{G}_j], j \in \{1, 2, \ldots, M\} \tag{14}$$

$$\Delta X_i \in \left[\Delta \underline{X}_i, \Delta \bar{X}_i\right], i \in \{1,2,\ldots,N\} \tag{15}$$

$$0 \leq \Delta W \leq \Delta \bar{W} \tag{16}$$

If the current design is infeasible, namely:$\lambda 1$, the local search procedure tries to get a less infeasible solution allowing only a limited weight increment (decrement) in each iteration (see Lamberti and Pappalettere [11]):

$$\sum_{i=1}^{M}\left(\Delta \underline{\mathrm{G}}_{\mathrm{i}} + \Delta \bar{G}_i\right) \rightarrow \min \tag{17}$$

$$G_j(X) + \sum_{i=1}^{N} \frac{\partial G_j(X)}{\partial X_i} * \Delta X_i \in \left[\underline{G}_j - \Delta \underline{G}_j, \bar{G}_j + \Delta \bar{G}_j\right], j \in \{1,2,\ldots,M\} \tag{18}$$

$$\Delta X_i \in \left[\Delta \underline{X}_i, \Delta \bar{X}_i\right], i \in \{1,2,\ldots,N\} \tag{19}$$

$$\Delta W \in \left[\Delta \underline{W}, \Delta \bar{W}\right] \tag{20}$$

In the pure discrete case (when the cross-sections are taken from a catalogue) we have two possibilities to develop a local search procedure.

We can define a simple "thumb rule" used to improve the quality of the generated discrete solutions. The starting base of the thumb rule is a discrete solution given by applying the usual "rounding to the next catalogue value" rule. When the discrete solution is feasible (infeasible) then, in a cyclically repairable process, we try to decrease the cross-sectional areas step by step selecting always the "best" element (element group), where "best" means an element (element group) for which the element stress is minimal (maximal) in absolute value.

An improvement, namely a cross-sectional area decreasing (increasing) is accepted, when the starting design feasibility level is not decreased by the current modification. The process terminates, when no such an element exists. We have to emphasize that in the presented path following approach the design feasibility is measured by the maximal load intensity factor, and therefore, the designs satisfy the stress constraints up to the maximal load intensity factor computed by the applied path following method.

The other possibility would be a "locally exact" binary formulation.The proposed binary linear (or quadratic) programming (BLP or BQP) approach exploits the fact, that using a "state-of-the-art" solver the solution time of a local BLP (or BQP) problem is competitive with the solution time of the "thumb rule" heuristic.

Naturally, a local BLP (BQP) formulation can give better results, as a pure heuristic approach. Using a "dense" catalogue the problem can be managed as linear programming problem, when the catalogue is "sparse", we have to use a quadratic formulation to describe the possible stress changes accurately, in the function of the "local" catalogue values. The immediate predecessor (successor) of the current catalogue value defines the “local catalogue”, for each element (element group), if such a value exists. According to the "local environment", an element (element group) can be described by at least three binary variables.

Naturally, using the standard trick (special ordered set (SOS) constraint management) of the operations research (OR), the formulation which has at least three binary variables, can be replaced by an equivalent formulation which has only at least two binary variables. Let $g, \; g \in \{1, 2, \ldots, G\}$ the member-group index and $c, \; c \in \{1, 2, \ldots, C\}$the catalogue index, where G is the number of elements (member-groups) and $C$is the size of the discrete catalogue of possible cross-sectional areas:$\{C_1, C_2 \ldots, C_C\}$.

Let $\{B_{g\,j}^{i} \mid j \in J^{i}\}$be the set of the binary variables needed to describe the possible movement and A_g^i the cross-sectional area for element (member-group)$g, \; g \in \{1, 2, \ldots, G\}$ in iteration $i, \; \{i = 1,2, \ldots, MI\}$. The "local catalogue" and the constraints connected to the local binary variables which describe the possible movements are presented in Figure 6-7. In iteration $i, \; \{i = 1,2, \ldots, MI\}$the local environment is defined by the result of the previous iteration.

In the local model exact analytical derivatives were used. To generate the symbolic derivatives, optimized to speed, Wolfram Mathematica 8.0 was used. Naturally, a linearized model can be replaced by a quadratic one, and the simplified assumption that the stress change of member-group $g$can be described by its cross-section change.

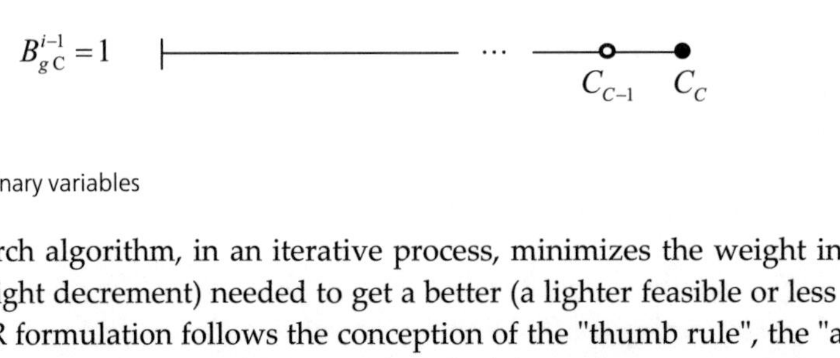

Figure 6. Local binary variables

The local search algorithm, in an iterative process, minimizes the weight increment (maximizes the weight decrement) needed to get a better (a lighter feasible or less unfeasible) solution. The OR formulation follows the conception of the "thumb rule", the "at least as good" quality requirement is managed by non-smoothed formulation, namely in the formulation the maximal constraint violation is constrained.

Naturally, the non-smooth $max()$ function can be replaced by an equivalent smooth formulation, by omitting the function and introducing additional constraints. In other words, when the starting base of an iteration is unfeasible ($\lambda 1$), than the local search algorithm generates a "mini-max" model, in which the maximal slack of the constraint set will be minimized according to the allowed maximal structural weight increase.

$$
\textit{if} \begin{cases}
B_{g1}^{i-1}=1 & B_{g1}^{i}+B_{g2}^{i}=1 \\
& A_g^i = C_1 B_{g1}^i + C_2 B_{g2}^i \\
& S_g^i = S_g^{i-1} B_{g1}^i + \left(S_g^{i-1} + \frac{\partial S_g^{i-1}}{\partial A_g^{i-1}} (C_2 - C_1) \right) B_{g2}^i \\
& B_{g\,k-1}^{i} + B_{g\,k}^{i} + B_{g\,k+1}^{i} = 1 \\
B_{g\,k}^{i-1}=1 \quad \textit{then} & A_g^i = C_{k-1} B_{g\,k-1}^i + C_k B_{g\,k}^i + C_{k+1} B_{g\,k+1}^i \\
& S_g^i = S_g^{i-1} B_{g\,k}^i + \left(S_g^{i-1} + \frac{\partial S_g^{i-1}}{\partial A_g^{i-1}} (C_{k-1} - C_k) \right) B_{g\,k-1}^i + \left(S_g^{i-1} + \frac{\partial S_g^{i-1}}{\partial A_g^{i-1}} (C_{k+1} - C_k) \right) B_{g\,k+1}^i \\
& B_{g\,C-1}^{i} + B_{g\,C}^{i} = 1 \\
B_{g\,C}^{i-1}=1 & A_g^i = C_{C-1} B_{g\,C-1}^i + C_C B_{g\,C}^i \\
& S_g^i = S_g^{i-1} B_{g\,C}^i + \left(S_g^{i-1} + \frac{\partial S_g^{i-1}}{\partial A_g^{i-1}} (C_{C-1} - C_C) \right) B_{g\,C-1}^i
\end{cases}
$$

Figure 7. Local binary constraints

4. Numerical example

4.1. Sizing optimization with buckling constraints - 120-bar truss dome

In this paper, in order to demonstrate the proposed solution method a well-known space dome structure is presented as a simple sizing problem, where two basic sub problems, continuous and discrete optimization problems are distinguished.

Saka and Ülker [12], as a continuous optimization problem, have introduced first time the 120-bar example. The minimal weight design subjected to structural constraints imposed on the member stress and nodal displacements based on linear and non-linear analysis. Subsequently, Soh and Yang [14] have been analyzed the same structure to obtain the optimal design related to sizing and configuration variables Kaveh and Talatahari [7] presented a heuristic method where the particle swarm optimizer, ant colony strategy and harmony search are hybridized.Therefore, several techniques have been incorporated to handle the constraints. Similar to Lee and Geem [10], Kelesoglu and Ülker [9], only sizing variables are considered to minimize the structural weight. According to the complexity of the concerned problems, another method has been proposed by Kaveh and Talatahari [8], namely a hybrid big bang–big brunch (HBB–BC) algorithm.The comparisons of numerical results using the HBB–BC method with the results obtained by other heuristic approaches are performed to demonstrate the robustness of the present algorithm. With respect to the big bang–big brunch (BB–BC) approach, HBB–BC has better solutions and standard deviations. In addition, HBB–BC has low computational time and high convergence speed compared to BB–BC. However, when the number of design variables increases the hybrid BB–BC shows better performance. The effects of nonlinear behavior to the optimal results have been investigated by Hadi and Alvani [19] and Lemonge and Barbosa [21].

The geometry and nodal coordinates are presented in Figure 8 and in Table 1. According to the structural symmetry, truss members are grouped into seven member-groups (see in Table 2). The truss is subjected to the given applied external loads in Table 3. The truss members as design variables are grouped into seven group variables (Table 4).

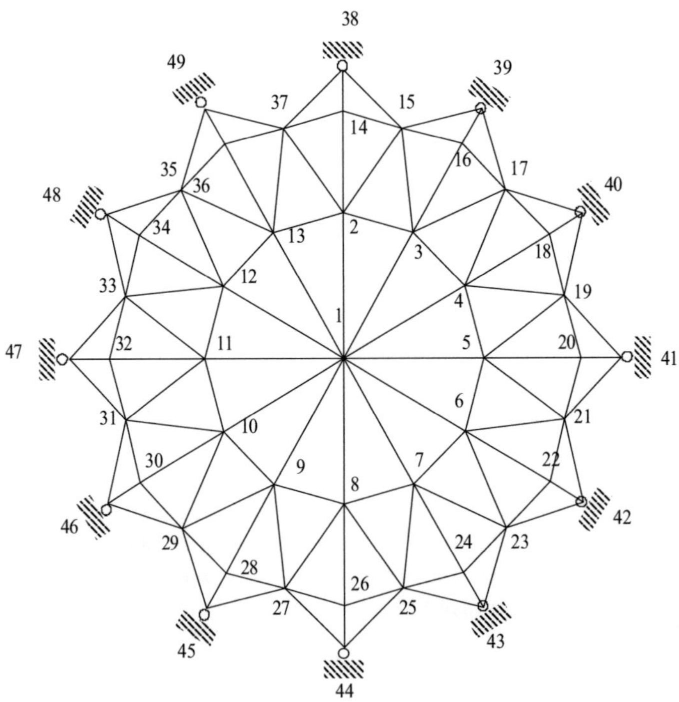

Figure 8. The layout of the 120-bar shallow truss dome

Nodes	X [*m*]	Y [*m*]	Z [*m*]
1	0.	0.	7.000
4	6.01108	3.4705	5.850
5	6.94100	0.	5.850
18	10.82532	6.2500	3.000

Nodes	X [*m*]	Y [*m*]	Z [*m*]
19	11.66266	3.1250	3.000
20	12.50000	0.	3.000
40	13.76114	7.9450	0.
41	15.89000	0.	0.

Table 1. The geometry of the 120-member truss dome

Node	1	2-13	14-37
Load [*kN*]	60	30	10

Table 2. The load condition of the 120-bar truss dome

Modulus of elasticity	$E = 210000 / MPa$
Material density	$\rho = 7850 / kg/m^3$
Stress constraints for tension	$\sigma_e^U = 140 / MPa$
Stress constraints for compression	$\sigma_e^L = -140 / MPa$

Table 3. Properties of the applied material

Groups	Truss members					
G_1	1-2	1-3	1-4	1-5	1-6	1-7
	1-8	1-9	1-10	1-11	1-12	1-13
G_2	2-3	3-4	4-5	5-6	6-7	7-8
	8-9	9-10	10-11	11-12	12-13	13-2
G_3	2-14	3-16	4-18	5-20	6-22	7-24
	8-26	9-28	10-30	11-32	12-34	13-36
G_4	2-15	3-17	4-19	5-21	6-23	7-25
	3-15	4-17	5-19	6-21	7-23	8-25
	8-27	9-29	10-31	11-33	12-35	13-37
	9-27	10-29	11-31	12-33	13-35	2-37
G_5	14-15	16-17	18-19	20-21	22-23	24-25
	15-16	17-18	19-20	21-22	23-24	25-26
	26-27	28-29	30-31	32-33	34-35	36-37
	27-28	29-30	31-32	33-34	35-36	37-14

Groups	Truss members					
G_6	14-38	16-39	18-40	20-41	22-42	24-43
	26-44	28-45	30-46	32-47	34-48	36-49
G_7	15-38	17-39	19-40	21-41	23-42	25-43
	15-39	17-40	19-41	21-42	23-43	25-44
	27-44	29-45	31-46	33-47	35-48	37-49
	27-45	29-46	31-47	33-48	35-49	37-38

Table 4. Groups of truss elements

Refer to the formerly presented papers (e.g. [16-18]), in this study, stainless steel tubular cross-sections are considered as design variables.According to the thin-wall pipe structural behavior, the following local stability constraints are proposed. The stress constraint for against of Euler-buckling or peripheral shell-like buckling is given in terms of the thickness ratio:

$$\sigma_e^E = \frac{\pi E}{4 L^2} \cdot \frac{0.5 - \alpha + \alpha^2}{\alpha(1-\alpha)} \cdot G_e \tag{21}$$

$$\sigma_e^B = KE\alpha \tag{22}$$

where$\alpha = T / D$ is the ratio of the wall-thickness and diameter of the applied G_e group elements.In the present study, since continuous and discrete design variables are considered as well we applied tubular cross sections with given α=0.05 thickness ratio. Cross sectional variables are changing from G_{min}=5.0cm^2 up to G_{max}=50.0cm^2. In this paper, only stress and buckling constraints are considered.

The obtained results for continuous problem using linear and non-linear structural model are compared are presented in Table 5 and in Table 6. Comparing with the results of continuous optimizations shows that GA based approach [19] gives a better minimum weight than the optimality criteria approach [12]. It is observed that further reduction is possible in the weight of the space truss considering the geometrically nonlinear analysis as compared to linear one.

Worthy of note, that the optimal design obtained by the proposed hybrid ANGEL seems much better than the results of previously presented compared methods. Remarkable in this study - using the formula (9)- that the related fitness value is Φ= 1.928 i.e. very close to the defined maximal fitness value. In the resulted optimal design only one buckling constraint is active, namely in the member-group 6.

In this paper for discrete optimization problem two types of catalogue values are distinguished, a sparse (case 1) and a dense (case 2) with the following cross sections:

Case 1: {5.0; 10.0; 15.0; 20.0; 25.0;…; 50.0}

Case 2: {5.0; 7.5; 10.0; 12.5; 15.0; 17.5; 20.0; 22.5; 25.0;…; 50.0}

We have to note that the related fitness value is Φ= 1.889 (Case 1) and Φ = 1.922 (Case 2), i.e. in case a sparse catalogue we obtained a bit worst fitness value than in case of dense catalogue values, but the difference is natural and both adjacent to the continuous one Φ = 1.928.

Groups / cm2	Saka,Ulker* [12]		Hadi, Alvani* [19]	Proposed method
Linear	Non-linear	Non-linear	Non-linear	
G_1	16.66	17.50	10.85	12.968
G_2	44.89	45.56	38.70	8.282
G_3	24.89	25.45	35.40	13.325
G_4	9.66	8.44	5.23	7.964
G_5	21.93	22.30	27.37	8.316
G_6	16.59	15.96	15.30	7.776
G_7	11.74	3.90	3.90	7.990
W / kg	8511	7587	7158.6	4650.659

Table 5. The best results of the continuous problem (*Note: section shape is not available)

Using a state-of-the-art callable BLP (BQP) solver, for example: CPLEX 12.0, the time requirement of the improved local search is compatible with the time requirement of the traditional "thumb rule" like approach. However, the improved approach is more efficient, because it is able to modify more than one cross-sectional area in one iteration.

In the presented computational test, ANGEL was run with the following parameters:

- the population size was 100,
- the number of generations was 10, and
- the maximal number of local search iterations was 10.

We note, that the maximal number of iterations does not necessarily mean that the number of iterations always 10.

4.2. Sizing-shaping optimization with stability constraints -24-bar truss dome

This academic example has been analyzed by the author previously [17] to demonstrate the difficulties of the stability investigation. The layout and the initial data are presented in Figure 9 and Table 7-8. At the central node, the load is 0.5, while at nodes 2-7 it is 1.0 unit.

Groups / cm2	Hadi, Alvani* [19]		Proposed method (Case 1)	Proposed method (Case 2)
	Linear	Non-linear	Non-linear	Non-linear
G_1	15.00	12.30	10.0	10.0
G_2	46.70	46.70	10.0	10.0
G_3	27.00	27.00	15.0	12.5
G_4	7.05	5.33	10.0	7.5
G_5	27.60	24.70	5.0	5.0
G_6	11.10	17.80	10.0	10.0
G_7	1.82	1.53	10.0	7.5
W / kg	7264.6	7229.0	4979.681	4242.075

Table 6. The best results of the discrete problem(*Note: section shape is not available)The local search terminates when, according to the given "play-field", in the current step no improvement can be reached without affecting the maximal allowable weight increase or the maximal allowable constraint violation defined by the previous step.

Nodes	X [*cm*]	Y [*cm*]	Z [*cm*]
1	0	0	8.216
2	12.50	21.65063509	6.2.16
3	25.00	0	6.216
8	0	50.00	0
9	43.330127019	25.00	0

Table 7. Initial coordinates of 24-bar shallow space truss

The equilibrium path that involves in this case four critical points has been determined inside of the optimization process. First is a single bifurcation (λ_1=8.68), while the following two are double bifurcation points (λ_2=10.26;λ_3=15.67). The fourth is a simple limit point (λ_4=18.40).We have to note that only the fourth singular point is a simple limit point. With the help of this simple example easy to confirm the hazardous of the theories and methods which are able to tackle only snap-through phenomenon.

In this paper, a weight optimization is considered subjected to global stability constraints. The cross-sections as design variables are involved into three groups (Figure 9). The load intensity factor is changing from zero to one.

Using the proposed hybrid metaheuristic method, where the number of generations is 10 and the population size is 100, two optimization problems are considered.

Case 1:

In first case, a sizing optimization problem is solved for minimal volume optimization subjected to structural stability. The structure is loaded up to the maximal load intensity factor while the smallest eigenvalue becomes zero. The obtained best solution for the grouped design variables are the following:A_1=1.000;A_2=1.321;A_1=1.119. The optimal volume in this case isV_{opt}=773.127.

Case 2:

In the second case, a sizing-shaping optimization problem is presented. The three sizing variables are extended with three shift variables namely the vertical position of all free joints (Z_i;i=1, 2, ..., 7), and the horizontal position of the joints 2-7 (R_j; j=2, ..., 7). In this case, the same proposed hybrid metaheuristic method has been applied, with the number of generations 10 and the population size 100. The obtained best solution is the following:A_1=1.000; A_2=1.378;A_1=1.084;Z_1=7.685;Z_{2-7}=6.121;R_{2-7}=24.665. The optimal volume is V_{opt}=765.699 and the lowest eigenvalue is zero for three digits in the best solution.

Design variables	**$A_i \in [1.00;2.00]$ (cm²); $i \in \{1, 2, 3\}$**	
Load cases	Nodes	Z
1	1	−5.00 *kN*
	2, 3, 4, 5, 6, 7	−10.00 *kN*
Material properties	Modulus of elasticity	$E = 10000\ kN / cm^2$

Table 8. Initial data of 24-bar shallow space truss

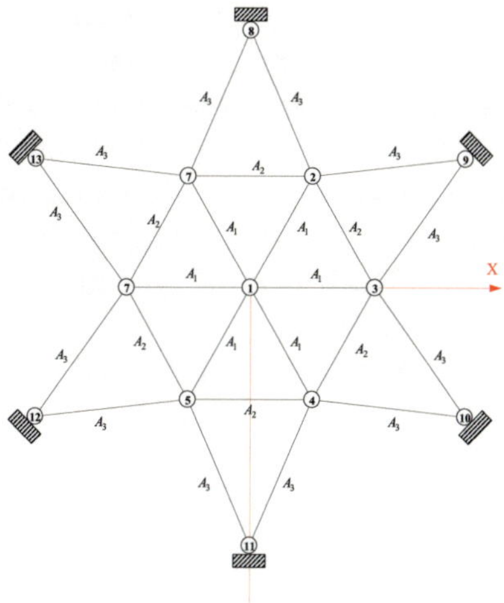

Figure 9. The layout of the 24-bar truss dome

5. Conclusion

The weight minimization of the shallow truss structures is a challenging but sometimes frustrating engineering optimization problem. Theoretically, the optimal design searching process can be formulated as an implicit nonlinear mixed integer optimization problem with a huge number of variables. The flexibility of the shallow truss structures might causes different type of structural instability. According to the nonlinear behavior of the resulted lightweight truss structures, a special treatment is required in order to tackle the "hidden" global stability problems during the optimization process. Therefore, we have to replace the traditional "design variables → response variables" like approach with a more time-consuming "design variables → response functions" like approach, where the response functions describe the structural response history of the loading process up to the maximal load intensity without constraint violation.

In this study, a higher order path-following method was embedded into a hybrid heuristic optimization frame in order to tackle the global structural stability constraints within the truss optimization. The proposed path-following method is based on the perturbation technique of the stability theory and a non-linear modification of the classical linear homotopy method.

In this chapter we presented a simple but very efficient hybrid metaheuristic for truss weight minimization with continuous and discrete design variables, and local and global stability constraints. The presented "supernatural" ANGEL method combines ant colony optimization (AN), genetic algorithm (GE) and gradient-based local search (L) strategy. In the algorithm, AN and GE search alternately and cooperatively in the design space. The powerful L algorithm, which is based on the local linearization of the constraint set, is applied to yield a more feasible or less unfeasible solution, when AN or GE obtains a solution.

The highly nonlinear and non-convex large-span and large-scale shallow truss examples with continuous and discrete design variables and non-linear response curves show that ANGEL may be more efficient and robust than the conventional gradient based deterministic or the traditional population based heuristic (metaheuristic) methods in solving explicit (implicit) optimization problems. ANGEL produces highly competitive and from engineering point of view safe and accurate results in significantly shorter run-times than the previously described pure approaches. The benefit of synergy was demonstrated by standard statistical tests. To the best of our knowledge, no such work has been done in the literature for truss weight minimization with non-linear response curves so far.

Author details

Anikó Csébfalvi

Department of Structural Engineering, University of Pécs, Hungary

References

[1] Csébfalvi, A. (1998). A nonlinear path-following method for computing the equilibrium curve of structures. *Annals of Operations Research*, 15-23, 10.1023/A:1018944804979.

[2] Csébfalvi, A. (2007). Angel method for discrete optimization problems. *Periodica Polytechnica Civil Eng*, 51/2, 37-46, 10.3311/pp.ci.2007-2.06.

[3] Csébfalvi, A. (2007). Optimal design of frame structures with semi-rigid joints. *Periodica Polytechnica Civil Eng*, 51/1, 9-15, 10.3311/pp.ci.2007-1.02.

[4] Csébfalvi, A. (2009). A hybrid meta-heuristic method for continuous engineering optimization. *Periodica Polytechnica, Ser Civ Eng*, 53(2), 93-100, 10.3311/pp.ci.2009-2.05.

[5] Csébfalvi, A. (2011). Multiple constrained sizing-shaping truss-optimization using ANGEL method. *Periodica Polytechnica Civil Engineering*, 55/1, 81-6, 10.3311/pp.ci. 2011-1.10.

[6] Csébfalvi, A. (2012). Kolmogorov- Smirnov Test to Tackle Fair Comparison of Heuristic Approaches in Structural Optimization. *Int. J. Optim. Civil Eng*, 2(1), 135-150.

[7] Kaveh, A., & Talatahari, S. (2009). Particle swarm optimizer, ant colony strategy and harmony search schemehybridized for optimization of truss structures. *Computers and Structures*, 87, 267-283.

[8] Kaveh, A., & Talatahari, S. (2009). Size optimization of space trusses using Big Bang-Big Crunch algorithm. *Computers and Structures*, 87, 1129-1140.

[9] Kelesoglu, O., & Ülker, M. (2005). Fuzzy optimization geometrical nonlinear space truss design. *Turkish Journal of Engineering &Environmental Sciences*, 29, 321-329.

[10] Lee, K. S., & Geem, Z. W. (2004). A new structural optimization method based on the harmony search algorithm. *Computers and Structures*, 82, 781-98.

[11] Lamberti, L., & Pappalettere, C. (2004). Improved sequential linear programming formulation for structural weight minimization. *Comput. Methods in Appl. Mech. Engrg.*, 193, 3493-3521.

[12] Saka, M. P., & Ülker, M. (1992). Optimum design of geometrically non-linear space trusses. *Computers and Structures*, 42, 289-299.

[13] Sivaraj, R., & Ravichandran, T. (2011). A review of selection methods in genetic algorithm. *International Journal of Engineering Science and Technology (IJEST)*, 0975-5462, 3(5), May.

[14] Soh, C. K., & Yang, J. (1996). Fuzzy controlled genetic algorithm search for shape optimization. *Journal of Computing in Civil Engineering, ASCE*, 10(2), 143-50.

[15] Tseng, L. Y., & Chen, S. C. (2006). A hybrid metaheuristic for the resource-constrained project scheduling problem. *European Journal of Operational Research*, 175, 707-721.

[16] Csébfalvi, A. (2003). Optimal design of space structures with stability constraints. *Bontempi F (ed) System-Based Vision for Strategic and Creative Design, Vols 1-3: 2nd International Conference on Structural and Construction Engineering, September 23-26, Rome, Italy, Leiden:Balkema Publishers*, 493-497, 9-05809-599-1.

[17] Csébfalvi, A. (2010). A Higher-Order Path-Following Method for Stability-Constrained Optimization of Geometrically Nonlinear Shallow Trusses. O Allix, P Wriggers (ed) ECCM 2010, IV European Conference on Computational Mechanics, Palais des Congrès, Paris, France, May 16-21,2010: European Committee on Computational Solids, 2010.05.16-2010.05.21. , 1-7.

[18] Csébfalvi, A. An Improved ANGEL Algorithm for the Optimal Design of Shallow Truss Structures with Discrete Size and Continuous Shape Variables and Stability Constraints. *Erik Lund (ed) 9th World Congress on Structural and Multidisciplinary Optimization: WCSMO-9. Shizuoka, Japan*, Shizuoka:paper ID: 100_1, 1-8.

[19] Hadi, M. N. S., & Alvani, K. S. (2003). Discrete Optimum Design of Geometrically Non-Linear Trusses using Genetic Algorithms, Seventh International Conference on The Application of Artificial Intelligence toCivil and Structural Engineering. *B.H.V. Topping (Ed.), Civil-Comp Press, Stirling, Scotland*, paper 37.

[20] Hanahara, K., & Tada, Y. Global Buckling Has to be Taken into Account for Optimal Design of Large-Scale Truss Structure. *Erik Lund (ed) 9th World Congress on Structural and Multidisciplinary Optimization: WCSMO-9. Shizuoka, Japan*, Shizuoka:paper ID: 142_1, 1-10.

[21] Lemonge, A. C. C., Barbosa, H. J. C., Fonseca, L. G., & Coutinho, A. L. G. A. (2010). A genetic algorithm for topology optimization of dome structures. *Helder C. Rodrigues (ed)2nd International Conference on Engineering Optimization, September 6-9, Lisbon, Portugal*, paper ID: 01284, 1-15.

Chapter 6

Scheduling in Manufacturing Systems – Ant Colony Approach

Mieczysław Drabowski and Edward Wantuch

Additional information is available at the end of the chapter

http://dx.doi.org/10.5772/51487

1. Introduction

Scheduling problems, also in manufacturing systems [4], are described by following parameters: the processing – computing – environments comprising processor (machines) set, other resources comprising transportations and executions devices, processes (tasks) set and optimality criterion. We assume that processor set consists of m elements. Two classes of processors can be distinguished: dedicated (specialized) processors and parallel processors.

In production systems machines are regarded as dedicated rather than as parallel. In such a case we distinguish three types of dedicated processor systems: flow-shop, open-shop and job-shop. In the flow-shop all tasks have the same number of operations which are performed sequentially and require the same sets of processors. In the open-shop the order among the operations is immaterial. For the job-shop, the sequence of operations and the sets of required processors are defined for each process separately.

In the case of parallel processors each processor can execute any task. Hence, a task requires some number of arbitrary processors. As in deterministic scheduling theory [12] parallel processors are divided into three classes: identical processors – provided that all tasks are executed on all processors with that same productivity, uniform processors – if the productivity depends on the processor and on the task, and unrelated processors – for which execution speed depends on the processor and on the task. In each of the above cases productivity of the processor can be determined.

Apart from the processors the can be also a set of additional resources, each available in m_i units.

The second parameter of the scheduling problem is the tasks system. The tasks correspond to the applications for manufactured goods. We assume that the set of tasks consists of n tasks. For the whole tasks system it is possible to determine such feature as preemptability (or nonpreemptability) and existence (or nonexistence) of precedence constraints.

Precedence constraints are represented as directed acyclic graphs (DAGs). Each task separately is described by a number of parameters. We enumerate tem in the following:

- Number of operations,
- Execution time,
- Ready time,
- Deadline,
- Resources requirements,
- Weight.

The optimality criteria constituting the third element of the scheduling problem are:

- Schedule length,
- Maximum lateness,
- Mean flow time,
- Mean tardiness.

Due to the fact that scheduling problems and their optimizations are general NP-complete [10,25] we suggest meta-heuristic approach: Ant Colony Optimization and its comparison with neural method and with polynomial algorithms for certain exemplary problems of task scheduling.

If a heuristic algorithm (such as ACO) finds an optimal solution to polynomial problems, it is probable that solutions found for NP-complete problems will also be optimal or least approximated to optimal. ACO algorithm was tested with known polynomial algorithms and all of them achieved optimal solutions for those problems.

The comparisons utilized such polynomial algorithms as [3,5,12]:

- Coffman-Graham Algorithm,
- Hu Algorithm,
- Baer Algorithm,

For non-polynomial problems of tasks scheduling ACO algorithm was tested with list algorithms [12] (HLFET, HLFNET, SCFET, SCFNET), with PDF/HIS [18] for STG tasks and neural approach [22].

2. Adaptation of ACO to solve the problems of scheduling

The Ant Colony Optimization (ACO) algorithm [2] is a heuristics using the idea of agents (here: ants) imitating their real behavior. Basing on specific information (distance, amount of pheromone on the paths, etc.) ants evaluate the quality of paths and choose between them with some random probability (the better path quality, the higher probability it represents). Having walked the whole path from the source to destination, ants learn from each other by leaving a layer of pheromone on the path. Its amount depends on the quality of solution chosen by agent: the better solution, the bigger amount of pheromone is being left. The pheromone is then "vapouring" to enable the change of path chosen by ants and let them ignore the worse (more distant from targets) paths, which they were walking earlier.

The result of such algorithm functioning is not only finding the solution. Very often it is the trace, which led us to this solution. It lets us analyze not only a single solution, but also permutations generating different solutions, but for our problems basing on the same division (i.e. tasks are scheduled in different order, although they are still allocated to the same processors). This kind of approach is used for solving the problems of synthesis, where not only the division of tasks is important, but also their sequence.

To adapt the ACO algorithm [24] to scheduling problems, the following parameters have been defined:

- Number of agents (ants) in the colony;
- Vapouring factor of pheromone (from the range (0; 1));

The process of choosing these parameters is important and should consider that:

- For too big number of agents, the individual cycle of algorithm can last quite long, and the values saved in the table ("levels of pheromone") as a result of addition will determine relatively weak solutions.
- On the other hand, when the number of agents is too small, most of paths will not be covered and as a result, the best solution can long be uncovered.

The situation is similar for the vapouring factor:

- Too small value will cause that ants will quickly "forget" good solutions and as a result it can quickly come to so called *stagnation* (the algorithm will stop at one solution, which doesn't have to be the best one).
- Too big value of this factor will make ants don't stop analyze "weak" solutions; furthermore, the new solutions may not be pushed, if time, which has passed since the last solution found will be long enough (it is the values of pheromone saved in the table will be too big).

The ACO algorithm defines two more parameters, which let you balance between:

- α – the amount of pheromone on the path;

- β – "quality" of the next step;

These parameters are chosen for specific task. This way, for parameters:

- $\alpha > \beta$ there is bigger influence on the choice of path, which is more often exploited,
- $\alpha < \beta$ there is bigger influence on the choice of path, which offers better solution,
- $\alpha = \beta$ there is balanced dependency between quality of the path and degree of its exploitation,
- $\alpha = 0$ there is a heuristics based only on the quality of passage between consecutive points (ignorance of the level of pheromone on the path),
- $\beta = 0$ there is a heuristics based only on the amount of pheromone (it is the factor of path attendance),
- $\alpha = \beta = 0$ we'll get the algorithm making division evenly and independently of the amount of pheromone or the quality of solution.

Having given the set of neighborhood *N* of the given point *i*, amount of pheromone on the path τ and the quality of passage from point *i* to point *j* as an element of the table η you can present the probability of passage from point *i* to *j* as [6,7]:

$$p_{ij}^{k} = \begin{cases} \dfrac{[\tau_{ij}]^{\alpha}[\eta_{ij}]^{\beta}}{\sum_{l \in N_i^k}[\tau_{il}]^{\alpha}[\eta_{il}]^{\beta}} & \text{When } j \in N_i^k \\ 0 & \text{Else} \end{cases}$$

Formula 1. Evaluation of the quality of the next step in the ACO algorithm

In the approach presented here, the ACO algorithm uses agents to find three pieces of information:

- the best / the most beneficial division of tasks between processors,
- the best sequence of tasks,
- searching for the best possible solution for the given distribution.

Agents (ants) are searching for the solutions which are the collection resulting from the first two targets (they give the unique solution as a result). After scheduling, agents fill in two tables:

- two-dimensional table representing allocation of task to the given processor,
- one-dimensional table representing the sequence of running the tasks.

The process of agent involves:

1. collecting information (from the tables of allocation) concerning allocation of tasks to resources and running the tasks;

2. drawing the next available task with the probability specified in the table of task running sequence;

3. drawing resources (processor) with the probability specified in the table of allocation the tasks to resources;

4. is it the last task?

To evaluate the quality of allocation the task to processor, the following method is being used:

1. evaluation of current (incomplete) scheduling;

2. allocation of task to the next of available resources;

3. evaluation of the sequence obtained;

4. release the task;

5. was it the last of available resources?

The calculative complexity of single agent is polynomial and depends on the number of tasks, resources and times of tasks beginning.

Idea of algorithm:

Algorithm:

1. Construct *G* – structure of tasks non allocation and *S* – structure of tasks, which may be allocation in next step (for ex ample: begin: $G = \{Z_1, Z_2, \dots, Z_7\}$ and $S = \{Z_1, Z_2, Z_3\}$); update range of pheromone and consideration of vapouring factor;

2. With *S* select of tasks with the most strong of trace;

3. Allocate available of task as soon as possible and in accordance with precedence constraints;

4. Remove selected of task with *G* and *S* and to add to list of tasks in memory of ant;

5. Update range of pheromone and remain of trace;

6. If $G = \emptyset$ END of algorithm;

7. Go to 1;

Example:

Two identical processors, digraph of seven tasks $Z_i(t_i)$, where t_i = time execution.

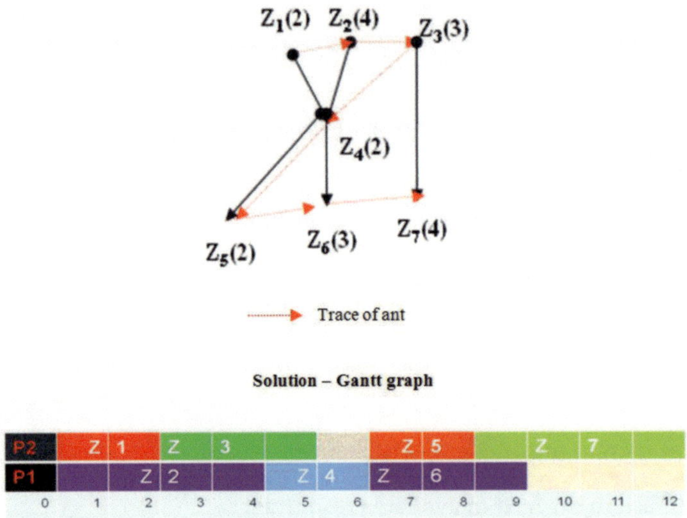

Parameters of ants' colony have been selected through experiments. Algorithm tuning is to select possibly best parameter values. This process demands many experiments which are conducted for different combinations of parameter values. For each combination of variable values, computation process has been repeated many times, and then an average result has been calculated. The same graphs type of STG, like at previous algorithms, have been applied [18,20].

Selected algorithm parameters:

- a – number of ants; for number of tasks n < 50, a = 75 and for n>= 50, a = 1,5 x n
- γ – the pheromone evaporation coefficient = 0,08.

3. Adaptation of neural method to solve the problems of scheduling

3.1. Neural network model

The starting point for defining the neural network model for solving the problems of task scheduling and resource allocation are the assumptions for the constraint satisfaction problem (CSP) [36,37]. CSP is the optimization problem which contains a certain set of variables, sets of their possible values and constraints forced on the values of these variables [14,15]. On the basis of this problem assumption a network model of the following features is suggested:

- A neural network consists of components; each of them corresponds to another variable.

http://dx.doi.org/10.5772/51487

- Each component contains such number of neurons which equals the number of possible values of each variable.
- Assigning a specified value to a variable is the process of switching on a relevant neuron (neurons) and switching off the remaining ones in the component corresponding to this variable.
- Switching on a neuron means assigning the value *"1"* to its output.
- Switching off a neuron means assigning the *"0"* to its output.
- Constraints to the network are introduced by adding a negative weight connection between neurons *('-1')*, symbolizing the variable values that cannot occur simultaneously.
- In the network there are additional neurons "the ones" that are switched on.

Each neuron has its own table of connections and each connection contains its weight and the indicator for the connected neuron. A characteristic feature of the network is the diversity of connections between neurons, but these never applied to all neurons [22,23]. It is a consequence of the fact that connections between neurons exist only when some constraints are imposed. The constraints existing in the discussed network model may be of the following types: resources, time, order.

The method of constraints implementation shall be discussed upon examples [22].

Example 1:

Such net (Fig. 1.) blocks solution, in which $Z_1 = 1$ as well as $Z_2 = 2$ or $Z_3 = 3$ as well as $Z_4 = 2$.

Example 2:

Let us have two operations with unit execution times. The operation Z_1 arrives at the system in time $t = 1$ and it is to be executed before the expiry of time $t = 4$. The operation Z_2 arrives in time $t = 1$ and may be executed after the completion of operation Z_1. A fragment of the net for his case including all the connections is shown by Fig. 2.

Neuron „one" ('1') – a special neuron switched on permanently – is responsible for time constraints. Introducing connections between such neuron and the relevant network neurons excludes a possibility of switching them on when searching for the solution. Task Z_1 cannot be scheduled in moment *0* and moment *4*, which corresponds to the assumption that this task arrives at the system at moment *1* and must be performed before moment *4*. Analogical process applies to operation Z_2. The sequence constraints are executed by the connections between the network neurons. The figure shows (with dotted line) all the connections making the performance of task Z_2 before task Z_1 impossible.

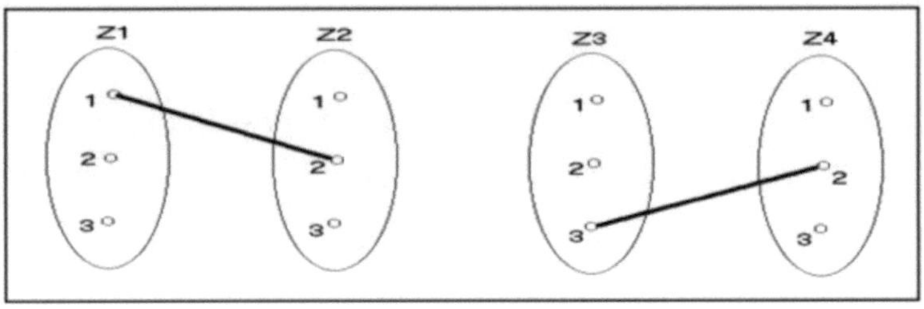

Figure 1. The example 1 of constraints.

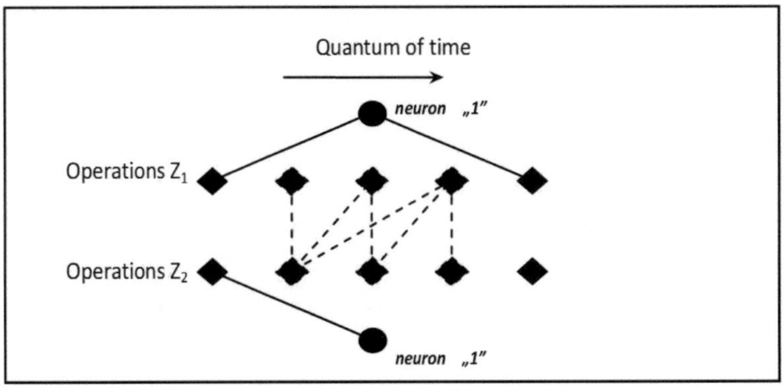

Figure 2. The example 2 of constraints.

3.2. The algorithm description

After entering the input data (the system specification), the algorithm constructs a neural network, the structure of which and the number of neurons composing it, depend upon the size and complexity of the instance of problem. We will name the part of the net allocated to this task – an area.

Constraints are introduced to the network by the execution of connections, occurring only between the neurons corresponding to the values of variables which cannot occur simultaneously.

The operation of the algorithm is the process of switching on appropriate neurons in each domain of network in order to satisfy the constraints imposed by the input data.

The algorithm course is as follows [36,38]:

1. *Allocating random values to consecutive variables.*
2. *Network relaxation:*

3. *Calculating the weighted sum of all neurons inputs.*

4. *Switching on the neuron with the highest input value.*

5. *Return to relaxation or – if there are no changes – exit from relaxation.*

6. *If there are connections (constraints) between the neurons that are switched on, each weight between two switched on neurons is decreased by 1 and there is a return to relaxation.*

The algorithm starts from allocating weight *'-1'* to all connections and then the start solution is generated. It is created by giving random values to the subsequent variables. This process takes place in a certain way: for each task i.e. in each area of the net such number of neurons is switched on as it is necessary for a certain task to be completed. The remaining, in the part which is responsible for its performance, neurons are being switched off. In the obtained result there are many contradictions, specified by switching on the neurons where the connections exist.

Therefore, the next step of the algorithm is the relaxation process, the objective of which is to "satisfy" the maximum numbers of limitations (backtracking). The objective is to obtain the result where the number of situations, where two switched on neurons of negative weight connection between them is the lowest. While switching on neurons with the biggest value at the start, in each area three instances may happen:

- If there is one neuron of the biggest value in the area, it is switched *on*; the remaining ones are switched *off*.

- If there are more neurons, among which there is a previously switched one, there is no change and it remains switched *on*.

- If there are more neurons, but there is no-one previously switched on, one of them is switched on randomly, the remaining ones are switched *off*.

A relaxation process finishes when the subsequent step does not bring any change and if all the requirements are met – the neurons between which a connection exist are not switched on – the right solution is found. If it is not still the case, it means that the algorithm found the local minimum and then the weight of each connection between two switched on neurons is decreased by *"1"* while its absolute value is being increased. It causes an increase in "interaction force' of this constraint which decreases the chance of switching *on* the same neurons in a relaxation process where we return in order to find the right solution.

After a certain number of iterations the network should consider all the constraints – providing that there is the right solution, it should be found. Another factor is worth pointing out: in a relaxation process such an instance may occur where changes always happen. Then, this process might never be completed. Then a problem is solved in such a way that relaxation is interrupted after a certain number of calls.

Search for a solution by algorithm consists of two stages. At the first one, which is described by the above presented algorithm, some activities are performed which lead to finding the right solution for the given specification. After finding such a solution, in consequence of purpose function optimization there is a change of values for a certain criterion – in this case, decrease – then, the subsequent search for the right solution occur. In this case the search aims at a solution which possesses bigger constraints as the criteria value is sharper. Two criteria are taken into consideration for which a solution is being searched. It may be a cost function – where at the given time criterion, we search for the cheapest solution, or time function – where at the given cost criterion, we search for the quickest solution. Thus, the run of the algorithm is to seek a solution for smaller and smaller value of a selected criterion. However, if the algorithm cannot find the right solution for the recently modified criteria value of the algorithm, it returns to the previous criteria value for which it has found the right solution and modifies it by a smaller value.

For instance, if an algorithm has found the right solution for cost criterion which is e.g. 10, and it cannot find it for cost criteria which are 9, it tries to find a solution for cost 9.5 etc. In this way the program never finishes work, but all the time it tries to find a better solution in sense of a certain criterion. The user/designer of the system can interrupt its work at any moment if he/she considers the current solution given by an algorithm to be satisfying.

In case of time criterion minimization, optimization goes at two planes. At the first one, subsequent neurons of the right side in task part of the network are connected to the neurons *"one"*, in this way fewer and fewer quanta is available for the algorithm of task scheduling which causes moving a critical line to the left and at the same time its diminishing. However, at the second, an individual quantum of time is being diminished; at each step an individual neuron will mean a smaller and smaller time passage.

The task part:

Each area corresponds to one task (Fig. 3.). For further area, the best possible setting for the task is selected. Which setting 'wins' at the given stage and in the given area – this shall be determined by the sum of neuron outputs in the setting, i.e. the one that introduces the smaller number of contradictions. Moreover, it is checked if among the found set of the best solutions there is no previous one, then it is left.

A neuron at the *[i, k]* position corresponds to the presence of *'i'* task on the processor at the *'k'* moment. Between these neurons there are suitable inhibitory connections *(-1.0).*

If, for example, task 1 must be performed before task 2, for all the neuron pairs

[1, k], [2, m] there are inhibitory connections (denoting contradictions), if $k >= m$ and if task 8 occurs in the system at moment 2, *„one"* neuron is permanently connected to neurons *[8, 0] and [8, 1]* (neuron which has 1.0 at the start which is permanently contradictory) and guarantees that in the final solution there is no quantum at moment 0 or 1.

We also take critical lines into account, which stand for time constraints that cannot be exceeded by any allocated tasks – connecting 'one' will apply to the neurons of the right side of the network outside the critical line.

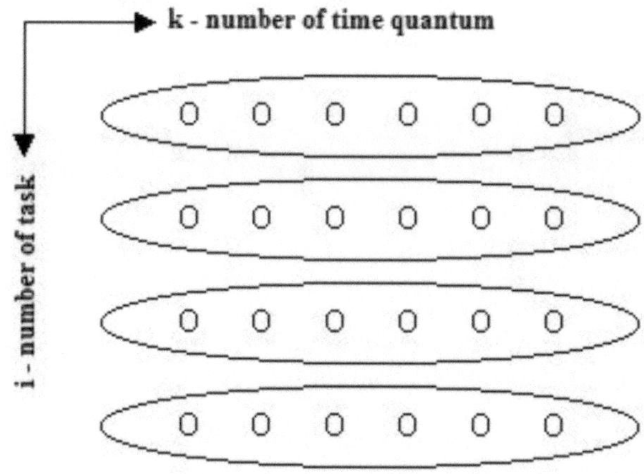

Figure 3. The task part for scheduling problems.

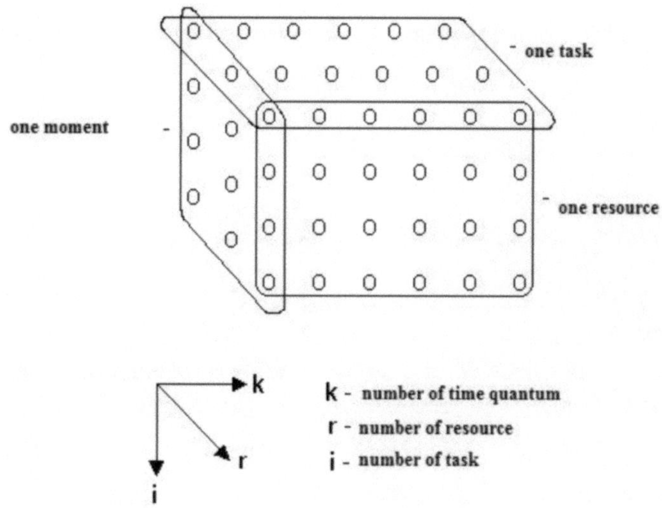

Figure 4. The resource part for scheduling problems.

The resource part:

Before selecting the quanta positions in the areas, algorithm has to calculate inputs for all the neurons. The neurons of the resource part are also connected to these inputs, as the number and the remaining places in recources have an impact on the setting which is going to "win" at a certain stage of computation. Thus, before an algorithm sets an exact task, it calculates the value of neuron inputs in resource part. The [r, i, k] neuron is switched on if at 'k' moment the resource 'r' is overloaded (too many tasks are using t), or it is not overloaded, but setting the task of part 'i' at the moment defined by *'k'* would result in overloading. Neurons in resource part (Fig. 4.) respond by their possible connection, resource overloaded, if part of the task were set and at moment *'k'*; therefore, neurons of resource part are connected to task inputs.

When in the resource part the neuron " *'r' resource overload'* is switched *on*, as task *'i'* is set at moment *'k'* ", its signal *(1.0)* is transferred by weight (-1.0) to the neuron existing in the task part, which causes the negative input impulse (-1.0 * 1.0) at the input which results in a contradiction.

In other words – it "disturbs" function *'compute_in'* to set the task and at moment "k". Thus, in the network there are subsequent illegal situations implemented (constraints).

Each neuron *[r, i, k]* of the resource part is connected with neuron *[i, k]* from the task part, so a possibility of task existence at a given moment with concurrent resource overloading is 'inhibited'.

Example:

Let us assume that there are five operations *A, B, C, D, E.*

Task part works as follows (a letter means a neuron switched on, sign '-' means a switched off neuron):

```
operation A:|---AAAA--AA-----
operation B:|--BBB-------BB--
operation C:|-C--------------          each line
operation D:|DDDDDD-----------         corresponds to available quanta
operation E:|---------EEEEE---         of subsequent tasks

   moment 0 |_________________________> time
```

These operations should be allocated to a certain number of processors, so that one only operation would be performed on one processor at an exact moment:

1. Algorithm allocates (at moment 0) fragment DDDDDD, adds a new processor (the first) and allocates on it:

   DDDDDD-----------

2. Allocation -C: for this moment (1) there is no place on the first processor, so algorithm adds the next processor and allocates an operation:

   DDDDDD-----------

   -C---------------

3. Allocation BBB: there is place on the second processor:

   DDDDDD-----------

   -C-BBB-----------

4. Allocation AAAA: there is no place at quantum 4 –algorithm adds the third processor and allocates:

DDDDDD-----------

-C-BBB-----------

----AAAA---------

5. Allocation EEEEE: there is place on the first processor :

DDDDDD---EEEEE---

-C-BBB-----------

----AAAA---------

6. Allocation AA there is place on the second processor

DDDDDD---EEEEE---

-C-BBB----AA------

----AAAA---------

7. Allocation BB: there is place on the second processor:

DDDDDD---EEEEE---

-C-BBB----AA-BB—

----AAAA---------

The result of the operations on the processors is as follows:

P1:DDDDDD---EEEEE---

P2:-C-BBB----AA-BB--

P3: ----AAAA---------

Computational complexity of neural algorithm for task scheduling

An algorithm gives the right solution for the problems of known multi-nominal algorithms and also may be used for problems NP-complete. The complexity of one computation step may be estimated as follows:

$$i * (1 + p * k + k * (1 + k * p) * m + k * r * i * p) + p \tag{2}$$

Where:

i – Number of tasks.

p – Number of processors.

k – Number of time quanta.

m – Number of all consecutive depend abilities between tasks.

r – Number of resources.

The largest complexity is generated by the process of increasing the number of tasks and an increase in the number of time quanta. Also, maximum number of processors and number of constitutive depend abilities in the introduced graph have a powerful effect on computation. It is a pessimistic estimation; in practice, real complexity may be slightly smaller, but proportional to that. An algorithm itself is convergent i.e. step by step generates better and better solutions.

4. Tests of task scheduling algorithms

4.1. The comparison with polynomial algorithms

To show convergence of ACO algorithm towards optimum, one can compare their results with optimal results of already existing, precise, polynomial algorithms for certain exemplary problems of task scheduling. If a heuristic algorithm finds an optimal solution to polynomial problems, it is probable that solutions found for NP-complete problems will also be optimal or at least approximated to optimal. Heuristic algorithm described herein was tested with known polynomial algorithms and all of them achieved optimal solutions for those problems. The comparisons utilized such polynomial algorithms as:

- Coffman – Graham Algorithm,
- Hu Algorithm,
- Baer Algorithm,

Comparisons of ACO solutions with selected precise polynomial algorithms will be presented as an example.

Coffman and Graham algorithm

Scheduling of tasks which constitute a discretionary graph with singular performance times on two identical processors in order to minimize $C_{max.}$ Calculation complexity of the algorithm is $O(n^2)$.

Test problem no 1:

- 2 identical processors (a), 3 identical processors (b).
- 15 tasks with singular performance times.
- Graph with tasks:

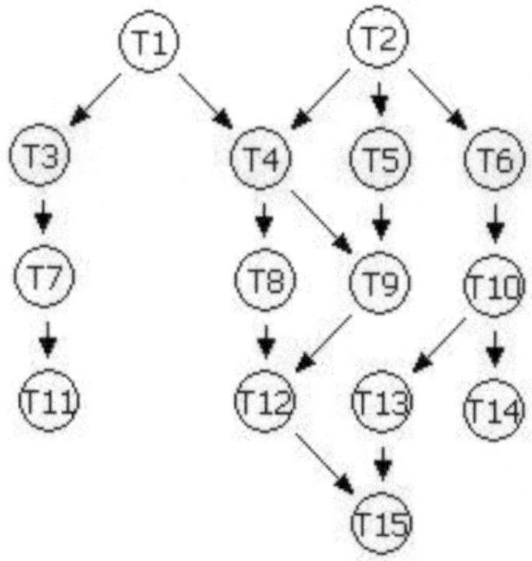

Figure 5. Graph of tasks used for the comparison of ACO algorithm with Coffman and Graham algorithm (test problem no 1).

- Optimal scheduling for two processors obtained as a result of Coffman and Graham algorithm use (1a).

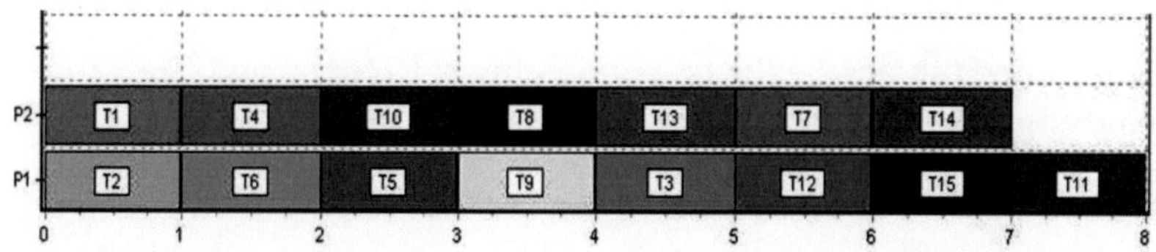

Figure 6. Optimal scheduling for two processors - Coffman and Graham algorithm (1a).

- Optimal scheduling for two processors obtained as a result of ACO algorithm use (1a).

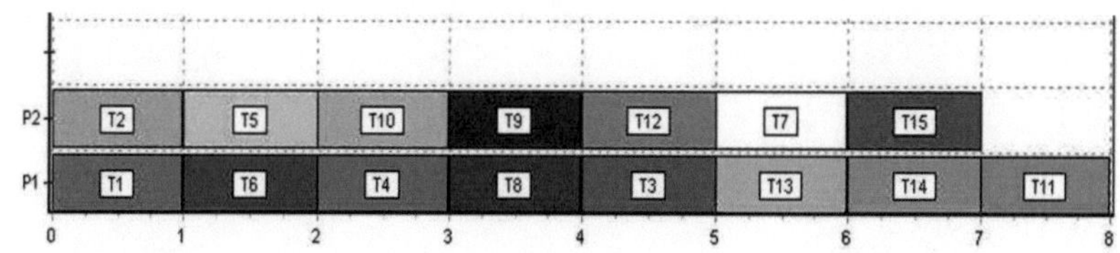

Figure 7. Optimal scheduling for two processors - ACO algorithm (1a).

- Scheduling for three processors obtained as a result of Coffman and Graham algorithm use (1b).

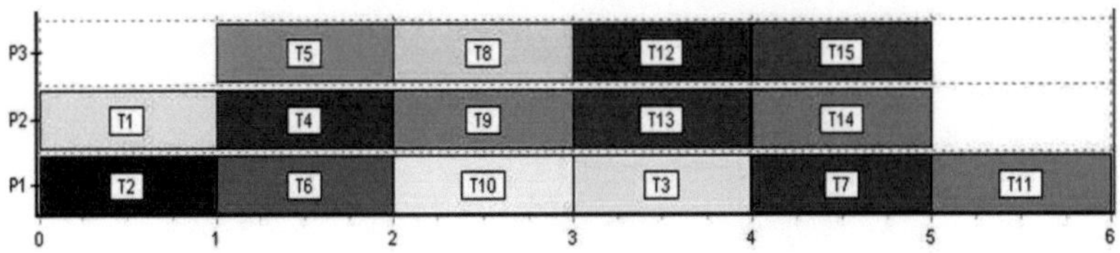

Figure 8. Problem scheduling for 3 processors - Coffman and Graham algorithm use (1b).

- Scheduling for three processors obtained as a result of ACO algorithm use (1b).

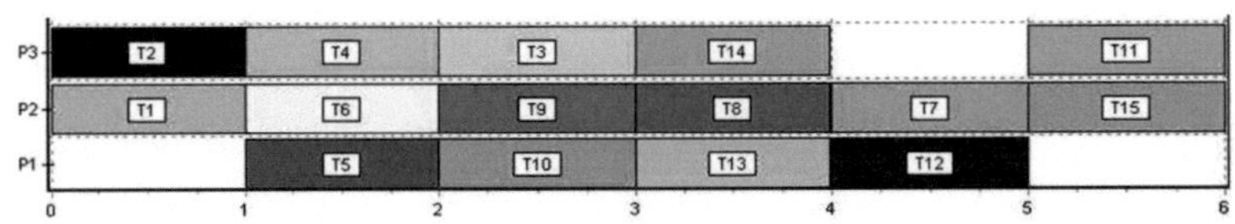

Figure 9. Optimal problem scheduling for 3 processors – ACO algorithm (1b).

For two processors (1a) ACO algorithm identical to Coffman and Graham algorithm obtained optimal scheduling. It was the same in the case of three processors (1b) – both algorithms obtained the same scheduling. Coffman and Graham algorithm is optimal only for two identical processors. For task graph under research it also found optimal scheduling for 3 identical processors.

Another test problem is shown by the non-optimality of Coffman and Graham algorithm for processor number greater than 2.

Test problem no 2:

- 2 identical processors (a), 3 identical processors (b)
- 12 tasks with singular performance times.
- Graph of tasks:

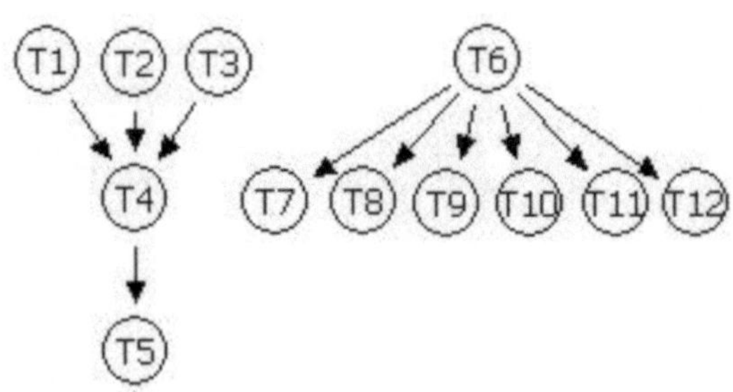

Figure 10. Graph of tasks used for the comparison of ACO algorithm with Coffman and Graham algorithm (test problem no 2).

• Optimal scheduling for two processors obtained as a result of Coffman and Graham algorithm use (2a).

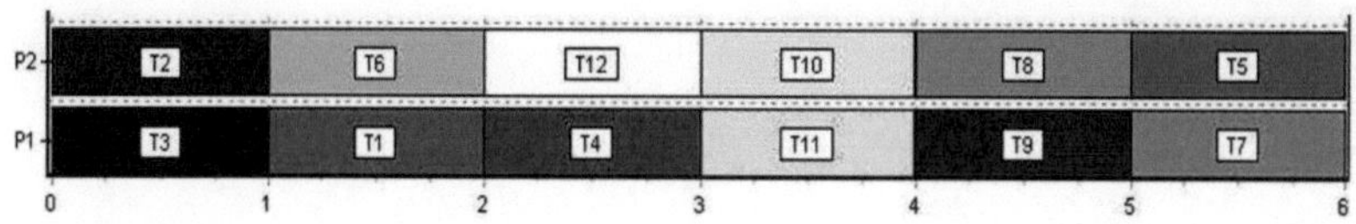

Figure 11. Optimal scheduling for 2 processors - Coffman and Graham algorithm (2a).

• Optimal scheduling for two processors obtained as a result of ACO algorithm use (2a).

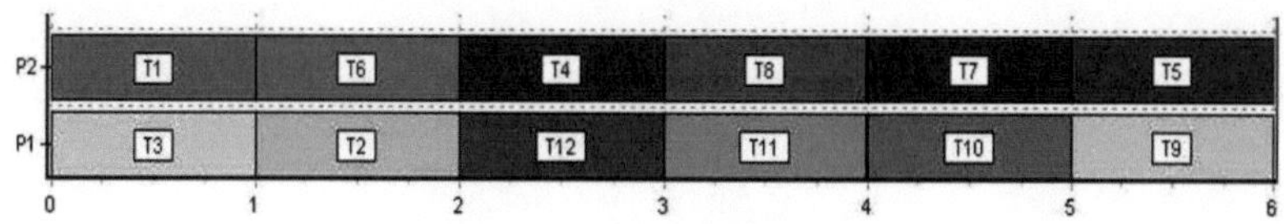

Figure 12. Optimal scheduling for 2 processors - ACO algorithm (2a).

• Non-optimal scheduling for three processors obtained as a result of Coffman and Graham algorithm use (2b).

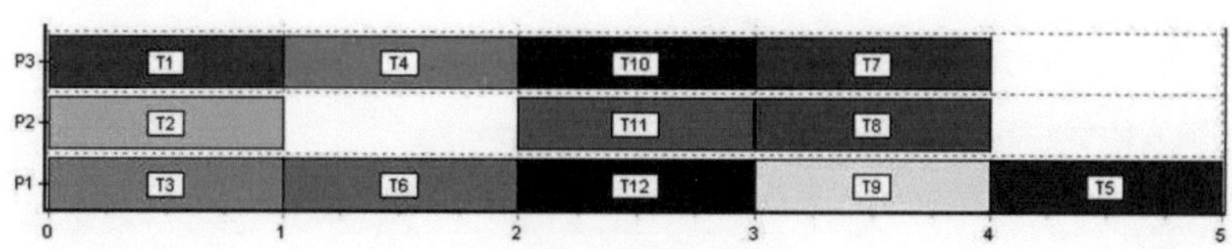

Figure 13. Non-optimal scheduling for 3 processors – Coffman and Graham algorithm (2b).

• Optimal scheduling for three processors obtained as a result of ACO algorithm use (2b).

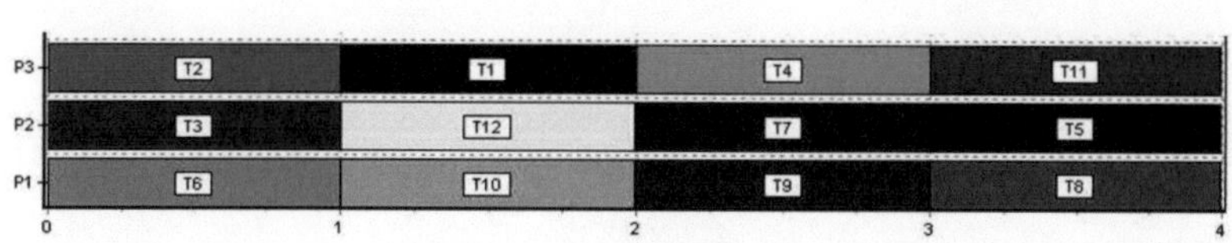

Figure 14. Optimal scheduling for 3 processors - ACO algorithm (2b).

For the problem of two processors (2a) both algorithms obtained optimal scheduling. In the case of three processors (2b) the Coffman and Graham algorithm did not find optimal scheduling, whereas the ACO algorithm did find it without any difficulty.

In another test example both algorithms were compared for the problem of task scheduling on two identical processors with singular and different performance times.

Test problem no 3:

- 2 identical processors.
- 5 tasks with singular performance times (a), 5 tasks with different performance times (b)
- Graph of tasks:

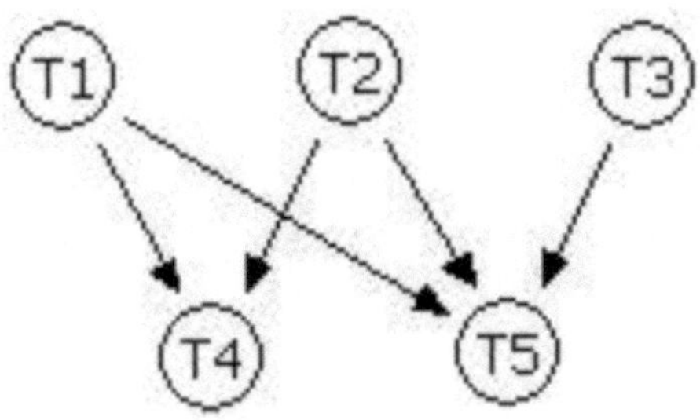

Figure 15. Graph of tasks used for the comparison of ACO algorithm with Coffman and Graham algorithm (test problem no 3)

- Optimal scheduling for singular task performance times obtained as a result of Coffman and Graham algorithm use (3a).

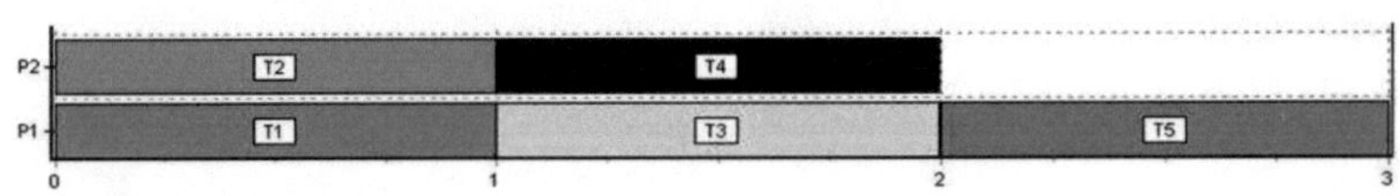

Figure 16. Optimal problem scheduling for singular task performance times – Coffman and Graham algorithm (3a)

- Optimal scheduling for singular task performance times obtained as a result of ACO algorithm use (3a).

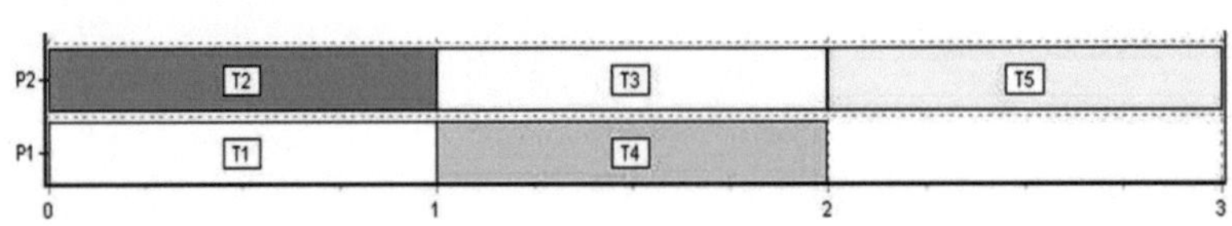

Figure 17. Optimal problem scheduling for singular task performance times – ACO algorithm (3a)

- Non-optimal scheduling for irregular task performance times obtained as a result of Coffman and Graham algorithm use (3b).

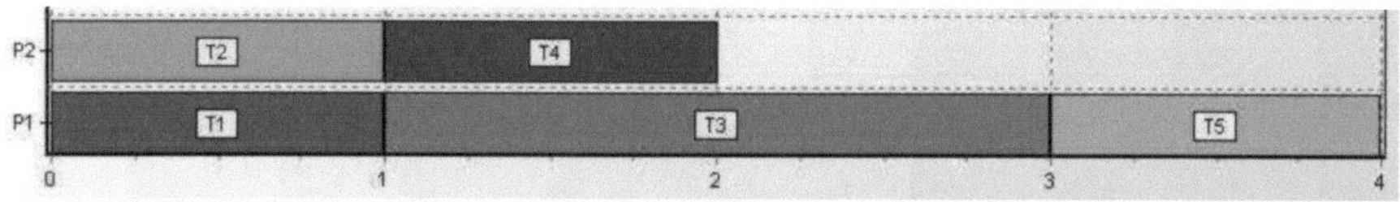

Figure 18. Non-optimal problem scheduling for irregular task performance times – Coffman and Graham algorithm (2b)

- Optimal scheduling for irregular task performance times obtained as a result of ACO algorithm use (3b):

Figure 19. Optimal problem scheduling for irregular task performance times – ACO algorithm (3b)

Both compared algorithms obtain optimal scheduling for the problem with regular (singular) task performance times (3a). For different task performance times (3b) the Coffman and Graham algorithm does not obtain optimal scheduling, whereas the ACO algorithm does obtain.

Hu algorithm

Scheduling of tasks with singular performance times which create a digraph of anti-tree type on identical processors in order to minimize C_{max}. Algorithm complexity is O(n).

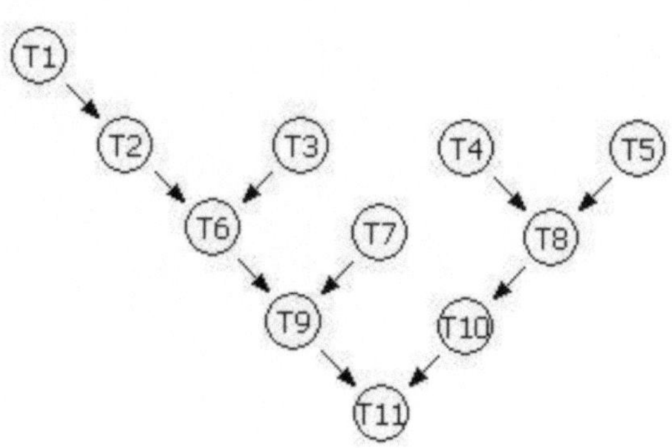

Figure 20. Graph of tasks used for the comparison of ACO and Hu algorithms.

Test problem no 1:

- 3 identical processors,
- 11 tasks with singular performance times,

- Graph of tasks (anti-tree):
- Optimal scheduling for problem 1 obtained as a result of Hu algorithm use:

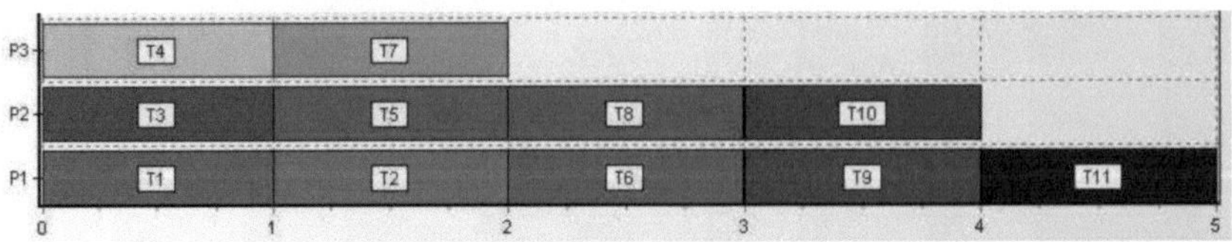

Figure 21. Optimal scheduling for problem 1 solved with Hu algorithm.

- Optimal scheduling for problem 1 obtained as a result of ACO algorithm use.

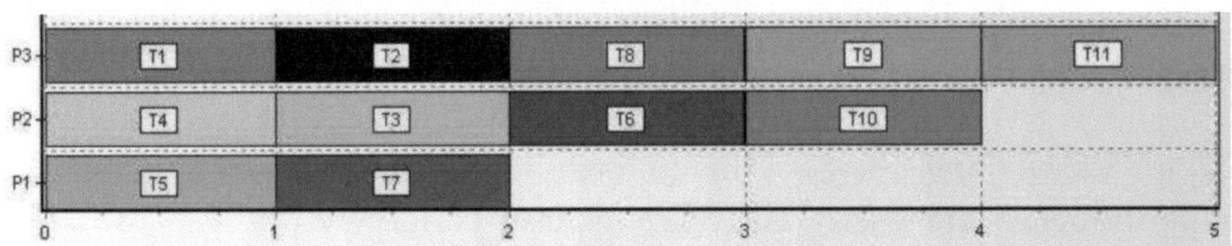

Figure 22. Optimal scheduling for problem 1 solved with ACO algorithm.

Test problem no 2:

- 3 identical processors,
- 12 tasks with singular performance times,
- Graph of tasks (anti-tree):

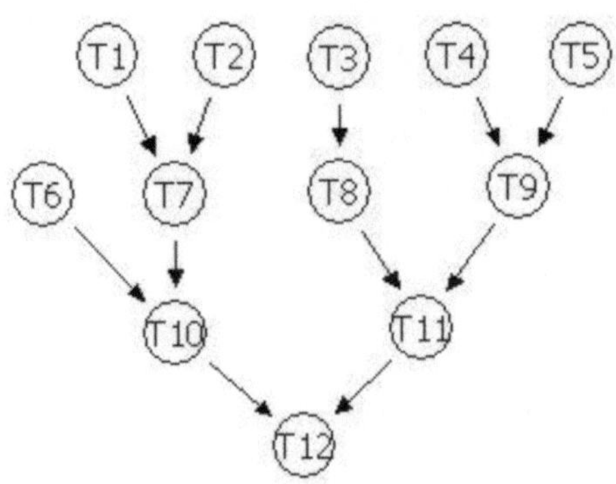

Figure 23. Graph of tasks used for the comparison of ACO and Hu algorithms (test problem no 2)

- Optimal scheduling for problem 2 obtained as a result of Hu algorithm use.

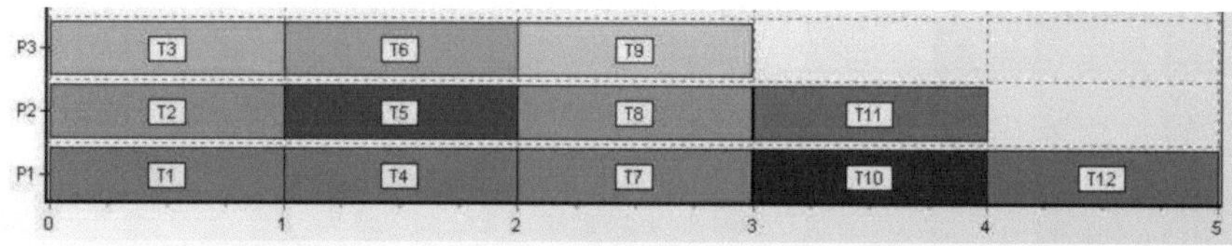

Figure 24. Optimal scheduling for problem 2 solved with Hu algorithm

- Optimal scheduling for problem 2 obtained as a result of ACO algorithm use.

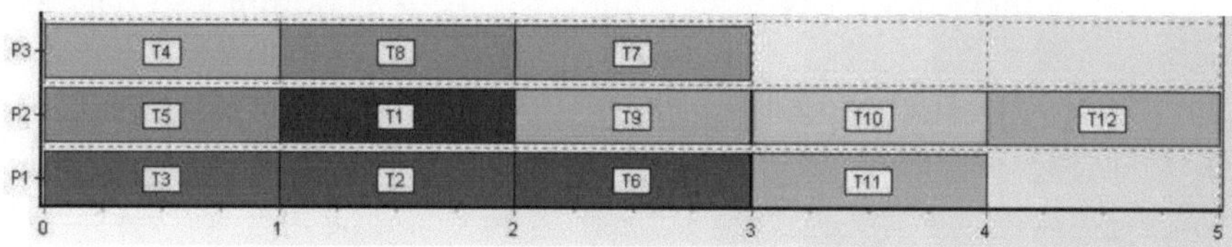

Figure 25. Optimal scheduling for problem 2 solved with ACO algorithm

Both problems solved with Hu algorithm were also solved easily by ACO algorithm. Scheduling obtained is optimal.

Baer algorithm

Scheduling of indivisible tasks, with singular performance times, which create a graph of anti-tree type on two uniform processors in order to minimize C_{max}.

Test problem:

- 2 uniform processors with speed coefficients $b_1 = 2$, $b_2 = 1$.
- 11 tasks with singular performance times.
- Graph of tasks (anti-tree):

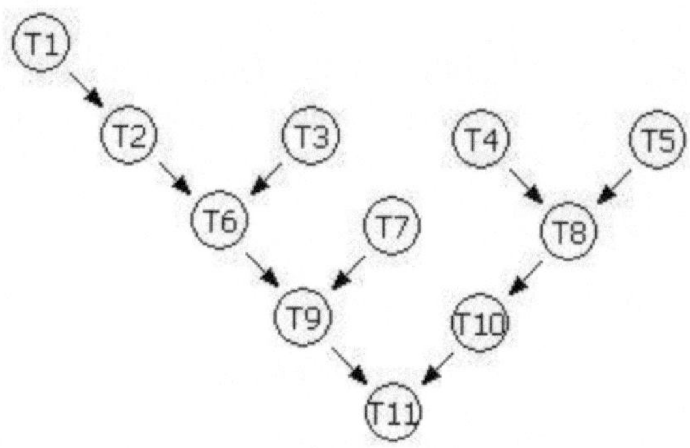

Figure 26. Graph of tasks used for the comparison of ACO and Baer algorithms.

- Optimal scheduling for the problem solved with Baer algorithm, obtained as a result of ACO algorithm use.

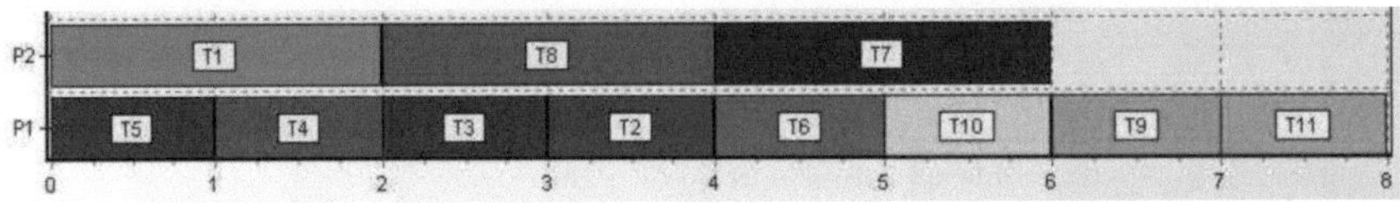

Figure 27. Optimal scheduling for the problem solved with Baer algorithm, obtained as a result of ACO algorithm use

For the problem optimized with Baer algorithm, the ACO algorithm also obtains optimal solution.

4.2. Comparison of algorithms for non-polynomial problems of task scheduling

4.2.1. NP- complete problem no 1:

Scheduling *nonpreemptive,* independent tasks on identical processors for C_{max} minimization.

Number of tasks	Number of processors	Cmax Neural Algorithm	Cmax ACO Algorithm
5	3	4	4
10	3	9	8
10	6	4	4
20	3	15	16
20	6	9	8
20	8	7	6

Table 1. Scheduling nonpreemptive, independent tasks on identical processors.

For all problems under research algorithms found similar solutions. Only neural algorithm did worse – for the problem of scheduling 10 tasks on 3 identical processors, 20 tasks on 6 processors and 20 tasks on 8 processors as well ACO algorithm for the problem of scheduling 20 tasks on 3 identical processors.

4.2.2. NP-complete problem no 2:

List scheduling with various methods of priority allocation

Because in general case the problem of scheduling dependent, nonpreemptable tasks is highly NP-complete, in some applications one can use polynomial approximate algorithms. Such algorithms are list algorithms.

In the chapter five types of list scheduling rules were compared: HLFET (Highest Levels First with Estimated Times), HLFNET (Highest Levels First with No Estimated Times), RANDOM, SCFET (Smallest Co-levels First with Estimated Times), SCFNET (Smallest Co-levels First with No Estimated Times) [12].

The number of cases, in which the solution differs less than 5% from optimal solution, is accepted as an evaluation criterion for the priority allocation rule. If for 90% of examined examples the sub-optimal solution fit in the above range, the rule would be described as "almost optimal". This requirement is met only by HLFET rule, which gives results varying from optimum by 4,4% on average.

Example:

- 2 identical processors.
- 12 tasks with different performance times: (Z0,1), (Z1,1), (Z2,7), (Z3,3), (Z4,1), (Z5,1), (Z6,3), (Z7,2), (Z8,2), (Z9,1), (Z10,3), (Z11,1).
- Graph of tasks:

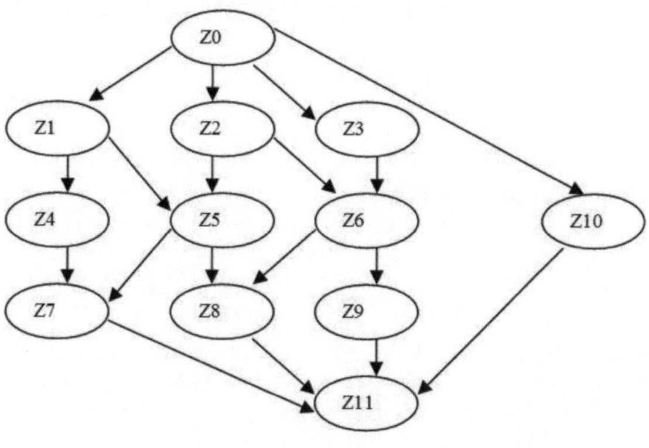

Figure 28. The graph of tasks used for the comparison of ACO and list algorithms

Scheduling obtained as a result of ACO algorithm operation.

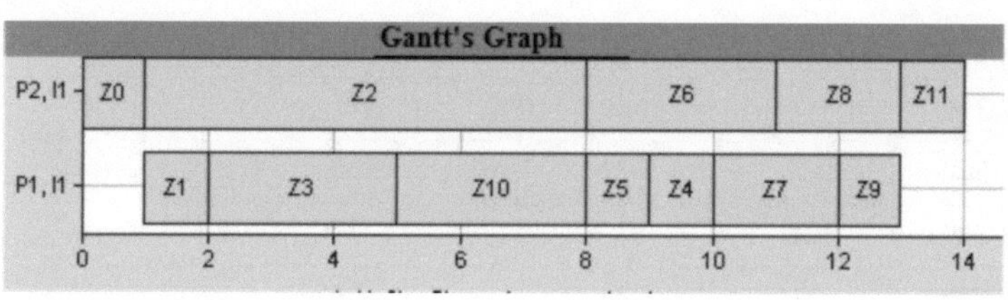

Figure 29. Scheduling obtained with ACO algorithm.

The length of obtained scheduling is compliant with the scheduling which was obtained by means of the best list scheduling available for this case and which is HLFET ("almost optimal").

4.2.3. Comparison with PDF/HIS algorithm

For research purposes a set of graphs was utilized from the website below: http://www.kasahara.elec.waseda.ac.jp/schedule/index.html. Task graphs made available therein were divided into groups because of the number of tasks. Minimum scheduling length was calculated by means of PDF/HIS algorithm (Parallelized Depth First/ Implicit Heuristic Search) for every tasks graph. STG graphs are vectored, a-cyclic tasks graphs. Different task performance times, discretionary sequence constraints as well as random number of processors cause STG tasks scheduling problems to be NP-complete problems. Out of all solved problems heuristic algorithms under research did not find an optimal solution (assuming this is the solution obtained with PDF/IHS algorithm) only for three of them. However, results obtained are satisfactory, because the deviation from optimum varies from 0,36% to 4,63% (table Tab 2).

STG	**Num-ber of tasks**	**Number of processors**	**PDF/ IHS**	**Ant colony**			**Neural**		
			C_{max}	C_{max}	Number of iterations	Diffe-rence [%]	C_{max}	**Number of itera-tons**	Diffe-rence [%]
rand0008	50	2	281	281	117	0	281	80	0
rand0038	50	4	114	114	1401	0	114	818	0
rand0107	50	8	155	155	389	0	155	411	0
rand0174	50	16	131	131	180	0	131	190	0
rand0017	100	2	569	569	171	0	569	92	0
rand0066	100	4	253	253	4736	0	257	3644	1,58
rand0106	100	8	205	205	861	0	205	927	0
rand0174	100	16	162	162	265	0	162	216	0
rand0020	300	2	827	846	5130	2,30	830	4840	0,36
rand0095	300	8	382	394	5787	3,14	384	5253	0,52
rand0136	300	16	324	339	2620	4,63	324	3067	0

Table 2. Comparison with PDF/IHS algorithm – the influence of tasks number

Algorithms were investigated by scheduling tasks represented with the same graph (50 STG tasks) on a different number of processors.

Number of tasks	**Number of processors**	**PDF/IHS**	**Ant colony**		**Neural**	
		C_{max}	C_{max}	Number of iterations	C_{max}	Number of iterations
50	2	228	228	132	228	92
50	4	114	114	1401	114	925
50	8	57	61	4318	58	4442
50	16	48	48	58	48	33

Table 3. Minimization of C_{max} of dependent tasks (STG rand0008.stg)

Number of tasks	**Number of processors**	**PDF/IHS**	**Ant colony**		**Neural**	
		C_{max}	C_{max}	Number of iterations	C_{max}	Number of iterations
50	2	267	267	388	267	412
50	4	155	157	4487	160	3339
50	8	155	154	89	155	112
50	16	155	155	10	155	8

Table 4. Minimization of C_{max} of dependent tasks (STG rand0107.stg)

In all researched problems algorithms under comparison found optimal solution. The only difference can be observed in the number of iterations needed to find an optimal solution. ACO algorithm needed less iterations than neural one to find the solution.

5. Comparing ACO algorithm and neural algorithm

For multiple criteria optimization in the following tests comparisons were made of compromise solutions for ACO algorithm with the results of neural algorithm. Optimization criteria were: time, cost and power consumption. Additional requirements and constraints were adopted: maximum number of processors – 5, maximal cost – 3, maximal time – 25.

Number of tasks	Ant colony			Neural		
	Cost	Time	Power consumption	Cost	Time	Power consumption
5	1,75	6,75	9,26	1,00	3,90	4,39
10	1,50	6,20	35,47	1,50	8,50	11,61
15	2,75	18,00	22,96	2,00	16,00	17,85
20	1,75	12,83	35,45	2,00	22,50	20,31
25	2,00	14,50	51,25	2,00	22,00	28,93
30	2,75	16,90	63,58	2,50	23,00	35,01
35	2,00	18,00	78,30	2,50	24,67	36,12
40	2,75	17,75	104,68	2,50	17,00	72,52
45	2,25	21,75	99,50	2,50	18,67	79,02
50	2,25	23,88	113,26	2,50	21,00	88,57
55	2,50	25,00	164,58	2,50	22,50	95,33

Table 5. Comparison of Ant Colony and neural for minimization of time, cost and power consumption.

Results were illustrated on the following charts – Chart: 30, 31, and 32.

When comparing solutions obtained by the algorithms one cannot provide an unequivocal answer which of the optimization methods is better. Greater influence on the quality of offered solutions has the algorithm itself, especially its exploration capacity of admissible solutions space. When analyzing the graphs of interdependence between cost and task number, it appears that neural algorithm is more stable i.e. attempts to maintain low cost, despite an increase in the number of tasks. This results in worse task performance time what is very visible on the graph where time is contingent on the number of tasks. From power consumption analysis it is evident that ACO algorithm solutions are more beneficial.

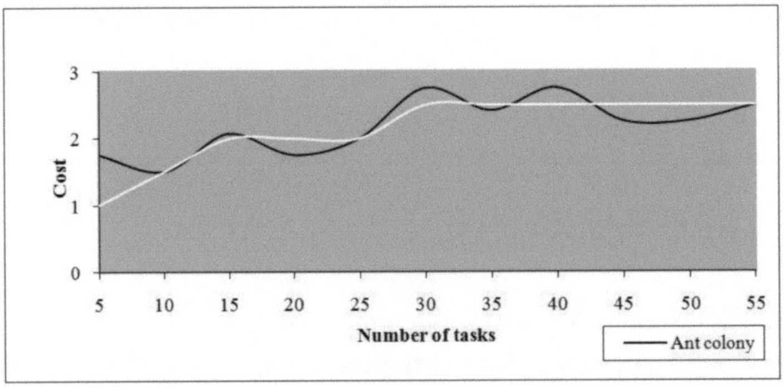

Chart 30. Influence of number tasks on cost – minimization of time, cost and power consumption .

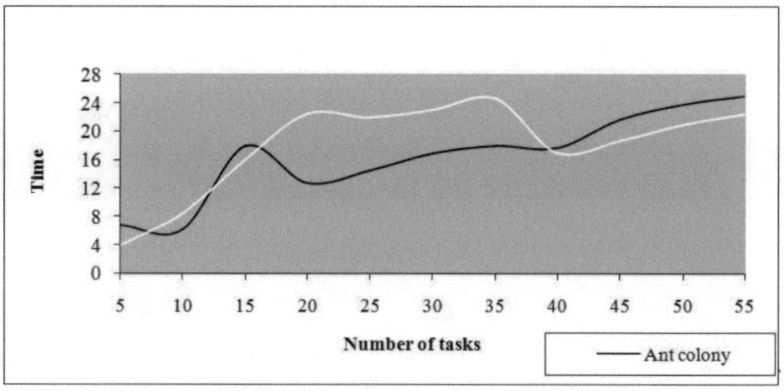

Chart 31. Influence of number of tasks on time – minimization of time, cost and power consumption.

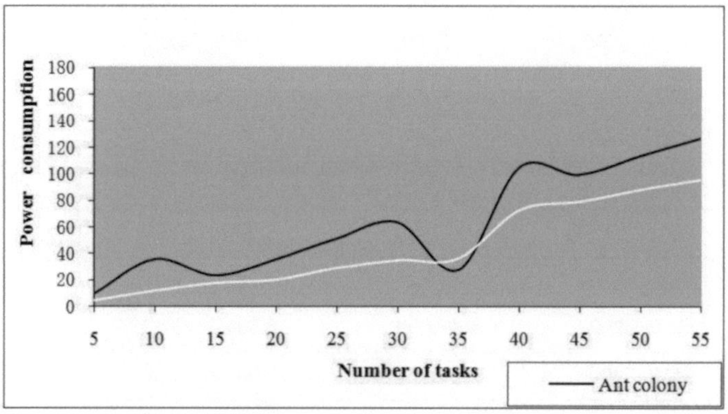

Chart 32. Influence of number of tasks on power consumption – minimization of time, cost and power consumption.

Additional requirements and constraints were adopted: maximum number of processors: 5, maximal cost: 8, maximal time: 50.

Results were illustrated in the following charts - Chart: 33, 34, and 35.

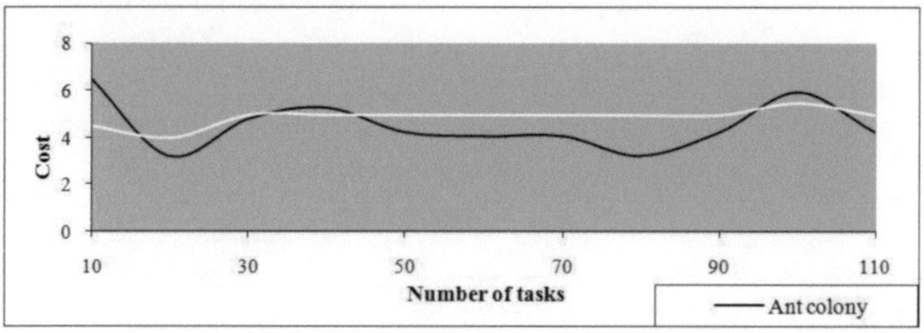

Chart 33. Influence of number of tasks on cost – minimization of time, cost and power consumption with of cost of memory.

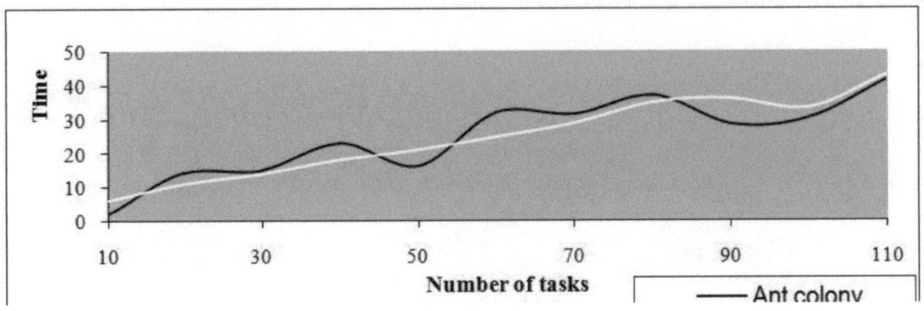

Chart 34. Influence of number of tasks on time – minimization of time, cost and power consumption with of cost of memory.

Number of tasks	Ant colony			Neural		
	Cost	Time	Power consumption	Cost	Time	Power consumption
10	6,50	2,00	37,99	4,50	6,00	7,52
20	1,50	18,50	33,15	4,00	11,00	19,07
30	5,90	23,00	82,41	5,00	14,00	30,98
40	7,00	23,00	121,56	5,00	18,00	37,33
50	4,25	16,20	186,05	5,00	21,00	49,99
60	2,50	32,00	175,24	5,00	25,00	60,20
70	2,50	38,00	167,59	5,00	29,00	69,35
80	3,25	37,00	183,67	5,00	32,00	79,19
90	4,25	28,60	328,73	5,00	36,00	98,39
100	6,75	30,33	336,36	5,50	39,00	101,62
110	4,25	41,80	435,77	5,00	43,00	115,53

Table 6. Comparison of Ant colony and neural for minimization of time, cost and power consumption.

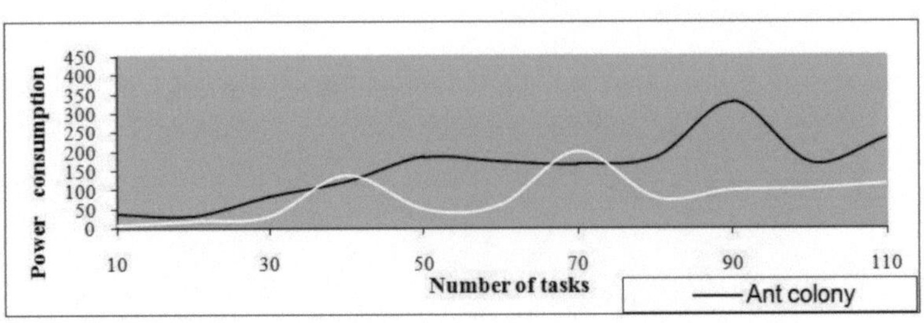

Chart 35. Influence of number of tasks on power consumption – minimization of time, cost and power consumption with memory cost

http://dx.doi.org/10.5772/51487

6. Conclusions

Conducted research shows that presented algorithms for task scheduling obtain good solutions - irrespectively of investigated problem complexity. These solutions are considered optimal or sub-optimal whose deviation from optimum does not exceed 5%. Heuristic algorithms proposed for task scheduling problems, especially ACO, should be a good tool for supporting planning process.

One should indicate a possible and significant impact of anomalies in task scheduling on the quality of the obtained results. The following examples [12] show a possibility of appearing such anomalies. Take an example of this digraph of tasks:

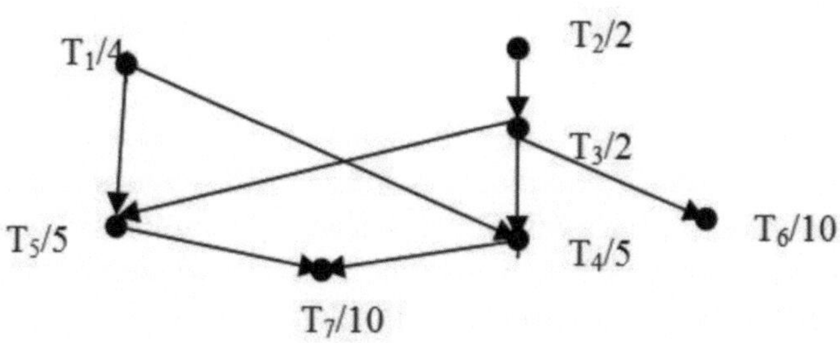

•

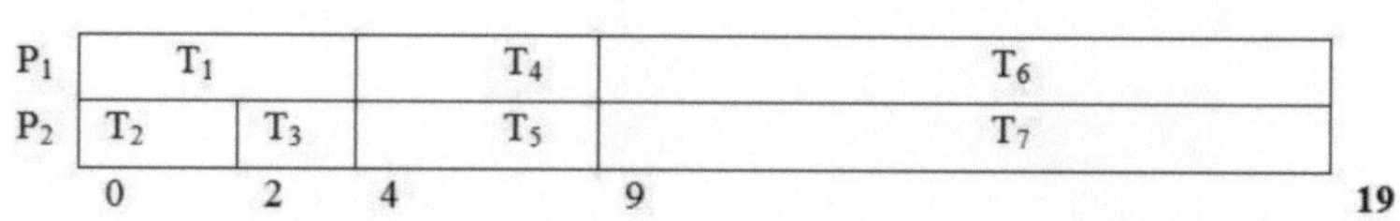

- Diminishing of performance time for all the tasks $t_i' = t_i - 1$ and the scheduling is longer than optimum scheduling (independently from choice list!):

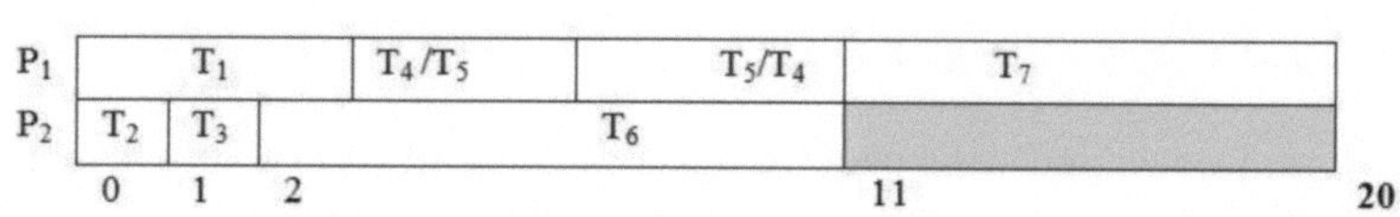

For different problem instances, particular algorithms may achieve different successes; others may achieve worse results at different numbers of tasks. The best option is to obtain results of different algorithms and of different runs.

The goal of this scheduling is to find an optimum solution satisfying the requirements and constraints enforced by the given specification of the tasks and resources as well as criteria.

As for the optimality criteria for the manufacturing system for better control, we shall assume its minimum cost, maximum operating speed and minimum power consumption.

We will apply multi-criteria optimization in sense of Pareto. The solution is optimized in sense of Pareto if it is not possible to find a better solution, regarding at least one criterion without deterioration in accordance to other criteria. The solution dominates other ones if all its features are better. Pareto ranking of the solution is the number of solutions in a pool which do not dominate it. The process of synthesis will produce a certain number of non-dominated solutions. Although non-dominated solutions do not guarantee that they are an optimal Pareto set of solutions; nevertheless, in case of a set of suboptimal solutions, they constitute one form of higher order optimal set in sense of Pareto and they give, by the way, access to the problem shape of Pareto optimal set of solutions.

Let's assume that we want to optimize a solution of two contradictory requirements: the cost and power consumption Fig. 36.

While using a traditional way with one optimization function, it is necessary to contain two optimal criteria in one value. To do that, it is advisable to select properly the scales for the criteria; if the scales are selected wrongly, the obtained solution will not be optimal. The chart in the illustration shows where, using linearly weighed sum of costs, we will receive the solution which may be optimizes in terms of costs.

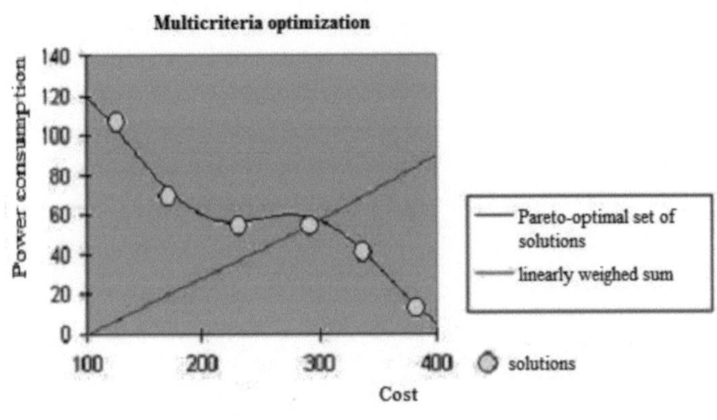

Figure 36. Set of optimal solutions in sense of Pareto.

Cost optimization, power and time consumption in the problem of scheduling is, undoubtedly, the problem where the potential number of solutions in sense of Pareto is enormous.

Future research: others of instances of scheduling problems, and additional criteria, especially in sense of Pareto and for dependable systems, are still open and this issue is now studied.

Author details

Mieczysław Drabowski[1*] and Edward Wantuch[1,2]

*Address all correspondence to: drabowski@pk.edu.pl

1 Cracow University of Technology, Poland

2 AGH University of Science and Technology, Poland

References

[1] Aggoune, R. (2004). Minimizing the makespan for the flow shop scheduling problem with availability constraints. *Eur. J. Oper., Res.*, 153, 534-543.

[2] Ostfeld, Avi. (2011). Any Colony Optimization. *Rijeka, Croatia, InTech.*

[3] Błażewicz, J., Drabowski, M., & Węglarz, J. (1984). Scheduling independent 2-processor tasks to minimize schedule length. *Inform. Proce. Lett.*, 18, 267-273.

[4] Błażewicz, J., Ecker, K., Pesch, E., Schmidt, G., & Węglarz, J. (1996). Scheduling Computer and Manufacturing Processes. *Springer.*

[5] Błażewicz, J., Ecker, K., Pesch, E., Schmidt, G., & Węglarz, J. (2007). Handbook on Scheduling, From Theory to Applications. *Springer-Verlag Berlin Heidelberg.*

[6] Blum, C. (2005). Beam-ACO- Hybridizing ant colony optimization with bean search: An application to open shop schedling. *Comput. Oper. Res.*, 32, 1565-1591.

[7] Blum, C., & Sampels, M. (2004). An ant colony optimization algorithm for shop scheduling problems. *Journal of Mathematical Modeling and Algorithm*, 3, 285-308.

[8] Breit, J., Schmidt, G., & Strusevich, V. A. (2003). Non-preemptive two-machine open shop scheduling with non-availability constraints. *Math. Method Opr. Res.*, 57(2), 217-234.

[9] Brucker, P. (2004). Scheduling Algorithms. *Springer.*

[10] Brucker, P., & Knust, S. (2006). Complex Scheduling. *Springer.*

[11] Cheng, T. C. E., & Liu, Z. (2003). Approximability of two-machine no-wait flowshop scheduling with availability constraints. *Opr. Res. Lett.*, 31, 319-322.

[12] Coffman, E. G. Jr. (1976). Computer and Job-shop scheduling theory. *John Wiley&Sons, Inc. New York.*

[13] Colak, S., & Agarwal, A. (2005). Non-greedy heuristiad augmented neural networks for the open-shop scheduling problem. *Naval Res. Logist.*, 52, 631-644.

[14] Dechter, R., & Pearl, J. (1988). Network-based heuristic for constraint satisfaction problems. *Artificial Intelligence*, 34, 1-38.

[15] Dorndorf, U., Pesch, E., & Phan-Huy, T. (2000). Constraint propagation techniques for disjunctive scheduling problems. *Artificial Intelligence*, 122, 189-240.

[16] Drabowski, M., & Wantuch, E. (2006). Coherent Concurrent Task Scheduling and Resource Assignment in Dependable Computer Systems Design,. *International Journal of Reliability Quality and Safety Engineering, World Scientific Publishing,*, 13(1), 15-24.

[17] Drabowski, M. (2007). Coherent synthesis of heterogeneous system- an ant colony optimization approach. *Proceedings of Artificial Intelligence Studies, Vol.4 (89)/2007, supported by IEEE, Siedlce*, 65-74.

[18] Drabowski, M. (2007). The ant colony in par-synthesis of computer system. *Proceedings of the 11th IASTED International Conference on Artificial Intelligence and Soft Computing, Palma de Mallorca, ACTA Press, Anaheim, USA*, 244-249.

[19] Drabowski, M. (2007). Coherent synthesis of heterogeneous system- an ant colony optimization approach. *Studia Informatica*, 2.

[20] Drabowski, M. (2007). An Ant Colony Optimization to scheduling tasks on a grid. *Polish Journal of Environmental Studies*, 16(5B).

[21] Drabowski, M. (2008). Solving Resources Assignment and Tasks Scheduling Problems using Neural Networks. *Artificial Intelligence Studies*, 2.

[22] Drabowski, M. (2008). Neural networks in optimization scheduling resources and processes for management on a grid. *Polish Journal of Environmental Studies*, 17(4C).

[23] Drabowski, M. (2009). Ant Colony and Neural method for scheduling of complex of operations and resources frameworks- comparative remarks. *Proceedings of the IASTED International Conference on Computational Intelligence, Honolulu, USA, ACTA Press, Anaheim, USA*, 91-97.

[24] Drabowski, M. (2011). Ant Colony Optimization for coherent synthesis of computer system. *Ostfeld A., (ed.) Ant Colony Optimization, InTech, Croatia, Austria, India*, 179-204.

[25] Garey, M. R., & Johnson, D. S. (1979). Computers and intractability: A guide to the theory of NP-completeness,. *San Francisco, Freeman.*

[26] Ha, S., & Lee, E. A. (1997). Compile-Time Scheduling of Dynamic Constructs in Dataflow Program Graphs,. *IEEE Trans. On Computers*, 46(7).

[27] Leung, J. Y. T. (2004). Handbook on Scheduling: Algorithms, Models and Performance Analysis,. *Chapman&Hall, Boca Raton.*

[28] Lee, C. Y. (1996). Machine scheduling with an availably constraint. *J. Global Optim.*, 9, 363-384.

[29] Lee, C. Y. (2004). Machine scheduling with availably constraints. *Leung J.Y.T. Handbook of Scheduling, CRC Press*, 22, 1-22.

[30] Meseguer, P. (1989). Constraint satisfaction problems: An overview. *AICOM*, 2, 3-17.

[31] Montgomery, J., Fayad, C., & Petrovic, S. (2006). Solution representation for job shop scheduling problems in ant colony optimization. *LNCS*, 4150, 484-491.

[32] Morton, T. E., & Pentico, D. W. (1993). Heuristic Scheduling System. *Wiley, New York.*

[33] Nuijten, W. P. M., & Aarts, E. H. L. (1996). A computational study of constraint satisfaction for multiple capacitated job shop scheduling. *European J. Oper. Res.*, 90, 269-284.

[34] Pinedo, M. (2001). Scheduling Theory, Algorithms, and Systems,. *Prentice Hall, Englewood Cliffs, N.J.*

[35] Taillard, E. (1993). Benchmarks for basic scheduling problems. *European J. Oper. Res.*, 64, 278-285.

[36] Tsang, E. (1993). Foundations of Constraint Satisfaction. *Academic Press, Essex.*

[37] Wang, C. J., & Tsang, E. P. K. (1991). Solving constraint satisfaction problems using neural-networks,. *IEEE Second International Conference on Artificial Neural Networks.*

[38] Xu, J., & Parnas, D. L. (1993). On Satisfying Timing Constraints in Hard-Real-Time Systems. *IEEE Trans. on Software Engineering*, 19(1), 70-84.

Chapter 7

Traffic-Congestion Forecasting Algorithm Based on Pheromone Communication Model

Satoshi Kurihara

Additional information is available at the end of the chapter

http://dx.doi.org/10.5772/52563

1. Introduction

The growth of **i**ntelligent **t**ransport **s**ystems (ITS) has recently been quite fast and impressive, and various kinds of studies on ITS from the viewpoint of artificial intelligence have also been done [1][2][3][4][5]. However, there are still many problems that need to be solved and alleviating traffic congestion is one of the main issues. Reducing traffic congestion is quite urgent because the amount of money lost due to congestion within only 1 km in Tokyo has reached as much as 400 million yen per year. To alleviate this situation, two traffic-control systems called the "**V**ehicle **I**nformation and **C**ommunication **S**ystem (VICS)" and "the probe **c**ar **s**ystem (PCS)" are currently in operation in Japan.

VICS is a telecommunication system that transmits information such as that on traffic congestion and the regulation of traffic by detecting car movements with sensors installed on the road [6]. Information on car movements and that on forecasting traffic congestion are analyzed at the VICS center in real time and then the information from the center is displayed on equipment, such as car-navigation systems installed in individual cars (see Fig. 1).

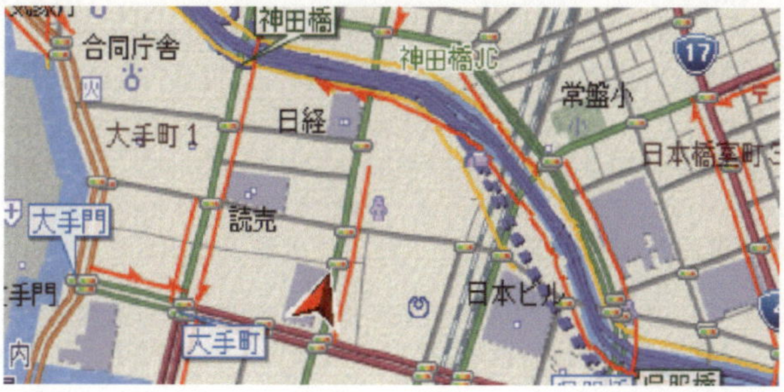

Figure 1. VICS

INTECH
open science | open minds

PCS also provides information on car movements and that on forecasting traffic congestion to individual drivers the same as VICS does. Different from VICS, this system collects traffic information from all cars, which are considered to be movable sensor units. Each car has a telecommunication unit and transmits several kinds of information such as position, velocity, and the status of the car to the central server. Then, the calculated car-movement and traffic-congestion-forecasting information are analyzed and the information from the center is displayed on equipment, such as car-navigation systems.

Though these two systems are currently operated in Japan, the system structure of both systems is top down and centralized, so the reaction to dynamic changes in traffic congestion and occurrence of accidents is usually delayed and serious problems can occur when the central server is down. In other words, there is a lack of real-time features and of robustness in these systems.

On the other hand, traffic-control systems like ITS and PCS essentially have interesting features for the coordination mechanisms of multi-agent systems (MASs). The coordination mechanisms of MAS can generally be divided into two types: direct and indirect. In the former, precise coordination can be achieved, but when the number of agents becomes excessive the load of coordination becomes extreme. The coordination for the latter is usually called "stigmergy". Stigmergy is a generic name for mechanisms that provide spontaneous, indirect coordination between agents, where the influence in the environment left by the behavior of one agent stimulates the performance of a subsequent action of this agent or a different agent [7]. Since direct coordination is unnecessary in stigmergy, this mechanism can work in situations with massive numbers of agents. However, there is no guarantee that optimal coordination can be achieved. Therefore, how to create optimal coordination using stigmergy is an ambitious topic for research.

Moreover, traffic-control systems essentially have an interesting feature for the system architecture of MASs. Each agent in a MAS usually behaves to achieve a MAS goal regardless of its local or global views, and no agent behaves selfishly for its own gain. Of course, the goal of agents in a market-based environment is their own gain and basically they do behave selfishly. However, in the MAS for traffic-control systems, two competitive goals need to be achieved: the "goal of each agent" and the "goal of the MAS".

In the MAS for a traffic-control system each agent, which controls each car[1], wants to behave selfishly to achieve its goal, e.g., optimal-route navigation by considering the shortest route and the avoidance of congestion. Therefore, each agent in the ITS is in a competitive situation similar to the conventional game environment in a MAS. However, the goal for the MAS itself is stability and optimizing the traffic-control system. That is, eliminating traffic congestion and minimizing the average travel time of all cars to attain a smooth traffic flow. To achieve these goals, it may be necessary to restrict the behavior of each agent. Consequently, the goal of each agent and the goal of the MAS have a competitive relation, and ITS is a very interesting application for the MAS.

In the VICS and PCS currently operated in Japan, congestion information and congestion-forecasting information are updated every 5 min. In other words, VISC or PCS cannot forecast less than five minutes ahead. Since traffic data from sensors and cars are collected at the central server and calculations are done by using all the data, this process

[1] A system that interacts with a human driver to lead him to a destination as in a car-navigation system.

http://dx.doi.org/10.5772/52563

needs a certain amount of time. Therefore, we propose a new congestion-forecasting system that can react to dynamically changing traffic conditions based on a coordination mechanism using the pheromone-communication model. Its main feature is to be able to forecast short-term congestion one or two minutes ahead. There have been many studies on ITS [8][9][10], but there have been few on the forecasting of short-term congestion.

Section 2 discusses traffic-congestion information for car agents and proposes a method of forecasting congestion that uses a multi-agent coordination mechanism for road agents set up at intersections based on a pheromone-communications model, which adaptively responds to increasing amounts of congestion. Section 3 discusses our tests to verify the basic effectiveness of this method. Finally, we conclude this paper in Section 4.

2. Method of forecasting congestion based on pheromone-communications model

Congestion-forecasting technology is one of the main elements of ITS. Up to now, several methods have been proposed, two of which are classified below.

- Long-term forecasting of congestion: A method of statistically analyzing past traffic data, and discovering a pattern where congestion has occurred [13].
- Short-term forecasting of congestion: A method of forecasting congestion a few minutes ahead by using real-time information.

Although it can effectively make forecasts under regular-congestion conditions that have originated from car and road situations, a large amount of past data is necessary for analysis. Moreover, it has weaknesses in forecasting under irregular-congestion conditions, such as those experienced during the Golden-week holidays in Japan and the Christmas-holiday season in the U.S.

VICS and PCS essentially belong to the second classification, and is excellent at short-term forecasting of congestion. Yet, in the current VICS and PCS that is operating in Japan, data from each car is collected at the central server and all calculations are done there. Consequently, it is difficult to supply real-time information due to bottlenecks and time lags in communicating information and the centralized calculations.

For solving these problems, a short-term system of forecasting congestion based on distributed processing is adequate. This paper focuses on "roads", and we propose a MAS consisting of many road agents. These road agents are set up at every intersection, and they coordinate locally with one another to forecast congestion. In this research, we adopted the pheromone-communications model as the mechanism for coordination.

Pheromone communications are based on the behavior of social insects like ants and bees and are applied as a model that is used to adaptively respond to dynamic changes in the environment in various applications [12] (see Fig. 2). Our method is an effective way of forecasting congestion in which each road agent generates pheromone information on its own road unit and exchanges this information with its neighboring agents. In a related study, Ando et al. investigated the forecasting of congestion in a local area a short time after pheromones had evaporated and diffused [11]. However, all drivers need to have the same probe-car system installed in their vehicles. Even though there has been some discussion on

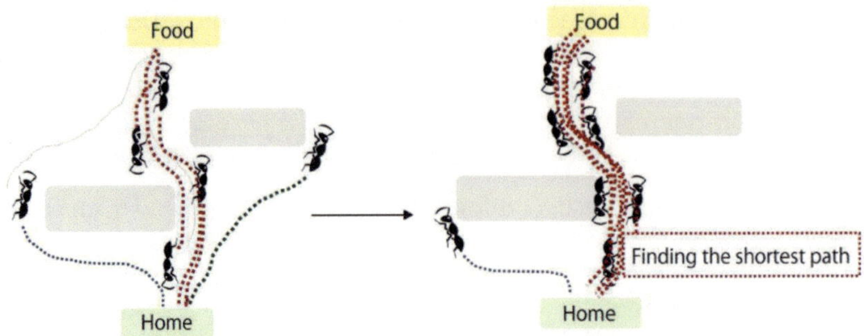

When one ant finds an advantageous path from the colony to food, others are more likely to follow that path, and positive feedback eventually leads all the ants to follow a single path.

Figure 2. Ant-colony optimization

information being shared, individual automobile manufacturers are currently developing their own probe-car systems and consequently the rate of diffusion of these probe-car systems is quite low. Therefore, we decided to develop a more realistic and universal system by focusing on the road and not the cars.

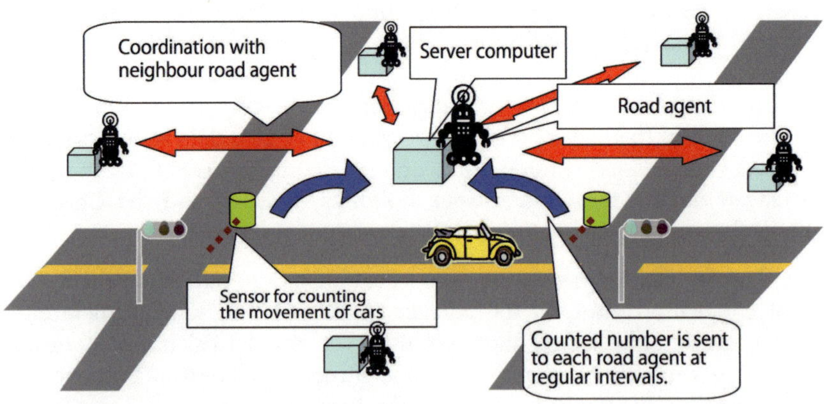

Figure 3. Structure of road environment

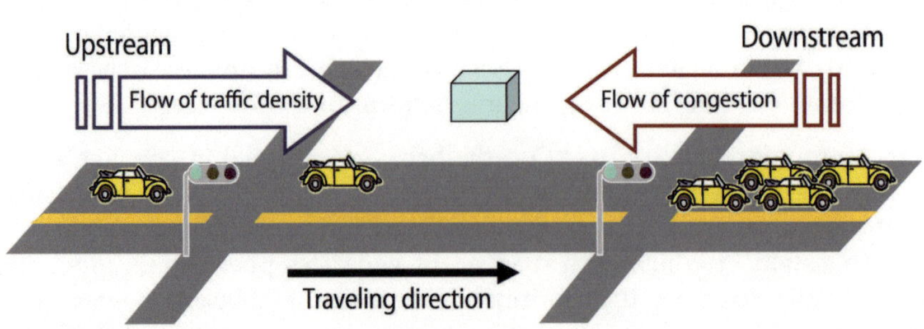

Figure 4. Two important flows in congestion dynamics

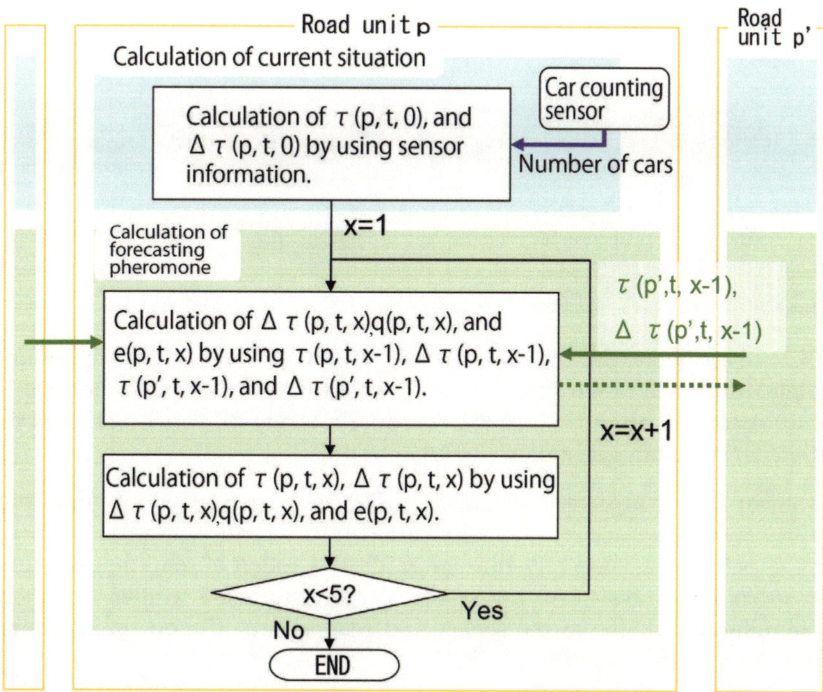

Figure 5. Flow chart for forecasting congestion

2.1. Congestion-forecasting algorithm

First, we will define the road environment as follows (see Fig. 3):

- A road unit is a section between two connected intersections. Each road unit consists of several lanes, usually in both directions, with no branching.
- The number of cars going through an intersection is counted by a sensor installed at each intersection, and this number is sent to each road agent installed on roadside server computers at regular intervals.
- The road agent installed in each roadside server computer calculates and forecasts the traffic congestion.

Therefore, central servers and probe-car systems are not necessary with our method.

A road unit on which a car is currently traveling is called "upstream", and a road unit that will be reached in the future is called "downstream". We focused on two important car-flow dynamics to investigate traffic congestion (see Fig. 4). The first was the flow in traffic density, which spreads from upstream to downstream, corresponding to the movement of cars. The second was the flow in traffic congestion, which spreads from downstream to upstream. At this point, the traffic congestion is defined as follows: a certain road unit becomes bottle-necked blocking the flow of cars. This blocking generates a queue of cars from downstream to upstream.

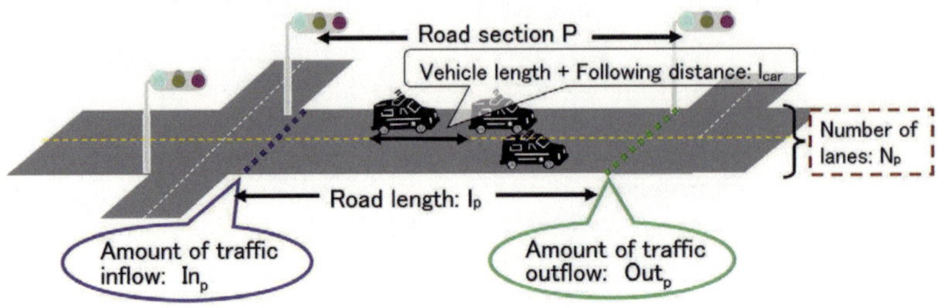

Figure 6. Calculation of current traffic situation

In this paper, we formulate the flow of traffic density using "traffic-density pheromones $\Delta\tau$" and formulate the growth of the queue using "congestion-diffusion pheromones q". To make forecasts more accurate, we introduce the "evaporation rate e", which indicates the change in congestion density from generation to dissolution.

Each road agent in our algorithm forecasts traffic congestion at one minute intervals, as shown in Fig. 5, where $\tau(p,t,x)$ is the forecasted traffic density of a road unit s at time t and $\Delta\tau(p,t,x)$ is the forecasted transition in traffic congestion of road unit s at time t. Even though the calculation interval for forecasting can be shortened further, this increases the load of communication between the sensor and road agent. The one-minute intervals are much shorter than the five minutes of VICS.

Forecasting one minute ahead is calculated through coordination between each agent and their adjacent neighbouring agents. And forecasting two or more minutes ahead is calculated through coordination between each agent and more dispersed neighbouring agents.

2.2. Calculation of the current traffic situation

The inflowing amount, $I(p,t)$, and outflowing number, $O(p,t)$, of cars at regular intervals t are measured with a sensor and are sent to road agents. $I(p,t)$ indicates how many cars flowed into a road unit, p, and $O(p,t)$ indicates how many flowed out of it. First, the road agent that receives this information calculates the traffic density as

$$N(p,t) = N(p,t-1) + I(p,t) - O(p,t) \tag{1}$$

$$d(p,t) = \frac{N(p,t) \times l_{car}}{l_p \times L_p} \tag{2}$$

where $N(p,t)$ is the number of cars, $d(p,t)$ is the traffic density at intervals t of a road unit, p, l_{car} is the length of a car[2], l_p is the length of the road unit, p, and L_p is the number of lanes of p (see Fig. 6).

[2] More precisely, the length of a car + the distance between two cars.

http://dx.doi.org/10.5772/52563

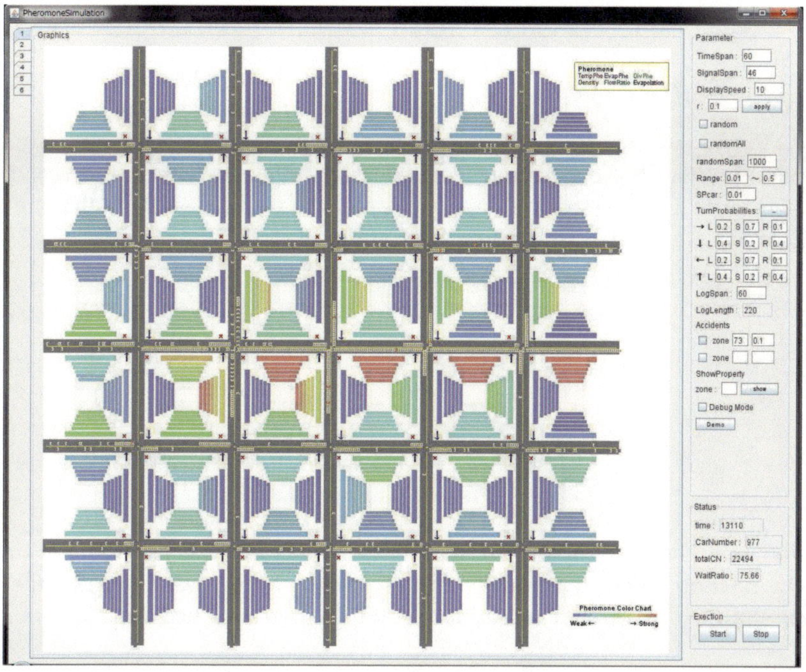

Figure 7. Traffic simulator

2.3. Calculation of congestion forecasting pheromone

Each road agent calculates the congestion forecasting pheromone, τ, which indicates the forecasted congestion density that will occur a few minutes ahead the current situation. $\tau(p,t,0) = d(p,t)$ and $\Delta\tau(p,t,0) = I(p,t) - O(p,t)$ are the initial values for this calculation. As Fig. 5 shows, the traffic-density pheromones $\Delta\tau(p,t,x)$, congestion-diffusion pheromones $q(p,t,x)$, and evaporation rate $e(p,t,x)$ are calculated using $\tau(p,t,x-1)$, $\Delta\tau(p,t,x-1)$, $\tau(p',t,x-1)$, and $\Delta\tau(p',t,x-1)$. At this point, $\tau(p',t,x-1)$ and $\Delta\tau(p',t,x-1)$ are given from the neighbouring road unit. Then, $\tau(p,t,x)$ is calculated.

(a) Calculation of traffic-density pheromones

As previously mentioned, the traffic density spreads from upstream to downstream, corresponding to the movement of cars. What is important is how fast this flow is transmitted, and we define the transmitting velocity of traffic density as $S(p,t,x)$.

$$S(p,t,x) = s_p \times bs_p \times jf(p,t,x) \tag{3}$$

Here, s_p is the distance that a car moves during a certain time span and this is calculated from the maximum legal speed limit of road unit p. bs_p is the proportion of time green lights are displayed in a signal cycle in the traveling direction of the car on this road. Moreover, $jf(p,t,x)$ is a congestion factor that shows the decreasing ratio of the transmitting velocity of traffic density due to the congestion.

$$jf(p,t,x) = \begin{cases} 1.0 & (\tau(p,t,x-1) < \alpha) \\ 1.0 - \tau(p,t,x-1) & (\tau(p,t,x-1) \geq \alpha) \end{cases} \tag{4}$$

α is a threshold where the congestion factor demonstrates the effect, and $\alpha = 0.5$ is used here. $S(p,t,x)$ indicates the transmission distance of the traffic density in the one time span, so the ratio of $S(p,t,x)$ and l_p is important.

$$\Delta\tau(p,t,x) = \sum_{p' \subset N_b} f(p,p') \times \Delta\tau'(p',p,t,x) \tag{5}$$

$$\Delta\tau'(p,t,x) = \begin{cases} \Delta\tau(p,t,x-1) \& (S(p,t,x) > l_p) \\ \frac{S(p,t,x)}{l_p} \times \Delta\tau(p,t,x-1) \& (S(p,t,x) \leq l_p) \end{cases} \tag{6}$$

where N_b indicates the set of upstream road units p and $f(p,p')$ is a parameter that changes based on the relation between p and p'. In this study, $f(p,p')$ was 0.7 when the road unit, $p' \rightarrow p$, was straight, 0.2 when it turned left, and 0.1 when it turned right.

(b) Calculation of congestion diffusion pheromones

As previously mentioned, traffic congestion spreads from downstream to upstream. Therefore, the congestion diffusion pheromones are defined based on the difference between the congestion level of the current road unit and the congestion level of the next road unit.

$$q(p,t,x) = \sum_{p'' \subset N_f} g(p,p'') \times q'(p'',p,t,x) \tag{7}$$

$$q'(p'',p,t,x) = \{\tau(p'',t,x-1) - \tau(p,t,x-1)\} \tag{8}$$

where N_f indicates the set of downstream road unit p, and $g(p,p'')$ is a parameter that changes based on the relation between p and p'', which is the same as $f(p,p')$.

	1 min ahead	3 min ahead	5 min ahead
Forecasting with pheromone method	0.98	0.94	0.91
Conventional forecasting	0.95	0.88	0.79

Table 1. Comparison of correlation coefficient between forecast and actual values due to changes in traffic density (forecasting 1 min ahead).

(c) Calculation of evaporation rate

As previously mentioned, the evaporation rate indicates the change in congestion density due to its generation and dissolution. That is, by referring to the degree of traffic change,

http://dx.doi.org/10.5772/52563

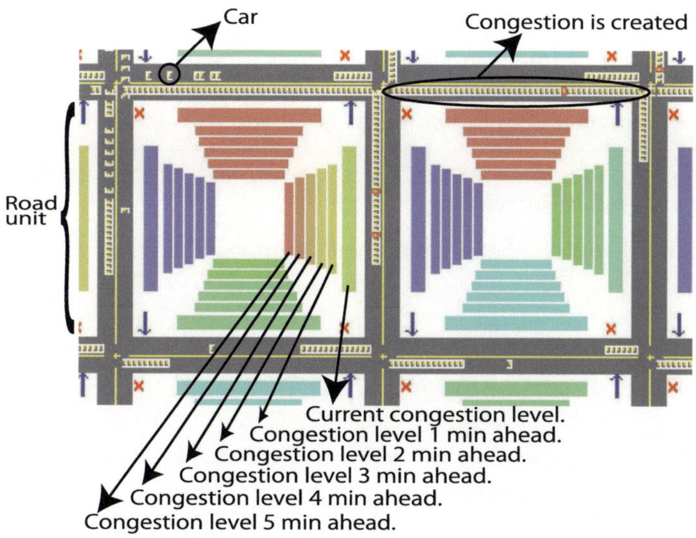

Figure 8. Forecasting scenario in simulator

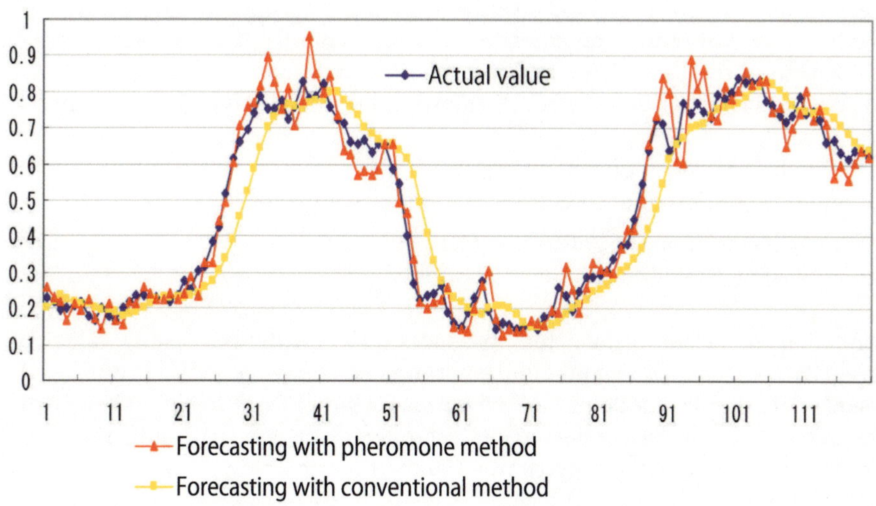

Figure 9. Comparison of congestion forecasting due to changes in traffic density (forecasting 1 min ahead).

$\Delta\tau(p,t,0) = I(p,t) - O(p,t)$, $\Delta\tau$ becoming larger than normal means that traffic congestion will occur. However, $\Delta\tau$ becoming smaller than normal means that traffic congestion is "evaporating". To determine the amount of normal traffic change on the road unit p, the decentralization, v_p, of this change is calculated using the data from a previous day.

$$e(p,t,x) = \begin{cases} \beta_1 \& (v(p,t,0) > x \times v_p) \\ 1.0 \& (-x \times v_p < v(p,t,0) < x \times v_p) \\ \beta_2 \& (v(p,t,0) < -x \times v_p) \end{cases} \tag{9}$$

The above expression shows that when the difference between the observed amount of traffic and the amount of traffic in normal conditions increases, the degree of congestion generation and congestion evaporation becomes big. β_1 and β_2 are parameters that indicate the degree of evaporation and in this study, β_1 is 1.1 and β_2 is 0.9.

(d) Calculating congestion-forecasting pheromones

The forecasting of congestion pheromones after x minutes is calculated from the above value as follows.

$$\tau(p,t,x) = e(p,t,x) \times \tau(p,t,x-1) + \Delta\tau(p,t,x) + q(p,t,x) \tag{10}$$

Each road agent forecasts short-term traffic congestion by sequentially and repeatedly calculating (a) to (d) from the above.

2.4. Simulations

To experimentally verify the basic effectiveness of our proposed forecasting model, we implemented a simple simulation environment and compared the accuracy of forecasting a few minutes ahead (i.e., one, three, and five minutes) with the proposed and a conventional method. We especially verified the effectiveness of our methodology in two respects, i.e.,

1. The forecasting accuracy of generation/dis-solution of congestion due to changes in traffic density and
2. The forecasting accuracy of generation/dis-solution of congestion due to sudden accidents.

The correlation coefficient of the actual measurements and the forecasting values was used for the evaluation, and the simulation environment shown in Fig. 7 was used for the experiment. This simple simulator had a 5 x 5 lattice structure with single-lane roads. There was one traffic signal at each intersection. The length of one road unit, i.e., the distance between two consecutive intersections, was 400 m.

In this experiment, we set $1time - step$ to $1sec$ and $1time - span$ to $60time - steps$. Each road agent calculated the traffic density on its own road unit every minute, and forecasted until 5 minutes ahead. To evaluate the effectiveness of the proposed method, we used a conventional method of short-term forecasting based on a statistical approach [8] and made forecasts 1, 3, and 5 min ahead.

This conventional forecasting approach was based on the assumption that the current congestion situation would generally continue for a few minutes. The current VICS and PCS update their congestion information every five minutes, so if we used this conventional method to forecast five minutes ahead, it could basically be thought of as using the same approach as VICS and PCS.

Fig. 8 is an expansion of part of the simulator used in executing the forecasts. We can see that one road agent forecasts congestion of its road unit that will not occur within 5 min but

http://dx.doi.org/10.5772/52563

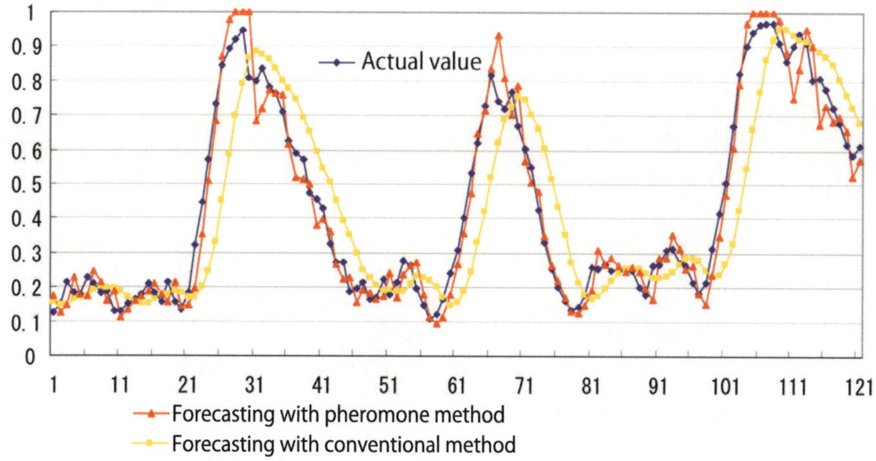

Figure 10. Comparison of congestion forecasts due to sudden accidents (forecasting 1 min ahead)

occur after this. On the other hand, we can also see that one agent forecasts congestion of its road unit that will continue for longer than 5 min.

	1 min ahead	3 min ahead	5 min ahead
Forecasting with pheromone method	0.98	0.94	0.86
Conventional forecasting	0.86	0.66	0.45

Table 2. Comparison of correlation coefficient between forecast and actual values due to sudden accidents

2.4.1. Congestion due to changes in traffic density

Traffic congestion is usually generated when more than the acceptable number of cars moves into a road unit. We carried out the simulation for about 2 hours and generated and evaporated congestion several times by changing the traffic density. We then compared our proposed method with the conventional approach by forecasting 1, 3, and 5 min ahead.

As a result, our proposed approach had a higher accuracy than the conventional method (Table 1). Fig. 9 shows the change in the actual traffic-congestion level (blue line) and the forecast congestion level 1 min ahead by using the conventional (yellow line) and our approach (red line). The change in the red line is similar to that in the blue line. The change in the yellow line, on the other hand, is delayed. Therefore, our proposed method can forecast congestion more accurately than the conventional approach.

2.4.2. Congestion due to sudden accidents

Next, we evaluated how accurately congestion could be forecast when sudden accidents occurred. This type of congestion does not happen based on changes in traffic density, but it occurs due to the decreased capacity of the roads to accommodate cars traveling along them. Since this decrease in capacity happens suddenly, the speed at which congestion is diffused is very rapid. In our simulation, we compared the effectiveness of our proposed method with that of the conventional approach by quickly changing the traffic density of a certain road unit. As Table 2 and Fig. 10 show, our proposed method is more accurate than the conventional scheme. Forecasting accuracy particularly worsened with the conventional method during long-term forecasts. However, we were able to maintain accurate forecasts with our method.

3. Conclusion

We proposed a method of forecasting congestion using a multi-agent coordination mechanism. A road agent installed at each intersection coordinates with its neighboring road agents based on the pheromone-communications model to adaptively respond to dynamically arising congestion and forecasts congestion a few minutes ahead. Here, we tested and verified the basic effectiveness of this method using simple simulation.

It is unnecessary in our approach to utilize a sufficient number of cars with the same probe system [8], or to upgrade the central server. At the very least, it needs to have simple sensors installed to count the number of cars moving through intersections, and small computers for road agents at these intersections. However, we have assumed that various kinds of computers, servers, and sensors will be installed in various locations to gather large amounts of information from the real world in about 5-10 years as part of urban scanning. Actually, small-scale real-world experiments are now being conducted in several locations throughout Japan [17]. These are based on the development of ubiquitous-information-communication technologies such as sensor-networks and wireless communication devices. In such situations, our method is expected to be quite practical. This evaluation was only done through simulation, and the road map used had a simple lattice structure. However, as we have already obtained detailed road data and VICS/PCS data throughout the entire country of Japan, we can shortly begin to evaluate our method using these real-world data.

As for traffic light control, all traffic lights need to react to dynamic changes in traffic in real time [14][15][16] in traffic-light-control systems, which are also the primary systems for controlling traffic. However, the current system cannot respond to dynamic changes in road conditions in real time even though some automatic control occurs according to the traffic flow. We also plan to develop a new traffic-light-control algorithm based on a MAS.

Author details

Satoshi Kurihara

Osaka University, Japan

References

[1] V. R. Tomás and L. A. Garcia: A Cooperative Multiagent System for Traffic Management and Control, The Fourth International Joint Conference on Autonomous Agents and Multiagent Systems (AAMAS-06), 2006.

[2] T. Nakata and J. Takeuchi: Mining Traffic Data from Probe-Car System for Travel Time Prediction, KDD'04, pp. 22-25, 2004.

[3] X.-H. Yu and W. W. Recker: Stochastic adaptive control model for traffic signal systems, Transportation Research Part C 14, pp. 263-282, Elsevier, 2006.

[4] K. Tufte, J. Li, D. Maier, V. Papadimos, R. L. Bertini, and J. Rucker: Travel Time Estimation Using NiagaraST and latte, SIGMOD'07, pp. 1091-1093, 2007.

[5] J.-D. Schmocker, S. Ahuja, and M. G. H. Bell: Multi-objective signal control of urban junctions - Framework and a London case study, Transportation Research Part C 16, pp. 454-470, 2008.

[6] http://www.vics.or.jp/english/index.html

[7] "Definitions of stigmergy." From a special Issue of Artificial Life on Stigmergy. Volume 5, Issue 2 / Spring 1999.

[8] P. G. Balaji, G. Sachdeva, D. Srinivasan, Multi-agent System based Urban Traffic Management, IEEE Congress on Evolutionary Computation 2007, pp. 1740–1747, 2007.

[9] Ana L. C. Bazzan, Opportunities for multiagent systems and multiagent reinforcement learning in traffic control, Autonomous Agents and Multi-Agent Systems, Vol. 18, No. 3, pp. 313–341, 2009.

[10] J. J. Sánchez-Medina and M. J. Gálan-Moreno and E. Rubio-Royo", Traffic Signal Optimization in La Almozara District in Saragossa Under Congestion Conditions, Using Genetic Algorithms, Traffic Microsimulation, and Cluster Computing, IEEE Transaction on Intelligent Transportation Systems, Vol. 11, No. 1. pp. 132–141, 2010.

[11] Y. Ando, Y. Fukazawa, O. Masutani, H. Iwasaki, and S. Honiden: Performance of Pheromone Model for Predicting Traffic Congestion, The Fifth International Joint Conference on Autonomous Agents and Multiagent Systems (AAMAS-06), 2006.

[12] M. Dorigo and G. di Caro: The ant colony optimization meta-heuristic, New ideas in optimization, McGrawHill, pp. 11-32, 1999.

[13] E. Chung: Classification of traffic pattern. Proceedings of the 11th World Congress on ITS, 2003.

[14] M. Wiering: Multi-Agent Reinforcement Learning for Traffic Light Control, Machine Learning, *Proceedings of the Seventeenth International Conference (ICML'2000)*, pp. 1151-1158, 2000.

[15] D. Oliveira, A. L. C. Bazzan, B. C. Silva, E. W. Basso, L. Nunes, and R. J. F. Rossetti, E. C. Oliveira, R. Silva, and L. C. Lamb: Reinforcement learning based control of traffic lights in non-stationary environments: A case study in a microscopic simulator, *Proc. of EUMAS06*, pp. 31-42, 2006.

[16] D. Oliveira, P. Ferreira, and A. L. C. Bazzan: Reducing traffic jams with a swarm-based approach for selection of signal plans, *Proc. ANTS 2004*, Vol. 3172 of LNCS, pp. 416-417, Berlin, Germany, 2004.

[17] http://uscan.osoite.jp/

Chapter 8

Ant Colony Algorithm with Applications in the Field of Genomics

R. Rekaya, K. Robbins, M. Spangler, S. Smith,
E. H. Hay and K. Bertrand

Additional information is available at the end of the chapter

http://dx.doi.org/10.5772/52051

1. Introduction

Ant colony algorithms (ACA) were first proposed by Dorigo *et al.* (1999) to solve difficult optimization problems, such as the traveling salesman, and have since been extended to solve many discrete optimization problems. As the name would imply, ACA are derived from the process by which ant colonies find the shortest route to a food source. Real ant colonies communicate through the use of chemicals called pheromones which are deposited along the path an ant travels. Ants that choose a shorter path will transverse the distance at a faster rate, thus depositing more pheromone. Subsequent ants will then choose the path with more pheromone creating a positive feedback system. Artificial ants work as parallel units that communicate through a cumulative distribution function (CDF) that is updated by weights, determined by the "distance" traveled on a selected "path", which are analogous to the pheromones deposited by real ants (Dorigo *et al.* 1999, Ressom *et al.* 2006). As the CDF is updated, "paths" that perform better will be sampled at higher likelihoods by subsequent artificial ants which, in turn, deposit more "pheromone", thus leading to a positive feedback system similar to the method of communication observed in real ant colonies. In the specific application of feature selection, the "path" chosen by an artificial ant is a subset of features selected from a larger sample space, and the "distance" traveled is some measure of the features performance.

The idea of selecting a sub-set of features capable of best classifying a group of samples can be, and has been, viewed as an optimization problem. The genetic algorithm (GA), simulated annealing (SA), and other optimization and machine learning algorithms have been applied to the problem of feature selection (Lin et al., 2006; Ooi and Tan, 2003; Peng et al., 2003; Albrecht et al., 2003). Though these methods are powerful, when dealing with thousands of features across multiple classes, the computational cost of these methods can be prohibitive. Previous results obtained with these methods when dealing with large numbers of features, utilized filters to reduce the dimension of the datasets prior to implementation (Lin et al., 2006; Peng et al., 2006), or have produced relatively low prediction accuracies (Hong and Cho, 2006). For ACA, the communication of the ants through a common memory has a synergistic effect that, when coupled with more efficient searching of the sample space though the use of prior information, results in optimal solutions being reached in far fewer iterations than required for GA or SA (Dorigo and Gambardella, 1997). The algorithm also lends itself to parallelization, with ants being run on multiple processors, which can further reduce computation time, making its use more feasible with high dimension data sets.

2. General presentation of ant colony algorithm

The ACA employs artificial ants that communicate through a probability density function (PDF) that is updated at-each iteration with weights or "pheromone levels", which are analogous to the chemical pheromones used by real ants. The weights can be determined by the strength of the association between selected feature and the response of interest. Using the notation in [Dorigo and Gambardella, 1997; Ressom et al., 2006], the probability of sampling feature m at time t is defined as:

$$P_m(t) = \frac{(\tau_m(t))^{\alpha} \eta_m{}^{\beta}}{\sum_{m=1}^{nf} (\tau_m(t))^{\alpha} \eta_m{}^{\beta}} \tag{1}$$

where $\tau_m(t)$ is the amount of pheromone for feature m at time t; $\eta_m$is some form of prior information on the expected performance of feature,α and β are parameters determining the weight given to pheromone deposited by ants and a priori information on the features, respectively.

Using the PDF as defined in equation (1), each of j artificial ants will select a subset S_k of n features from the sample space$S$ containing all features. The pheromone level of each feature m in S_k is then updated according to the performance of $S_k$as:

$$\tau_m(t+1) = (1-\rho) * \tau_m(t) + \Delta\tau_m(t) \tag{2}$$

where ρ is a constant between 0 and 1 representing the rate at which the pheromone trail evaporates; $\Delta\tau_m(t)$is the change in pheromone level for feature m based on the sum of accuracy of all S_k containing SNP m, and is set to zero if feature m was not selected by any of the artificial ants.

Although the general idea of the ACA is simple and intuitive, its application to solve real world applications requires some good heuristics in defining the pheromone functions and their updating. In this chapter, we are presenting three applications of the ACA in the field of genetics and genomics based on previously published research by our group [Robbins et al., 2007, Robbins et al., 2008; Spangler et al., 2008; Rekaya and Robbins, 2009; Robbins et al., 2011]. Specific implementation details for each application are added in the appropriate sections of the chapter.

2.1. Ant colony algorithm for feature selection in high dimension gene expression data for disease classification

The idea of using gene expression data for diagnosis and personalized treatment presents a promising area of medicine and, as such, has been the focus of much research (Bagirov et al., 2003; Golub et al., 1999, Ramaswamy et al., 2001). Many algorithms have been developed to classify disease types based on the expression of selected genes, and significant gains have been made in the accuracy of disease classification (Antonov et al., 2004; Bagirov et al., 2003). In addition to the development of classification algorithms, many studies have shown that improved performance can be achieved when using a selected subset of features, as opposed to using all available data (Peng et al., 2003; Shen et al., 2006; Subramani et al., 2006). Increases in accuracy achieved through the selection of predictive features can complement and enhance the performance of classification algorithms, as well as improve the understanding of disease classes by identifying a small set of biologically relevant features (Golub et al., 1999).

In this section the ACA was implemented using the high-dimensional GCM data-set (Ramaswamy et al., 2001), containing 16,063 genes and 14 tumor classes, with very limited pre-filtering, and compared to several other rank based feature selection methods, as well as previously published results to determine its efficacy as a feature selection method.

A.1 Latent variable model: A Bayesian regression model was used to predict tumor type in the form of a probability $p_{ic}(y_{ic}=1)$, with $y_{ic} = 1$ indicating that sample i is from tumor class c. The regression on the vector of binary responses y_c was done using a latent variable model (LVM), with l_{ic} being an unobserved, continuous latent variable relating to binary response y_{ic} such that:

$$y_{ic} = \begin{cases} 1 & \text{if } l_{ic} \geq 0 \\ 0 & \text{if } l_{ic} < 0 \end{cases}$$

The liability l_{ic} was modeled using a linear regression model as:

$$l_{ic} = \boldsymbol{X}_{ic}\boldsymbol{\beta}_c + e_{ic} \; E(l_{ic}) = \boldsymbol{X}_{ic}\boldsymbol{\beta}_c \; e_{ic} \sim N(0,\, 1)$$

where X_{ic} corresponds to row i of the design matrix X_c for tumor class c. The link function of the expectation of the liability $\boldsymbol{X}_{ic}\boldsymbol{\beta}_c$ with the binary response y_{ic} was constructed via a probit model (West, 2003) yielding the following equations:

$$p_{ic}(y_{ic}=1) = \boldsymbol{\Phi}(\boldsymbol{X}_{ic}\boldsymbol{\beta}_c) \text{ and } p_{ic}(y_{ic}=1) = 1 - \boldsymbol{\Phi}(\boldsymbol{X}_{ic}\boldsymbol{\beta}_c)$$

where Φ is the standard normal distribution function. Subject i was classified as having tumor class c if $p_{ic}(y_{ic}=1)$ was the maximum of the vector p_i, containing all $p_{ic}(y_{ic}=1)$ c=1,…, nc, where nc is the number of tumor classes in the data set.

A.2 Gene Selection: Filter and wrapper based methods were used to select features to form classifiers for each tumor class. Filter methods selected genes based on ranks determined by the sorted absolute values of fold changes (FC), t-statistics (T), and penalized t-statistics (PT) calculated for each gene for each tumor class. The wrapper method coupled the ACA with LVM (ACA/LVM) such that groups of genes were selected using the ACA and evaluated for performance using LVM.

A.3 Ant colony optimization: The general ACA presented in the previous section was used. The prior information, η_{mc}, was assumed as:

$$\eta_{mc} = \frac{\frac{f_{mc}-\min(\boldsymbol{f}_c)}{\max(\boldsymbol{f}_c)-\min(\boldsymbol{f}_c)} + \frac{t_{mc}-\min(\boldsymbol{t}_c)}{\max(\boldsymbol{t}_c)-\min(\boldsymbol{t}_c)} + \frac{pt_{mc}-\min(\boldsymbol{pt}_c)}{\max(\boldsymbol{pt}_c)-\min(\boldsymbol{pt}_c)}}{3}$$

where $\boldsymbol{f}_c$ is a vector of all fold change values for tumor class c; $\boldsymbol{t}_c$ is a vector of all t-statistic values for tumor class c; and $\boldsymbol{pt}_c$ is a vector of all penalized t-statistic values for tumor class c. After several trail runs the parameters α and β were set to 1 and.3 respectively.

The ACA was initialized with all features having an equal baseline level of pheromone used to compute $P_m(0)$ for all features. Using the PDF as defined in equation (1), each of j artificial ants will select a subset S_k of n features from the sample space S containing all features. The pheromone level of each feature m in S_k is then updated according to the performance of S_k following equation (2).

The procedure can be summarized in the following steps:

1. Each ant selects a predetermined number of genes.
2. Training data is randomly split into two subsets for training (TDS) and validation (VDS) containing ¾ and ¼ of the data, respectively (none of the original validation data (VD) is used at any point in the ACA).
3. Using the spectral decomposition of TDS, principle components are computed to alleviate effects of collinearity and selected for TDS and VDS by removing components with corresponding eigenvalues close to zero.
4. Using TDS, a latent variable model is trained for each tumor class, and $p_{ic}(y_{ic}=1)$ is predicted for every tumor class c for each sample i in VDS.
5. The accuracy for each tumor class c is calculated as:

$$acc_c = \frac{\sum_{i=1}^{nc} \Phi(\mathbf{P}_{ic}\beta_c) / nc + \sum_{i=1}^{nr} 1 - \Phi(\mathbf{P}_{ic}\beta_c) / nr}{2} \quad (3)$$

where $\boldsymbol{P}_{ic}$contains principle component values for sample i for tumor class c; $\boldsymbol{\beta}_c$is a vector of coefficients estimated using TDS; *nc* is the number of samples in VDS having tumor class *c*; and *nr* is the remaining number of samples in VDS.

6. The change in pheromone for each tumor class is calculated as:

$$\Delta \tau_{mc}(t) = acc_c^{(1-acc_c)}$$

where acc_c is the accuracy for tumor type c as calculated using equation (3).

Following the update of pheromone levels according to equation (2), the PDF is updated according to equation (1) and the process is repeated until some convergence criteria are met. As the PDF is updated, the selected features that perform better will be sampled at higher likelihoods by subsequent artificial ants which, in turn, deposit more "pheromone", thus leading to a positive feedback system similar to the method of communication observed in real ant colonies. Upon convergence the optimal subset of features is select based on the level of pheromone trail deposited on each feature.

A.4 GCM data set: The data set contained 198 samples collected from 14 tumor types: BR (breast adenocarcinoma), Pr (prostate adenocarcinoma), LU (lung adenocarcinoma), CO (colorectal adenocarcinoma), LY (lymphoma), BL (bladder transitional cell carcinoma), ML (melanoma), UT (uterine adenocarcinoma), LU (leukemia), RE (renal cell carcinoma), PA (pancreatic adenocarcinoma), OV (ovarian adenocarcinoma), ME (pleural mesothelioma), and CNS (central nervous system). The unedited data set contained the intensity values of 16063 probes generate using Affymetrix high density oligonucleotide microarrays, and calculated using Affymetrix GENECHIP software (Ramaswamy et al, 2001). Following the thresholding of intensity values to a minimum value of 20 and a maximum value of 16000, a log base 2 transformation was applied to the data set. Genes with the highest expression values being less than two times the smallest were removed, leaving 14525 probes for analysis.

A.5 Results and discussions: The GCM data set has been a benchmark to compare the performance of classification and feature selection algorithms. Table 1 shows the best prediction accuracies obtained by methods used in this study and several previous studies (GASS (Lin et al., 2006), GA/MLHD (Ooi and Tan, 2003), MAMA (Antonov et al., 2004), and GA/SVM (Liu et al., 2005)) using independent test, performed on the same training and validation data sets originally formed by Ramaswamy et al., 2001 (GCM split), and leave one out cross validation (LOOCV). The proposed ACA/LVM yielded substantial increases in accuracies over all other methods, with a 6.5% increase in accuracy over the next best results obtained using the GCM split (Antonov et al., 2004). Furthermore, the ACA/LVM achieved increases of 13.9%, 40%, and 16.6% in accuracy over the FC/LVM, T/LVM, and PT/LVM methods of feature selection, respectively.

GCM data set			
	GCM split[a]	Replicated splits	LOOCV[b]
ACA/LVM(14525[c])	90.7	84.8	___
FC/LVM(14525)	79.6	74.8	___
T/LVM(14525)	64.8	___	___
PT/LVM(14525)	77.8	74.4	___
AVG[d]/LVM(14525)	79.6	74.8	___
GASS(1000)	81.5	___	81.3
GA/MLHD(1000)	76	___	79.8
MAMA	85.2	___	___
GA/SVM(1000)	___	___	81

[a]Split used by Ramaswamy et al 2001; [b]Leave one out cross validation; [c]Number of genes selected prior to the implementation of feature selection algorithm; [d]Weighted average of scaled fold change, t-test, and penalized t-test values.

Table 1. Accuracy (%) of tumor class predictions using ant colony algorithm (ACA) and several previously published methods.

Due to its poor performance, the confusion matrix of predictions using T/LVM is not included, but matrices for the predictions obtained by the ACA/LVM, FC/LVM, and PT/LVM using the GCM split can be found in Tables 2-4. These tables show that the ACA/LVM performs as good or better than the rank based methods for every tumor type. Additionally the ACA/LVM correctly predicted 50% of the BR samples, a tumor class that has traditionally yielded very poor results (Bagirov et al., 2003; Ramaswamy et al., 2001). The ACA/LVM also achieved 100% prediction accuracy for 10 of the 14 tumor classes, as compared to only 7 and 8 when using FC/LVM or PT/LVM, respectively.

True\ Predicted	**BR**	**PR**	**LU**	**CO**	**LY**	**BL**	**ML**	**UT**	**LE**	**RE**	**PA**	**OV**	**ME**	**CNS**	
BR	2									1		1			4
PR	1	5													6
LU			4												4
CO				4											4
LY					6										6
BL		1				2									3
ML							2								2
UT								2							2
LE									6						6
RE										3					3
PA				1							2				3
OV												4			4
ME													3		3
CNS														4	4
	1	6	4	6	6	7	2	2	6	3	1	2	4	4	49/54

Table 2. Confusion matrix for predictions obtained for the GCM data set using genes selected by the ant colony algorithm.

True\ Predicted	**BR**	**PR**	**LU**	**CO**	**LY**	**BL**	**ML**	**UT**	**LE**	**RE**	**PA**	**OV**	**ME**	**CNS**	
BR	0					3		1							4
PR	1	5													6
LU			3							1					4
CO				4											4
LY					6										6
BL		1				2									3
ML							2								2
UT								2							2
LE									6						6
RE										2	1				3
PA				1		1					1				3
OV						1						3	1		4
ME													3		3
CNS														4	4
	1	6	4	6	6	7	2	2	6	3	1	2	4	4	43/54

Table 3. Confusion matrix for best predictions obtained for the GCM data set using genes selected by the fold change (50 genes)

True\ Predicted	**BR**	**PR**	**LU**	**CO**	**LY**	**BL**	**ML**	**UT**	**LE**	**RE**	**PA**	**OV**	**ME**	**CNS**	
BR	0					3				1					4
PR	1	5													6
LU			4												4
CO				4											4
LY					6										6
BL		1				2									3
ML							2								2
UT								2							2
LE									6						6
RE										2	1				3
PA				2		1					0				3
OV						1						2	1		4
ME													3		3
CNS														4	4
	1	6	4	6	6	7	2	2	6	3	1	2	4	4	42/54

Table 4. Confusion matrix for best predictions obtained for GCM data set using genes selected by the penalized t-test (10 genes)

To further evaluate performance, each of the feature selection algorithms was tested using four additional random splits of the data. The best classification accuracies obtained for each algorithm can be found in Table 5. The ACA/LVM algorithm yielded the best prediction accuracies for all replicates, with increases in accuracies ranging from 6.7% to 14% over the best accuracies obtained by filter methods. When looking at the three filter methods it can be seen that the best method varied depending on the replication. These findings are in agreement with Jefferey et al. (2006).

Replication	1	2	3	4	5
ACA/LVM	90.7	83.3	79.6	81.5	88.9
FC/LVM	79.6	77.8	68.5	72.2	75.9
PT/LVM	77.8	77.8	66.7	68.5	81.5
AVG[b]/LVM	79.6	70.4	70.4	70.4	83.3

[a] Split used by Ramaswamy et al 2001; [b]Weighted average of scaled fold change (FC),

t-test (PT), and penalized t-test values (PT).

Table 5. Classification accuracies using several feature selection methods

Due to a lack of any good criterion for determining an objective cut-off value for the rank based methods, several values were used and evaluated. Since the use of fewer features is desirable from a biological standpoint, an upper limit of 50 genes per tumor class was imposed on all methods. Table 6 shows the number of genes needed for each tumor type to achieve the best results, averaged across all replicates. It can be seen that, for 10 of the 14 tumor classes, the ACA/LVM selects fewer genes than the rank based methods.

The performance of the ACA/LVM model was superior, not only to the filter based methods used in this study, but also several reported results using the GCM data set. The ACA/LVM consistently yielded superior accuracies using fewer genes than the filter based methods, for which ranks varied with each replication. The breaks in pheromone levels observed with the most predictive genes also provided more objective selection criteria for identifying top features, unlike the filter methods in which truncation points were somewhat arbitrary. The objective selection criteria and robustness of the ACA, within the confines of the GCM data set, make it a superior method for clinical applications, as it could enable a single procedure to be effectively applied to varied applications. The use of filter based methods in such scenarios would require different combinations of truncation points and scoring methods for each data set, a highly impractical endeavor.

	BR	PR	LU	CO	LY	BL	ML	UT	LE	RE	PA	OV	ME	CNS
ACA	3.4	4.8	2	7.8	6.6	19.6	4.6	7.6	3.2	16	14.6	17.2	5	5.6
FC	18	18	18	18	18	18	18	18	18	18	18	18	18	18
PT	14	14	14	14	14	14	14	14	14	14	14	14	14	14
Average[a]	18	18	18	18	18	18	18	18	18	18	18	18	18	18

[a] Weighted average of scaled fold change (FC), t-test, and penalized t-test (PT) values

Table 6. Number of genes selected for each tumor type using ACA and other feature selection methods.

The superiority of the ACA/LVM when compared to models using GA indicates the ACA's utility, as compared to other optimization methods, when working with high dimension data sets. The ACA's ability to incorporate prior information in the optimization process provides several advantages over other optimization algorithms when dealing with large numbers of features. The inclusion of prior information in the pheromone function focuses the selection process on genes that should yield better results without the need for an explicit truncation of the data, which was needed to achieve good results with the GA (Hong and Cho, 2006; Lin et al., 2006; Liu et al., 2005; Ooi and Tan et al., 2003; Peng et al., 2003). Truncation of large numbers of genes could a priori eliminate genes from consideration that, though they may not have high predictive ability alone, could contribute to the predictive power of an ensemble of genes. Additionally, depending on the method of truncation, the reduced gene list could be highly redundant (Lin et al., 2006; Shen et al., 2006), further reducing the informativeness of pre-selected genes. Conversely, when removing a small number of features in a large data set, the truncated data set may be too large for efficient convergence of the algorithm (Lin et al., 2006). Additionally, the inclusion of prior information allows the ACA to be coupled with many other types of feature selection methods, making the ACA a versatile feature selection tool.

For LU tumors, the ACA identified two genes capable of classifying LU tumor samples with 100%, in each of the five replicates. The selected genes, SP-B and SP-A, both encode pulmonary surfactant proteins which are necessary for lung function. Another tumor class, with which the ACA was able to select a small number of highly predictive genes, was CNS. As with the LU tumor type, the genes selected by the ACA were very consistent from replication to replication. The gene encoding for APCL protein had the highest pheromone levels in all five replicates and was the only gene required to achieve 100% accuracy in replicate five. APCL protein is a homologue of APC, a known tumor suppressor that interacts with microtubules during mitosis (Akiyama and Kawasaki, 2006). The gene encoding MAP1B, a protein found to be important in synaptic function of cortical neurons, was also identified as being highly predictive of CNS tumor types. Several other genes selected by the ACA, found in *supplemental materials*, were identified in a previous study (Antonov et al., 2004).

In contrast to the LU and CNS tumor types, BR samples were consistently predicted with low accuracies. These findings are in agreement with previous results (Bagirov et al., 2003; Ramaswamy et al., 2001). Unlike the gene list obtained for BR and CNS tumor types, the gene lists for BR tumors were highly variable, suggesting potentially high heterogeneity in these tumor samples. Despite dissimilarities between the genes selected across replications, the ACA did identify SEPT9 as being highly predictive in four of the five replicates. The protein encoded by this gene has been shown to be involved in mitosis of mammary epithelial cells (Nagata et al., 2003) and has been associated with both ovarian and breast neoplasia (Scott et al., 2006). The identification of this gene by the ACA demonstrates its ability to identify biologically relevant features in challenging data sets.

2.2. The use of the ant colony algorithm for the detection of marker associations in the presence of gene interactions

With the advent of high-throughput, cost effective genotyping platforms, there has been much focus on the use of high-density single nucleotide polymorphism (SNP) genotyping to identify causative mutations for traits of interest, and while putative mutations have been identified for several traits, these studies tend to focus on SNP with large marginal effects [Hugot et al., 2001; Woon et al., 2007]. However, several studies have found that gene interactions may play important roles in many complex traits [Coutinho et al., 2007; Barendse et al., 2007]. Given the high density of SNP maker maps, examining all possible interactions is seldom possible computationally. As a result, studies examining gene interactions tend to focus on a small number of SNP, previously identified as having strong marginal associations. Using an exhaustive search of all two-way interactions, Marchini et al. achieved greater power to detect causative mutations than when estimating only marginal effects. Due to the high computational cost of this approach, a two-stage model was proposed, in which SNP were selected in the first stage based on marginal effects and then tested for interactions in the subsequent stage [Marchini et al., 2005]. This approach could, however, result in the failure to detect important regions of the genome in the first stage of the model. As such, there is a need for methodologies capable of identifying important genomic regions in the presence of potential gene interactions when large numbers of markers are genotyped.

One approach would be to view the identification of groups of interacting SNP as an optimization problem, for which several algorithms have been developed. These algorithms are designed to search large sample spaces for globally optimal solutions and have been applied to a wide range of problems [Shymygelska and Hoos, 2005; Ding et al., 2005]. Through the evaluation of groups of loci efficiently selected from different regions of the genome, optimization algorithms should be able to account for potential interactions.

In this section, a modified ACA, enabling the use of permutation testing for global significance, was combined with logistic regression and implemented on a simulated binary trait under the influence of interacting genes. The performance of the ACA was evaluated and compared to models accounting for only marginal effects.

B.1 Logistic regression: Groups of SNP markers were evaluated based in haplotype genotype effects estimated as log odds ratios (*lor*) using logistic regression (LR). The relationship between the *lor* and the binary response can be expressed as:

$$y_i = \begin{cases} 1 & \text{if } lor_i \geq 0 \\ 0 & \text{if } lor_i < 0 \end{cases}$$

The log odds ratio lor_i is modeled as:

$$lor_i = \ln(\frac{p_i}{1 - p_i}) = \boldsymbol{X}_i \boldsymbol{\beta} + e_i \tag{4}$$

where P_i = probability (y_i = 1) and X is a matrix containing indicator variables for the haplotypes formed from the selected SNP. Groups of SNP markers with less than two corresponding observations were discarded, and analysis was conducted on all remaining marker groups.

The link function of the log odds ratio $\boldsymbol{X}_i \boldsymbol{\beta}$with the binary response y_i gives the following equations:

$$p_i(y_i = 0) = \frac{1}{1 + \exp(\boldsymbol{X}_i \boldsymbol{\beta})} \text{ and } p_i(y_i = 1) = \frac{\exp(\boldsymbol{X}_i \boldsymbol{\beta})}{1 + \exp(\boldsymbol{X}_i \boldsymbol{\beta})} \tag{5}$$

yielding the following relationships:

$$y_i = \begin{cases} 1 & \text{if } \frac{\exp(\boldsymbol{X}_i \boldsymbol{\beta})}{1 + \exp(\boldsymbol{X}_i \boldsymbol{\beta})} \geq 0.5 \\ 0 & \text{if } \frac{\exp(\boldsymbol{X}_i \boldsymbol{\beta})}{1 + \exp(\boldsymbol{X}_i \boldsymbol{\beta})} < 0.5 \end{cases}$$

B.2 Marginal effects model: The genotype and haplotype association methods were implemented using R functions developed by [Gonzalez et al., 2007; Sinnwell and Schaid, 2005]. The haplotype analysis was implemented using a sliding window approach which utilizes a window of *k* SNP in width sliding across the genome *h* SNP at a time. Individual SNP scores were determined as the maximum average of all haplotypes containing a given SNP.

B.3 Ant colony algorithm: While the algorithm, in the aforementioned form can be used to subjectively identify markers, it is not well suited for the calculation of permutation p-values. When updating the pheromone function, as previously described in equation (2), the final pheromone levels are relative not only to prediction accuracy, but the number of times a SNP marker is selected. As a result, the amount of pheromone deposited on a feature depends greatly on the amount of pheromone deposited on all other SNP markers and can vary wildly from permutation to permutation. One obvious solution to this problem is to use the average accuracy of all S_k containing genotypes for SNP *m*; however, this approach substantially reduces the ACA's ability to efficiently burn in on good solutions, an attribute needed to detect unknown gene interactions in high-dimension data sets.

To overcome these limitations, a two-layer pheromone function was developed:

$$P_m(t) = \frac{\tau_m(t)^{\alpha}\tau 2_m(t)^{\alpha 2}\eta_m{}^{\beta}}{\sum_{m=1}^{nf}\tau_m(t)^{\alpha}\tau 2_m(t)^{\alpha 2}\eta_m{}^{\beta}} \tag{6}$$

where $\tau_m(t)$ is the first pheromone layer updated using the sum of accuracies for all S_k containing SNP m; $\tau 2_m(t)$is the second pheromone layer updated using the average accuracy of all S_k containing genotypes for SNP m; andη_m, α, $\beta$are as previously described. For the current study, $\alpha$and $\alpha 2$ were set to 1, $\beta$was set to.3 and the prior information (η_m) was the prediction the accuracy of SNP marker m, obtained using logistic regression on genotypes.

The pheromone for $\tau_m(t)$ was updated using equation (2) and $\tau 2_m(t)$ was updated using the following equation:

$$\tau 2_m(t+1) = [t * \tau_m 2(t) + \Delta\tau_m 2(t)] / (t + ns) \tag{7}$$

where t is the iteration number; $\Delta\tau_m 2(t)$is the change in pheromone level for feature m based on the sum of accuracy of all S_k containing genotypes for SNP m, and is set to zero if feature m was not selected by any of the artificial ants; and ns is the number of times SNP m was selected at iteration t. Permutation p-values were calculated using $\tau 2_m(t)$ only.

The procedure can be summarized in the following steps:

1. Each ant selects a predetermined number of SNP markers.
2. Using the selected SNP markers, accuracies are computed using logistic regression on haplotypes or genotypes.
3. The pheromone for each selected group of SNP, S_k, is calculated as:

$$pheromone_k = acc^{\,(1-acc)} \tag{8}$$

1. The change in pheromone at time t is then calculated using equations (2) and (7).
2. Following the update of pheromone levels according to equations (2) and (7), the PDF is updated according to equation (6) and the process is repeated until pheromone levels have converged.

B.4 Data simulation: Genotype data on 90 unrelated individuals from the Japanese and Han Chinese populations were downloaded from the HapMap ECODE project website. Each simulation scenario was replicated five times using two 500 Kbp regions on chromosome 2, comprising 2047 polymorphic SNP. All SNP haplotypes were assumed to be known without error. The binary disease trait was simulated under a two locus epistatic model as seen in Table 7.

	Scenario 1				Scenario 2			
	AB	aB	Ab	ab	AB	aB	Ab	ab
AB	1	1	1	1	1	1	1	1
aB	1	1	1	1	1	1	1	1
Ab	1	1	1	1	1	1	1	1
Ab	1	1	1	15	1	1	1	10

Table 7. Relative risk for simulated trait (relative to the aa/bb genotype)

The loci of the causative mutations were selected at random; with the frequencies of the causative mutations being.58 and.6. Although these frequencies might be considered high, it was necessary to restrict selection to SNP with mutant allele frequencies greater than.5. This was done to insure a reasonable simulated disease incidence of 15%. A plot illustrating the LD of all SNP with the two causative mutations is shown in Fig (1). The plot shows a large peak of high LD with rs2049736 (SNP 409), while the peak of high LD with rs28953468 (SNP 2041) is substantially narrower, and is preceded by a plateau of SNP in moderate LD with rs28953468.

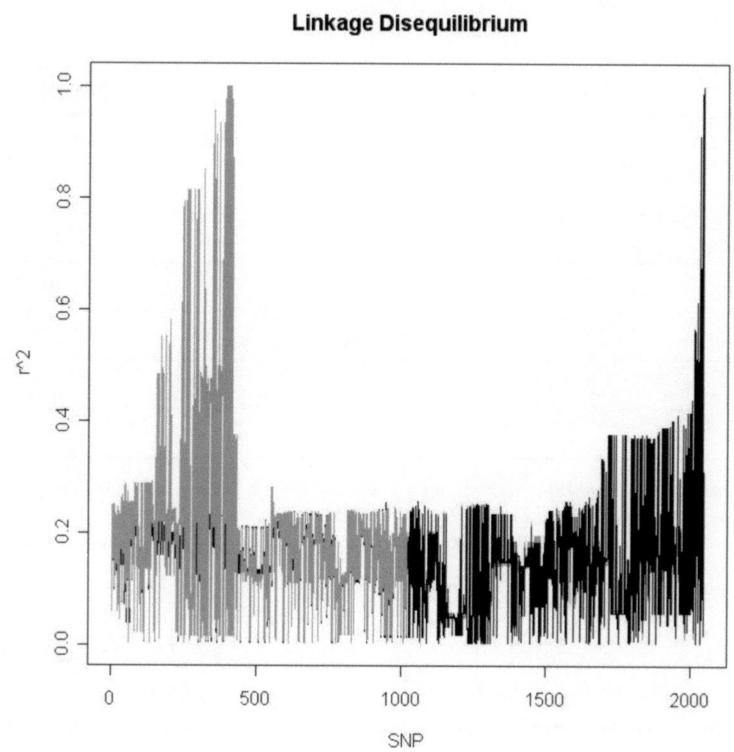

Figure 1. Plots of each marker's linkage disequilibrium (LD) with the two causative mutations. The light grey line represents LD with the causative mutation located at position 409. The black line represents LD with the causative mutation located at position 2041.

Permutation testing was used to access global significance for all models used in the study. Statuses were randomly shuffled amongst subjects, with haplotype effects, genotype effects and association p-values re-estimated for each new configuration of the response variables. The largest estimated haplotype/genotype effect or the smallest haplotype/genotype association p-value from each permutation was saved to form an empirical distribution used for calculation of p-values. One hundred permutations were performed, yielding p-values accurate to 1%. Power was calculated as the proportion of times a given method identified at least one SNP marker in high LD ($r^2 \geq .80$) with a causative mutation.

B.5 Results and discussions: Estimates of power for the three methods can be found in Table 8. Methods employing the ACA showed substantial increases in power when compared to the methods accounting for only marginal effects. Due to the fact that the trait was simulated under a dominance model, analysis of genotypes yielded superior results when compared to haplotype analysis. Despite the inherent advantage of genotype analysis using a dominance model, the ACA using haplotypes (ACA/H) still showed greater power than RG/D in both scenarios. For scenario 2, all models showed a reduction in power; however, the superiority of the ACA methodologies remained constant, with the ACA using LG on genotypes assuming a dominance model (ACA/G/D) yielding 66.7% increase in power for both scenarios when compared to the next best method, RG/D.

	Scenario 1			Scenario 2		
	1 locus	2 locus	3 locus	1 locus	2 locus	3 locus
ACA/G/D	___	1.00	0.90	___	0.50	0.40
ACA/G/C	___	0.70	0.80	___	0.40	0.40
ACA/HAP	___	0.60	0.70	___	0.50	0.40
RG/D	0.60	___	___	0.30	___	___
RG/C	0.30	___	___	0.30	___	___
SW/HAP	___	0.10	0.20	___	0.00	0.00

[a] Power was calculated as the proportion of times at least one SNP in high linkage disequilibrium (>.8) with a causative mutations was detected by the model at α=.05 for genome-wide significance

Table 8. Power calculations[a].

Plots of the associative effects, obtained using SW/H, ACA/G/D, and RG/D, are shown in Fig. (2) and (3). When compared to the LD plot (Fig. (1)) all methods show good correspondence for scenario 1, though only the ACA/G/D was able to identify markers for both causative mutations in all replicates. In scenario 2, where the genetic effect was greatly reduced, plots of associative effects tended to be noisier for all models, with the ACA/G/D again showing superior performance, identifying several SNP markers having only moderate LD with causative mutation rs28953468.

http://dx.doi.org/10.5772/52051

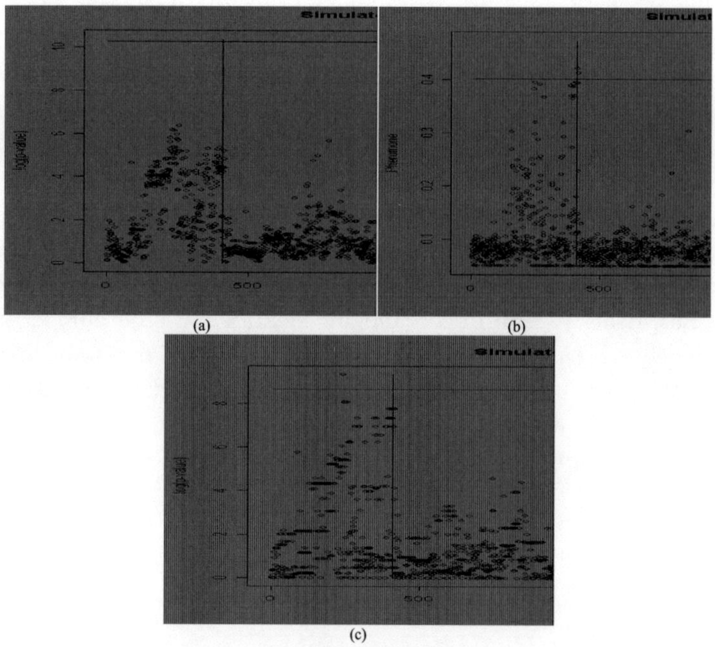

Figure 2. Association plots of SNP markers for the simulated trait under scenario 1. Plots were obtained using 2 SNP haplotypes analyzed by a. SW/LR and b. ACA/LR. Vertical lines represent the position of the two causative mutations, and horizontal lines represent the threshold at which associations are significant at α=. 05

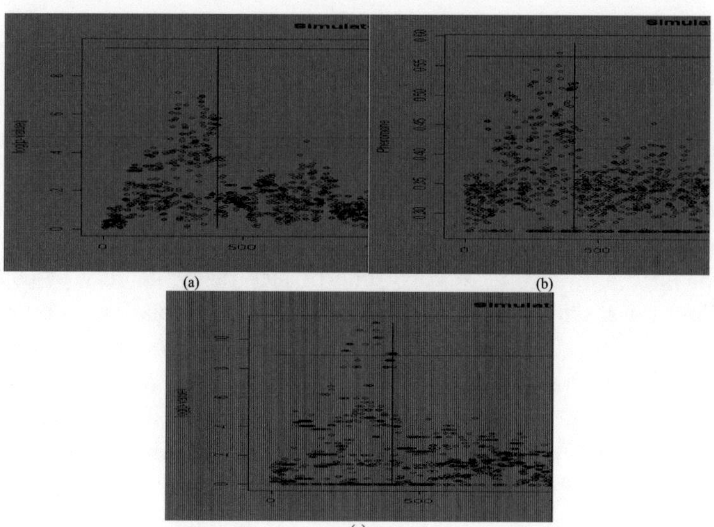

Figure 3. Association plots of SNP markers for the simulated trait under scenario 2. Plots were obtained using 3 SNP haplotypes analyzed by a. SW/LR, b. ACA/LR, and c. RG. Vertical lines represent the position of the two causative mutations, and horizontal lines represent the threshold at which associations are significant at α=.05.

To determine the effectiveness of the permutation on pheromone levels, the cumulative distribution, based on LD with causative mutations, of SNP identified as being significantly associated with simulated trait by ACA/G/D and RG/D were plotted and can be found in Fig. (4). Despite similarities in the average number of SNP identified by ACA/G/D (15.4) and RG/D (22), the distributions of these SNP, differed substantially. In contrast to RG/D, the ACA/G/D identified a large number of SNP having LD between.35-.45. These SNP corresponded to the broad plateau of SNP in LD with SNP 2041. Unlike RG/D, the ACA/G/D also identified several SNP (5.19%) having less than.10 LD with either of the causative mutations, an unexpected result given the strict family-wise significance thresholds (α=0.05) imposed on all models. Surprisingly, both methodologies identified a large number of SNP having LD of approximately ~.2. Upon closer examination it was found that these SNP had LD of ~. 2 with both causative mutations, likely artifacts of the data resulting from the relatively small sample size. The LD with both causative mutations imparted a portion of the epistatic effect on these SNP, resulting in significant associations with the simulated traits.

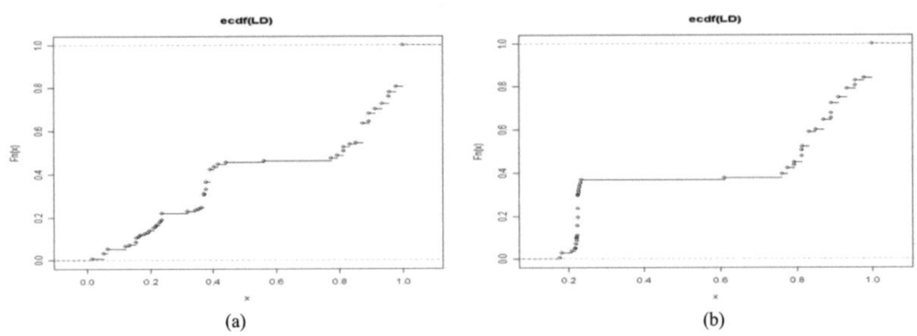

Figure 4. Plot of the cumulative distribution of SNP, identified as have significant associations when using a) ACA/G/D using 2 loci model (5.19%) b) RG/D, based on linkage disequilibrium with the causative mutations

2.3. Ant colony optimization as a method for strategic genotype sampling

Interest in identifying QTL of economic importance for marker-assisted selection (MAS) in livestock populations has increased greatly in the past decade. Yet, it may not be viable to genotype each animal due to cost, time or lack of availability of DNA. A method that would allow for a selected sample (e.g. 5%) of the population to be genotyped and at the same time inferring with high probability genotypes for the remaining animals in the population could be beneficial. By using such a method, fewer animals in a population would be needed for genotyping which would decrease the time and cost of genotyping. Theoretically the problem at hand is simple to solve. If it were possible to evaluate every possible subset of animals equal to the desired size (e.g. 5%) then the optimal solution could be found. However, this is computationally impossible at the current time. Consequently a more feasible solution is needed. An intuitive solution would be one that selects animals based on their relationship with other animals in the pedigree. However, the heterozygosity and the structure of the pedigree play important roles as well. Consequently, the problem is one of optimization.

http://dx.doi.org/10.5772/52051

In the case of genotyping, the ACA should select a subset of animals that, when genotyped, should give an optimal performance in terms of extrapolating the alleles of non-genotyped animals. Therefore, the objectives were to investigate the usefulness of a search algorithm as implemented by Ressom *et al.* (2006) to optimize the amount of information that can be extracted from a pedigree while only genotyping a small portion. The results of the proposed method are compared to other viable methods to ascertain any potential gain. The procedures were tested using simulated pedigrees and actual beef cattle pedigrees of varying sizes and structures.

C.1 *Ant colony optimization*: The ACA is initialized with all features having an equal baseline level of pheromone which is used to compute $P_m(0)$ for all features. Using the PDF as defined in equation (1), each of j artificial ants will select a subset S_k of n features from the sample space S containing all features.

Following the update of pheromone levels according to equation (2), the PDF is updated according to equation (1) and the process is repeated until some convergence criteria are met. Upon convergence the optimal subset of features is select based in the level of pheromone trail deposited on each feature.

In the specific case of selecting individuals for genotyping, the features are candidate animals for genotyping from a full or partial pedigree. The pheromone of some feature, m, in the current study was proportional to the sum of an animal's number of mates and number of offspring

$$\tau_m(t) = numoff_m + nummate_m \tag{9}$$

where $numoff_m$ and $nummate_m$ were the number of offspring and number of mates for animal m at time t, respectively. Consequently, the performance of a particular subset, S_k, is determined the by the cumulative sum as described above for each of n animals in the subset.

$$\tau_m(t) = \sum_{m=1}^{n} numoff_m + nummate_m \tag{10}$$

Outside of actual ant colonies, and with regard in particular to the current study, it is difficult to assign a biological explanation to the evaporation rate orρ. Consequently, a relatively small value of 0.01 was chosen in an attempt to reach convergence faster. For each of j artificial ants, a subset of animals was chosen equal to approximately 5% of the pedigree size.

For the five replicates of simulated pedigrees, 100 ants were used for each of 30,000 iterations. The evaporation rate was set equal to 0.01. The criterion used for evaluating candidates was a function of their number of mates and number of offspring. Each animal in the pedigree was randomly assigned to be either homozygous or heterozygous. The probability of an animal being assigned to one of these two groups was dependent on the allelic frequencies such that if the allele frequencies were assumed to be 0.7/0.3 then approximately 58% of the animals would be categorized as homozygous based off of Hardy-Weinberg Laws of equilibrium. The assignment of homozygous/heterozygous status was performed each iteration. If a selected animal 2was homozygous then his/her number of mates and number of offspring were corrected such that for every homozygous offspring he/she had the number of offspring was corrected accordingly so that the number of offspring only reflected the number of heterozygous offspring. The same correction was done for the number of mates. Similarly, if a selected animal was heterozygous, the number of offspring and the number of mates reflected a count of only homozygous individuals. An animal's probability of being selected was based off of maximizing the corrected sum of the animal's number of offspring and number of mates. The accuracy for evaluating a selected group of animals was proportional to this corrected sum. The uncorrected or original sum of each animal was used as prior information. Selected animals were chosen based off of their cumulative probability were assumed to have known genotypes for the peeling procedure. Simulated allele frequencies of 0.7/0.3 and 0.5/0.5 were used to assign genotypes to the animals in the pedigree.

In the case of the real pedigree the same parameters were used as in the simulated pedigrees with the following exceptions; 100 ants were used for each of 5,000 iterations. The top 1,455 animals out of 29,101 were selected (5% of the total pedigree) based off of their cumulative probability were assumed to have known genotypes for the peeling procedure. In the case of the research beef cattle pedigree, 100 ants were used for each of 20,000 iterations. The top 434 out of 8,688 animals were selected (5% of the total pedigree) based on the same criteria.

C.2 Peeling: Given that genotypes in this study were assigned at random in the population, it is possible to extract additional genotypic information from the pedigree. Animals with missing genotypic information can be assigned one or both alleles given parental, progeny, or mate information. Given this trio of information sources and following an algorithm similar to Qian and Beckmann (2002) and Tapadar et al. (2000), imputation on missing genotypes were made and additional genotypic information was garnered. For the current study it was assumed that there were no errors in the recorded pedigree resulting in all animals having known paternity and maternity. Whenever possible, maternal and paternal alleles were identified based on the inheritance. For the purpose of this study, the first allele was inherited from the sire and the second allele was inherited from the dam. If the parental origin of an allele was unclear, then allele was arbitrarily assigned as either the paternal or maternal allele.

After the peeling process, the number of animals with one or two alleles known was computed. This was done by simply counting the number of animals that were assigned either one or two alleles based on the peeling procedure described above. The percentage of alleles known based on the peeling procedure (AK_P) was then computed as follows:

$$AK_P = \left(\frac{(n_1 \times 2) + n_2}{n_a \times 2} \right) \times 100, \tag{11}$$

http://dx.doi.org/10.5772/52051

where n_1 and n_2 were the number of animals with 2 and 1 allele(s) known and n_a was the total number of animals in the population. Furthermore, $n_1$and n_a were multiplied by two since each animal has two alleles.

At the end of the peeling process those animals that had either one or two alleles known were retained for further analysis to determine the remaining unknown alleles in the population. In other words, those animals having one or two known alleles were used as prior information in the Gibbs sampling procedure for determining the remaining unknown alleles in the population.

C.3 Gibbs sampling: After the known alleles were determined by the peeling process described above, these alleles were used as prior information in the Gibbs Sampler to assign genotypes to the remaining animals in the population. For the base population animals, the unknown allele(s) were randomly sampled given the frequency of alleles in the population and the assumption of Hardy-Weinberg equilibrium. Unknown alleles for non-base population animals were randomly sampled from the parent's genotypes according to Mendelian rules. An equal weight was assumed for inheriting either the first or second allele from a parent. For a non-base population animal that had only one unknown allele, the unknown allele was sampled approximately half of the time from the sire's genotype and the remaining time from the dam's genotype. This was to compensate for incorrect assignment of the known allele as illustrated in the above example.

At the end of the sampling process, a benefit function that described the total number of alleles known in the population was computed. This function was computed from a combination of known alleles and the probability of unknown alleles assigned during the sampling process. In order to be included in the benefit function, an allele in a particular position had to be equal to the true allele of the same position (i.e., *Bb* and *bB* were not equal). The probability of allele$a_{i,j}$, (j = 1 or 2) being assigned as the true allele j for animal *i* was calculated as:

$$p(a_{i,j}) = \frac{\text{number of times } a_{i,j} \text{ was assigned}}{\text{number of iterations}}. \tag{12}$$

Using $p(a_{i,j})$ and the number of known alleles, the benefit function was then computed as

$$Benefit = n_1 \times 2 + \sum_{i=1}^{n_2} [1 + p(a_{i,j})] + \sum_{i=1}^{n_3} [p(a_{i,1}) + p(a_{i,2})], \tag{13}$$

wheren_1, n_2, and n_3 were the number of animals with 2, 1 or 0 alleles known, respectively, and $p(a_{i,j})$ as previously defined. The percentage of alleles known after the Gibbs sampling process, AK_G, was such that

$$\mathrm{AK_G} = \left(\frac{benefit}{n_a \times 2}\right) \times 100, \tag{14}$$

where *benefit* was the benefit function computed above and n_a was the total number of animals in the population.

During each round of the sampling process only one genotype of a given animal was assigned as the true genotype. Thus, at the end of the sampling process every animal had a probability of having the true genotype,PTG_{ig} , assigned as

$$\mathrm{PTG}_{ig} = \frac{\text{number of times genotype } g \text{ was assigned}}{\text{total number of samples}}, \tag{15}$$

where genotype g was the true genotype for animal$i$. The average probability of the true genotype being identified for every animal in the population (APTG) was computed using the following:

$$\mathrm{APTG} = \frac{\sum_{i=1}^{n_a} \mathrm{PTG}_{ig}}{n_a}, \tag{16}$$

where PTG_{ig} was defined as above and n_a was the total number of animals in the population. In contrast to the benefit function, APTG only required that the animal have the correct genotype—*Bb* was considered the same genotype as *bB*—and therefore was able to compensate for the incorrect allele position and sampling the correct unknown allele.

C.4 Simulation: A simulation using an animal model was carried out to investigate two methods of selecting animals for genotyping and two methods of maximizing the genetic information of the population. A pedigree with four over-lapping generations was simulated. The base population included 500 unrelated animals and subsequent generations consisted of 1,500 animals with a total of 5,000 animals generated. For the simulated pedigrees as well as the real pedigrees, one gene with two alleles was simulated for every animal in the pedigree file. Genotypes of the base population animals were assigned based on allele frequencies. For the subsequent generations, genotypes were randomly assigned using the parent's genotype, where an equal chance of passing either the first or second allele was assumed. Five replicates of the simulated data were generated.

Two different frequencies for the favorable allele were used in the simulation and analyses. The frequencies were 0.30, and 0.50. For the analyses using Gibbs sampling, a total chain length of 25,000 iterations of the Gibbs sampler was run, where the first 5,000 iterations were discarded as burn-in.

C.5 Results of simulated pedigrees: Table 9 presents results of the ACO and alternative methods for analysis of the simulated pedigrees (Spangler 2008). The ant colony optimization method (ACO) appeared to be the most desirable method of those discussed in the current study. Compared to selecting 5% of the animals at random, ACO showed gains in AK_P, AK_G, and APTG ranging from 261.09 to 262.93%, 19.97 to 26.04%, and 23.5 to 29.6%, respectively. As compared to the favorable method of the alternative approaches, selecting males and females based of off the diagonal element of the inverse of the relationship matrix, the increase in AK_P ranged from 4.98 to 5.16%. This gain is due to the amount of animals with both alleles known after the peeling process which was between 20.74 and 21.07% larger in favor of ACO. Admittedly, the gains in AK_G were slight as compared to selecting males and females based of off the diagonal element of A^{-1}, yet ACO still performed better. The increase in APTG ranged from 1.6 to 1.8% in favor of ACO over selecting males and females from their diagonal element.

	ACO		Random		Males		Males and females	
Parameter[b]	(0.30)	(0.50)	(0.30)	(0.50)	(0.30)	(0.50)	(0.30)	(0.50)
No. of animals with								
2 alleles known	811.20	787.20	258.20	259.60	250.00	250.60	670.00	652.00
1 allele known	2,166.80	2,063.00	527.80	485.60	2,939.80	2,793.00	2,262.60	2,152.80
Benefit function	8,055.01	7,550.36	6,713.56	6,007.02	7,943.67	7,401.57	8,019.88	7,497.70
AK_P	37.89	36.29	10.44	10.05	34.40	32.94	36.03	34.57
AK_G	80.55	75.71	67.14	60.07	79.44	74.02	80.20	74.98
APTG	0.63	0.57	0.51	0.44	0.59	0.52	0.62	0.56

[a] Random= 5% selected at random, Males= 5% of males selected from their diagonal element of A^{-1}, Males and females= 2.5% males and 2.5% females selected from their diagonal element of A^{-1}. Numbers in parenthesis are the true allele frequencies used in the simulation. [b] Descriptions of the parameters can be found in equations 5-10

Table 9. Number of animals with one or two alleles known, percentage of alleles known, and probability of assigning the true genotype using other approaches[a]

C.6 Real beef cattle pedigree: Results from the ACO analysis can be found in Table 10 along with results from alternative approaches. The largest gains were seen in AK_P which ranged from 150.00 to 171.62%, 2.95 to 3.04%, and from 1.80 to 1.94% as compared to random selection, selection of males and females from A^{-1}, and selection of males from A^{-1}, respectively. ACO also showed gains in AKG and APTG over random selection between 70.06 and 74.91% and between 14.3 and 15.4%, respectively. Table 3 shows advantages, although slight, of ACO over the methods using the diagonal element of A^{-1} for the parameters of AK_G and APTG.

C.7 Research beef cattle pedigree: Results from the ACO analysis and other approaches using the same pedigree can be found in Table 11. As compared to randomly selecting 5%

of the animals, ACO showed increases in AK_P, AK_G, and APTG ranging from 241.24 to 302.58%, 42.93 to 43.17%, and 20.9 to 38.0%, respectively. Realized gains in AK_P of ACO over selecting males from A^{-1} or males and females from A^{-1} ranged from 8.78 to 10.15%, and 2.04 to 3.40%, respectfully.

The results suggest that ACO is the most desirable method of selecting candidates for genotyping, particularly after peeling (AK_P). From these results it appears that the number of offspring and the number of mates along with the homozygosity of the genotyped animals is critical in the selection process. Consequently, in application it will be critical to have good estimates of allele frequencies prior to implementing the genotype sampling strategy proposed in the current study. Differences in performance of ACO do exist between the pedigrees explored in the current study. This is due to the proportion of sires and dams that have large numbers of offspring and/or mates. In the dairy industry, for example, there may be only a small number of sires in a pedigree but they may all be used heavily as in the case of the simulated pedigrees in the current study. In contrast, a pedigree from the beef industry may have a larger proportion of sires but a large number of them may be used less frequently.

	ACO		Random			Males	Males and females	
Parameter[b]	(0.30)	(0.50)	(0.30)	(0.50)	(0.30)	(0.50)	(0.30)	(0.50)
No. of animals with								
2 alleles known	1,767.00	1,706.00	1,505.00	1,501.00	1,473.00	1,470.00	2,086.00	1,999.00
1 allele known	11,451.00	10,382.00	2,508.00	2,144.00	11,756.00	10,607.00	10,376.00	9,398.00
Benefit function	34,977.61	32,547.06	20,569.53	18,609.00	34,876.62	32,282.40	34,005.21	31,456.36
AK_P	25.75	23.70	9.48	8.84	25.26	23.28	24.99	23.02
AK_G	60.10	55.92	35.34	31.97	59.92	55.47	58.43	54.05
APTG	0.45	0.40	0.39	0.35	0.44	0.39	0.44	0.40

[a] Random= 5% selected at random, Males= 5% of males selected from their diagonal element of A^{-1}, Males and females= 2.5% males and 2.5% females selected from their diagonal element of A^{-1}. Numbers in parenthesis are the true allele frequencies used in the simulation. [b] Descriptions of the parameters can be found in equations 5-10.

Table 10. Number of animals with one or two alleles known, percentage of alleles known, and probability of assigning the true genotype using other approaches from a real beef cattle pedigree [a]

	ACO		Random		Males		Males and females	
Parameter[b]	(0.30)	(0.50)	(0.30)	(0.50)	(0.30)	(0.50)	(0.30)	(0.50)
No. of animals with								
2 alleles known	975.00	720.00	452.00	458.00	438.00	439.00	1,082.00	751.00
1 allele known	5,101.00	4,009.00	847.00	682.00	5,525.00	4,132.00	4,747.00	3,768.00
Benefit function	13,916.18	11,990.71	9,719.53	8,284.42	14,113.18	12,017.80	13,743.44	11,848.01
AK_P	40.58	31.36	10.08	9.19	36.84	28.83	39.77	30.33
AK_G	80.09	68.15	55.94	47.68	81.22	69.16	79.09	68.19
APTG	0.69	0.52	0.50	0.43	0.69	0.51	0.68	0.52

[a] Random= 5% selected at random, Males= 5% of males selected from their diagonal element of A^{-1}, Males and females= 2.5% males and 2.5% females selected from their diagonal element of A^{-1}. Numbers in parenthesis are the true allele frequencies used in the simulation. [b] Descriptions of the parameters can be found in equations 5-10.

Table 11. Number of animals with one or two alleles known, percentage of alleles known, and probability of assigning the true genotype using other approaches from a real beef cattle research pedigree[a]

Furthermore, pedigrees from field data or from research projects will also have innate structural differences. Research projects may be limited by the size of the population and thus only use a small number of sires. In this scenario it would also be possible for higher rates of inbreeding and larger numbers of loops in a pedigree due to a large number of full sibs.

In the current study, the simulated pedigrees are composed of approximately 10% sires, while the large beef cattle pedigree and the small research beef cattle pedigree contain approximately 16 and 7% sires, respectively. Intuitively, as the proportion of sires goes up, the number of offspring per sire goes down. This explains the similarity of the results between the simulated pedigrees and the small research pedigree. Thus, it is expected that the ACO algorithm will be far superior to other alternatives when very small (few hundred animals) pedigrees are considered or in situations where more than 5% of animals are genotyped due to reduction in animal with large diagonal elements in A^{-1}.

Ant colony optimization offers a new and unique solution to the optimization problem of selecting individuals for genotyping. The heuristics used in the current study such as the number of ants, number of iterations, and the evaporation rate are unique only to the pedigrees used in the current study. Each pedigree will offer a different structure and thus require a different set of parameters.

3. Conclusions

When applied to the high-dimensional data sets, the ant colony algorithm achieved higher prediction accuracies than all other feature selection methods examined. In contrast to previous applications of optimization algorithms, the ant colony algorithm yielded high accuracies without the need to pre-select a small percentage of genes. Furthermore, the ant colony algorithm was able to identify small subsets of features with high predictive abilities and biological relevance. In the presence of simulated epistasis, the proposed optimization methodology obtained substantial increases in power, demonstrating the effectiveness of machine learning approaches for the analysis of marker association studies in which gene interactions may be present. Although the ACA methods identified more SNP markers that could be construed as false positives, the use of a more stringent threshold eliminated the problem without greatly reducing the advantage of the ACA, in terms of power, when compared to other methods. The results of this study provide compelling evidence that the ACA is capable of efficiently modeling complex biological problems, such as the model proposed in this study.

Author details

R. Rekaya[1,2,3*], K. Robbins[4], M. Spangler[5], S. Smith[1], E. H. Hay[1] and K. Bertrand[1]

*Address all correspondence to: rrekaya@uga.edu

1 Department of Animal and Dairy Science, The University of Georgia, Athens, Greece

2 Department of Statistics, The University of Georgia, Athens, Greece

3 Institute of Bioinformatics, The University of Georgia, Athens, Greece

4 Dow AgroSciences, Indianapolis, IN, USA

5 Animal Science Department, University of Nebraska, Lincoln, NE, USA

References

[1] Akiyama,T. and Y Kawasaki (2006) Wnt signaling and the actin cytoskeleton *Oncogene,* 25, 7538-7544.

[2] Albrecht, A., Vinterbo,S.A. and L. O. Machado 2003, 'An epicurean learning approach to gene-expression data classification', *Artif. Intell in Medicine,* 28, 75-87.

[3] Antonov,A.V., Tetko,I.V., Mader,M.T., Budczies,J. and H. W. Mewes (2004) Optimization models for cancer classification: extracting gene interaction information from microarray expression data *Bioinformatics,* 20, 644-652.

[4] Bagirov,A.M., Ferguson,B., Ivkovic,S., Saunders,G. and J. Yearwood (2003) New algorithms for multi-class cancer diagnosis using tumor gene expression signatures *Bioinformatics,* 19, 1800-1807.

[5] Barendse, W., Harrison, B. E., Hawken, R. J., Ferguson, D. M., Thompson, J. M., Thomas, M. B., and R. J. Bunch. 2007. Epistasis between Calpain 1 and its inhibitor Calpastatin within breeds of cattle. Genetics 176:2601-2610.

[6] Coutinho, A. M., Sousa, I., Martins, M. et al. 2007. Evidence for epistasis between SLC6A4 and ITGB3 in autism etiology and in the determination of platelet serotonin levels. Hum. Genet. 121:243-256.

[7] Ding, Y. P., Wu, Q. S., and Q. D. Su. 2005. Multivariate Calibration Analysis for metal porphyrin mixtures by an ant colony algorithm. Analytical Sciences. 21:327-330.

[8] Dorigo M., Di Caro G. & Gambardella L.M. (1999) Ant algorithms for discrete optimization. Artificial Life 5, 137–72.

[9] Dorigo, M. and L. M. Gambardella. 1997. Ant colonies for the travailing salesman problem. BioSystems. 43:73-81.

[10] Golub,T.R., Slonim,D.K., Tomayo,P., Huard,C., Gaasenbeek,M., Mesirov,J.P., Coller,H., Loh,M.L., Downing,J.R., Caligiuri,M.A., Bloomfield,C.D. and E. S. Lander (1999) Molecular classification of cancer: class discovery and class prediction by gene expression monitoring *Science,* 286, 531-537.

[11] Gonzalez, J. R., Armengol, L., Sole, X., Guino, E., Mercader, J. M., Estivill, X., and V. Moreno. 2007. SNPassoc: an R package to perform whole genome association studies. Bioinformatics. 23(5):644-645

[12] Hong,J. and S. Cho (2006) Efficient huge-scale feature with speciated genetic algorithm *Pattern Recognition Lett.,* 27, 143-150.

[13] Hugot, J. P., Chamaillard, M., Zouali, H. et al. 2001. Association of NOD2 leucine-rich repeat variants with susceptibility to Crohn's disease. Nature. 411:599-603.

[14] Jefferey,I.B., Higgins,D.G. and A. Culhane (2006) Comparison and evaluation of methods for generating differentially expressed gene lists from microarray data, *BMC Bioinformatics,* 7.

[15] Lin,T., Liu,R., Chen,C., Choa,Y. and S. Chen (2006) Pattern classificationin DNA microarray data of multiple tumor types *Pattern Recognition,* 39, 2426-2438.

[16] Liu,J.J., Cutler,G., Li,W., Pan,Z., Peng,S., Hoey,T., Chen,L. and X. B. Ling (2005) Multiclass cancer classification and biomarker discover using GA-based algorithms *Bioinformatics,* 21, 2691-2697.

[17] Marchini, J., Donnelly, P., and L. R. Cardon. 2005. Genome-wide stregies for detecting multiple loci that influence complex diseases. Nat. Genetics. 37:413-417.

[18] Nagata,K., Kawajiri,A., Matsui,S., Takagishi,M., Shiromizu,T., Saitoh,N., Izawa,I. Kiyono,T., Itoh,T.J., Hotani,H. and M. Inagaki (2003) Filament formation of MSF-A, a mammalan Septin, in human mammary epithelial cells depends on interactions with microtubules *J. of Biol. Chem.,* 278, 18538-18543

[19] Ooi,C.H. and P. Tan (2003) Genetic algorithms applied to multi-class prediction for the analysis of gene expression data *Bioinformatics,* 19, 37-44.

[20] Peng,S., Xu,Q., Ling,X.B., Peng,X., Du,W. and L. Chen Molecular classification of cancer types from microarray data using the combination of genetic algorithms and support vector machines *FEBS Letters,* 555, 358-362.

[21] Qian D. & Beckmann L. (2002) Minimum-recombinant haplotyping in pedigrees. American Journal of Human Genetics 70, 1434–45.

[22] Ramaswamy,S., Tamayo,P., Rifkin,R., Mukherjee,S., Yeang,C., Angelo,M., Ladd,C., Reich,M., Latulippe,E., Mesirov,J.P., Poggio,T., Gerald,W., Loda,M., Lander,E.S. and T. R. Golub (2001) Multiclass cancer diagnosis using tumor gene expression signatures *PNAS,* 98, 15149-15154.

[23] Rekaya, R, K. Robbins. (2009). Ant colony algorithm for analysis of gene interaction in high-dimensional association data. Revista Brasileira de Zootecnia. doi: 10.1590/S1516-35982009001300011.

[24] Ressom,H.W., Varghese,R.S., Orvisky,E., Drake,S.K., Hortin,G.L., Abdel-Hamid,M. Loffredo,C.A. and R. Goldman (2006) Ant colony optimization for biomarker identification from MALDI-TOF mass spectra *Proc. of the 28th EMBS Annual Inter. Conf.,* 4560-4563.

[25] Robbins, K. R., Zhang, W., R. Rekaya, and J. K. Bertrand. 2007. The use of the ant colony algorithm for analysis of high-dimension gene expression data sets. 58th Annual Meeting of the European Association for Animal Production (EAAP):167.

[26] Robbins, K. R., Zhang, W., J. K. Bertrand, R. Rekaya. 2008. Ant colony optimization for feature selection in high dimensionality data sets. Math Med Biol. 24(4):413-426.

[27] Robbins K, K. Bertrand, and R. Rekaya. 2011. The use of the ant colony algorithm for the detection of marker associations in the presence of gene interactions. International Journal of Bioinformatics Research, 2:227-235.

[28] Scott,M., McCluggage,W.G., Hillan,K.J., Hall,P.A. and S. E. H. Russell (2006) Altered patterns of transcription of th septin gene, SEPT9, in ovarian tumorgenesis *Int. J. Cancer,* 118, 1325-1329.

[29] Shen,R., Ghosh,D., Chinnaiyan,A. and Z. Meng Eigengene-based linear discriminant model for tumor classification using gene expression microarray data *Bioinformatics,* 22, 2635-2642.

[30] Shymygelska, A. and H. H. Hoos. 2005. An ant colony optimization algorithm for the 2D and 3D hydrocarbon polar protein folding program. BMC Bioinformatics. 6:30.

[31] Sinnwell, J. P. and D. J. Schaid. 2005. haplo.stats: Statistical Analysis of Haplotypes with Traits and Covariates when Linkage Phase is Ambiguous. R package version 1.2.2.

[32] Spangler, M. L., K. R. Robbins, J. K. Bertrand, M. MacNeil, and R. Rekaya. 2008. Ant colony optimization as a method for strategic genotype sampling. Animal Genetics 40: 308 – 314.

[33] Subramani,P., Sahu,R. and S. Verma, Feature selection using Haar wavelet power spectrum *BMC Bioinformatics,* 7:432.

[34] Tapadar P., Ghosh S. & Majumder P.P. (2000) Haplotyping in pedigrees via a genetic algorithm. Human Heredity 50, 43–56.

[35] West M. (2003) Bayesian factor regression models in the "Large p, Small n" paradigm, *Bayesian Statistics,* 7, 723-732.

[36] Woon , P. Y., Kaisaki, P. J., Braganca, J., Bihoreau, M. T., Levy, J. C., Farrall, M., and D. Gauguir. 2007. Aryl hydrocarbon receptor nuclear translocator-like (BMAL1) is associated with susceptibility to hypertension and type 2 diabetes. Proc. Natl. Acad. Sci. 104(36):14412-14417.